FABIO VIGHI

EMERGENCY CAPITALISM

Financial Hubris, Economic Collapse and Systemic Manipulation

sublation press

Emergency Capitalism

First Published by Sublation Media 2024
Copyright © 2024 Fabio Vighi

All Rights Reserved
Commissioned and Edited by Douglas Lain
Copy Editor: Konrad Jandavs

A Sublation Press Book
Published by Sublation Media LLC

Distributed by Ingramspark

www.sublationmedia.com

Print ISBN: 979-8-9901591-6-7
eBook ISBN: 979-8-9901591-7-4

Edited and typeset by Polifolia in Germany

Contents

Acknowledgments	v
Introduction: Adrift in the End-Times	vii
A social relation	viii
The paradigm shift	ix
From the great escape…	xi
… to the great bluff	xiii
Monetary dystopia	xv
Terminal sickness	xvii
A sin against the Holy Spirit	xix
Geopolitics of recession	xxi
1. Systemic Collapse and Pandemic Simulation	1
The great freeze	2
Follow the magic money!	7
Joining the dots	11
Doing capitalism differently?	18
2. A Self-Fulfilling Prophecy	24
The Covid symptom	24
Biopolitics on steroids	30
From conspiracy theory to successful paranoia	33
The morality ruse	38
3. Quo Vadis, Homo Pandemicus?	46
The absent cause	46
Obsolescence of valorization	51
Panic consumption and the new narcissists	56
Ideology today	61
Denkverbot and faceless humanity	64
4. When All Else Fails, They Take You to War	68
Monetary variants	69
The debt's unstoppable flight forward	73
Societal decomposition	76
The Putin virus	78
The tangled web we weave	82
Hyperreality and forever wars	87
The war dividend	91
Our Zone of Interest: The noise of permanent warfare	96

5. Perversions of Crisis Capitalism — 103
Calculated crises and selective defaults — 104
"Safe and effective" digital shots — 108
Choking on credit — 114
A new 9/11? — 120
A warlike enterprise — 127

6. The Great Denial — 132
The icesheet is cracking — 133
The empty ground — 138
Capital's perpetual motion machine — 145
A sense of perspective — 152

7. Welcome to "Lower Energy" Capitalism — 158
The inflation genie — 159
From denial to sacrifice — 164
Rolling out fear to rollover debt — 166
Poverty is the new green — 171

Conclusion: The One-Way Street of Capitalist Civilization — 181

Endnotes — 187

Acknowledgments

This book brings together, in a substantially expanded and revised form, my writings on "emergency capitalism" since the outbreak of the Covid-19 health crisis. Most of these writings appeared in the *Philosophical Salon* blog between 2021 and 2023. The book would therefore not have materialized without the generosity of Michael Marder, editor of *The Philosophical Salon*, who took the risk of publishing my texts at a time when the coronavirus narrative could hardly be questioned or challenged. I wish to thank Michael, as well as all those who followed my work over the last three years. My gratitude also goes out to Douglas Lain for his unwavering support and to Konrad Jandavs for the exceptional professionalism with which he oversaw the copy editing process. Finally, I like to think that this book would have been valued by my friend and comrade Achim Szepanski, a true master of dissent who recently passed away.

Introduction
Adrift in the End-Times

•

> The threat of one catastrophe is deferred by that of others.
> —Theodor Adorno[1]

> The West has become a totalitarian space—the space of a self-defensive hegemony defending itself against its own weakness.
> —Jean Baudrillard[2]

The age of crisis capitalism is characterized by two major socio-economic trends: (1) the addiction to credit creation, whose main purpose is to inflate and prop up the financial markets; (2) the controlled demolition of the real economy and the modern model of society organized around wage labor. These two tendencies are now tied together in an increasingly suffocating feedback loop, which remains impenetrable for most. The current finance- and debt-based constellation will only survive to the detriment of the work society, whose decay is managed from the top down via emergency-driven strategies of mass manipulation and control. While "elites" steer the implosive course of our civilization, this process is simultaneously reified into the impersonal code of crisis-to-crisis capitalism, which is becoming totalitarian. The puppeteers—the psychopathic functional managers of emergency capitalism—are both responsible for and defined by the destructive movement of capital.

A social relation

My argument is premised on the simple observation that, in capitalism, value is generated by living labor. Our social bond presupposes the mediation of wage labor, which is a "real abstraction":[3] it is *abstract* as it turns work into a commodity exchanged on the market; and it is *real* as it determines the conditions of possibility for our lives. Like any other social relation, capitalism is grounded in the successful naturalization of a symbolic narrative which "runs the show from behind our backs." At the heart of this narrative lies a social convention: the convertibility of labor power into a quantum of economic value. Establishing an equivalence between the concrete materiality of commodity-producing labor and a salary is the abstract practice that defines the historical specificity of capitalist modernity. In capitalist terms, freedom itself ultimately coincides with the freedom to sell one's labor power. In this respect, modernity sets itself up as a prodigious belief system. It relies, in other words, on the deep-seated persuasion that human work is computable as labor time and exchangeable for a sum of money. Capitalism converts lifetime into labor time.

Collective belief in the labor commodity validates capitalism as the historical formation that was able, around 500 years ago, to overcome the final crisis of the feudal system. Once the equivalence between labor time and money was established, the dynamism of modernity was secured by the self-expansion of economic value, which solidified into an axiomatic social discourse that gradually grew autonomous from official religions and political ideologies. The dominance of capital as a blind drive for profit making was achieved with the first industrial revolution in the second half of the eighteenth century. Essentially, modern capitalism is a compulsive disorder socialized via mass wage labor. In this respect, it can be argued that modernity thrived through its capacity to establish a secular link with eternity after dissolving the metaphysical anchoring of the feudal system: one assumes that capital is blessed with the divine attribute of perpetual motion and thus that nothing exists beyond it. As Walter Benjamin put it, "The transcendence of God has fallen. But he is not dead; he has been drawn into human fate."[4] This naturalization of capital as destiny hinders our ability to confront its terminal crisis, which I will now introduce in greater detail.

The paradigm shift

Capitalism is unwittingly destroying its own substance, the capacity for self-reproduction through labor-intensive value creation. The social narrative from which it emerged is no longer working, which translates into the following paradox: capital can only pursue profit making by disabling its source of valorization—commodity-producing labor. The main consequence of this momentous shift is that our societies are now forced to reproduce themselves by drawing on the purely speculative (fictitious) character of their economies. As technological productivity soars, a greater share of capital profitability heads toward the financial markets. Such a paradigm change requires a redefinition of the liberal ethos of our world, which is turning explicitly authoritarian to manage decline, immiseration, and protest. This also means that the function of "crisis" has mutated. While an economic slump led in the past to a new growth cycle, today we are faced with a slow-motion collapse accompanied by increasingly aggressive strategies of mass deception. Having exhausted both all remaining space for external development and the possibility of real economic valorization through "qualitative leaps" in productivity, capital today can only aim for a development-free mode of equilibrium. But this is against its nature as a self-expansive drive, and it can only be achieved via illiberal governance or openly autocratic political regimes.

The third industrial revolution, spearheaded in the 1970s by microelectronics and digitization, displaced labor on an unprecedented scale. This caused a tectonic shift within the core of the system. Following the implementation of large-scale technological automation in the 1980s, capital could no longer reabsorb the mass of productive labor it was rapidly eliminating. Thus, it began sinking under the weight of its own internal contradiction, the fact that labor is both its lifeblood and an annoying cost that must be reduced if enterprises are to compete successfully for market shares. Unable to create its socially necessary standards by engaging and exploiting labor, capital then began to desocialize society by fleeing *en masse* to the financial markets. Today, the outcome of this transformation appears before our eyes in the form of a crisis management regime wherein the middle classes are shrinking; the industrial working classes have fragmented into multitudes of unemployed, underemployed, self-employed, precarious, migrant, and flexible workers (or a huge mass of potential recruits who no longer even seek employment); and where the third world has plunged into a primitive economy of subsistence.

In short, there is no longer enough labor power to reproduce our societies but still too much of it for capital's absorption capacity. The widespread implementation of microelectronics pushed this contradiction beyond the point of no return, forcing more and more capitals to seek profitability in the financial markets (where money makes *money* work) rather than in the labor-based economy (where money makes *people* work). The neoliberal revolution provided the political validation for capital's financial escape from its broken engine—an escape route that, incidentally, was not available to the socialist work societies that collapsed in the late 1980s. Today, at the dawn of the fourth industrial revolution (artificial intelligence, genetic engineering, augmented reality, etc.), the destruction of labor-intensive production via technological automation is both irreversible and catastrophic for a system built on the extraction of value from the combustion of human energy. This is why the survival of ultrafinancialized capitalism depends on its capacity to keep what are in capitalist terms the unproductive and superfluous masses under control. The neoliberal flight of fancy is coming back down to earth as a resolutely dystopian nightmare: a fully digitized, neofeudal type of capitalist seigniorage wherein a small financial aristocracy rules over the heavily manipulated, confused, and immiserated plebs.

From the great escape…

It ought to be no surprise that global debt (currently around $313 trillion)[5] has since the 1980s risen at a much faster rate than economic output, with appetite for borrowing growing at an alarming pace and debt productivity declining steadily—to the extent that a "great reset" is now openly regarded as being inevitable.[6] Stated differently, capital's expansion can no longer be satisfied by labor exploitation alone, nor can state economies survive without grotesquely indebting themselves. Today's center of "wealth production" is neither the factory nor the tertiary sector but *the financial simulation of growth*. Financial "signs" (asset prices) are increasingly self-reflexive (referring to nothing other than themselves) while their fluctuations are guaranteed by the potentially infinite capacity of central banks to absorb increases in borrowing. The epicenters of our world-system are the bond markets, where sovereign and corporate debt securities (IOUs like US Treasury bills, notes, and bonds) are traded. When the appetite for these securities is low, the central bank cavalry is set in motion to "print" cash and swoop up the unloved debt certificates—now a permanent rescue operation. Our globalized world is held captive by the centralized management of a monstrous "debt bubble" acting as the ultimate backstop for stock markets and the underlying socioeconomic relations. But how does this mechanism work?

Financial speculation is supposed to anticipate future profits in the real economy. However, since the neoliberal "great escape" of the 1980s, we have been flying on borrowed wings, with speculative bets extended further and further into the future as they cannot be matched by corresponding returns in the work society. In this "all-hat-no-cowboy" type of debt-driven capitalism, financial bubbles are endemic and, strictly speaking, necessary. When the speculative frenzy sets in, bets and side bets quickly multiply, so that the market value of a given asset class (real estate, bonds, energy, cash, etc.) ends up vastly exceeding its intrinsic value. For instance, housing prices swelled by around 80% between 2000 and 2006, which was not matched by growth in real earnings. As a result, we now live in a "bubble-to-bubble" economy. The proliferation of financial bubbles over the past three decades has included the tech or dot-com bubble (1996–2000), the real estate bubble (2000–2007), and the bond bubble (2009–today)—each contained within the other like Russian dolls and depending on frantic liquidity creation and bond yield suppression courtesy of central banks.

The troubling implication is that financial bubbles are now *systemic* drivers where they used to be isolated phenomena in both time and space. With the popping of Dutch tulip mania in the 1630s and the South Sea bubble of 1720 (built on the slave trade), new accumulation cycles based on mass labor power ensued; by contrast, today's bubbles can only morph into larger bubbles. The key point here is not only that Wall Street's virtual economy has reached near-total autonomy from the automated assembly lines of Main Street but that an enormous share of real production has been *colonized* by the sprawling financial sector and its credit addiction. The wealth contained in financial bubbles has no intrinsic value, but since financial markets have taken over the running of our societies, all hell breaks loose when they burst. As we shall see, the most likely outcome of this imbalance is persistent and unforgiving currency devaluation.

... to the great bluff

It is no longer a secret that our virtualized economy is dominated by three giant asset managers (BlackRock, Vanguard, and State Street) that control around 90% of the largest US shareholding companies. Yet, we should not assume that the financial plutocracy is just a corrupt version of a healthy mode of production. Rather, we would do better to focus on the historical process that brought us to where we are. This process is entirely determined by the objective law of capital's self-expansion. The qualitative leap in the function of credit commenced in the early twentieth century, when additional liquidity began supplementing the mass of value generated through investment in productive labor. During Fordism, resorting to external credit transformed from a sporadic phenomenon to the condition of possibility for mass production itself, thanks especially to the technological impulse provided by the global industrial mass murder known as World War II. As technological productivity soared and profits from individual capitals struggled to cover investments in labor power and machines, credit injections became rampant, as exemplified by Keynesian economic models based on "deficit spending." The gold standard was then abandoned so that currencies could be deregulated into fiat money (inconvertible, government-backed paper money). After US President Richard Nixon closed the gold window for good on August 15, 1971, money broke free from its labor substance, losing its objective foundation as a store of value and inaugurating the era of structural inflation. Capitalism now turned increasingly into a great bluff: a brutal self-fulfilling prophecy requiring ever higher doses of mass deception to hide its implosion.[7]

Compensatory credit and the stifled mass of real value operate as communicating vessels. While individual capitals must continue to appropriate market shares to service their debts, growing portions of this value are already part of the expanding pool of credit. In other words, each increase in real valorization (such as industrial profits) is now merely the form of appearance for exponentially larger monetary expansions. This means that the profitability of individual capitals reflects a *contraction* of the total value produced relative to the additional money supply. Today, this condition manifests as irreversible currency debasement, the result of accumulated pressure from past extensions of the credit chain. Irrespective of the multipolar conflicts in the making (i.e., the West versus BRICS+), a ubiquitous economic model cannibalized by "easy money" is bound to debase its fiat currencies throughout the globe. Whether you are in the US, Europe, or China—whose monopoly on manufacturing is now increasingly dependent on financial bubbles and central bank stimulus—the erosion of your purchasing power will not stop.

Explaining inflation solely through discrete and quantifiable factors (Covid, war in Ukraine, supply bottlenecks, etc.) typifies the positivistic myopia of the dominant economic science, which has long since abandoned the concept of value in its nexus with labor and therefore peddles a hopelessly ahistorical view of capitalism. Such a view is buoyed by the illusion that money is not a manifestation of labor valorization but is instead capable of autonomous self-expansion. Today, the multiplication of money takes place at a much faster pace than the accumulation of labor-based economic value, to the extent that money capital is increasingly "without substance," dissociated from productive labor. More precisely, the system's dependence on an ever-growing supply of insubstantial credit (generated *ex nihilo*) has turned into a pathological and ultimately self-defeating ruse designed to compensate for vanishing surplus value creation. This also means that financial markets are no longer a reflection of the real economy. On the contrary, entire societies are held captive by the purely speculative character of financial markets and their existential requirements, including the release of wave after wave of emergency, fear, and destabilization.

Capitalism is now "repurposing" from a model based upon work ethics rewarded by hedonistic mass consumerism to a fear-and-control ideology aimed at wealth preservation for the 0.1 percenters and poverty management (or worse) for all the rest. Our "system" can only continue to reproduce itself by widening the gap between the handful of superrich and the impoverished populations, with the latter expected to "own nothing and be happy" (per the World Economic Forum's infamous slogan), sacrifice their personal freedoms (e.g., the freedom of speech, muzzled by censorship and a hyperregulated cultural discourse), and surrender to the state their right to exist (which the state administers on behalf of transnational capital).

Monetary dystopia

In terms of monetary policy, the managers of crisis capitalism are caught in a lose-lose scenario. On the one hand, they must find reasons to pull more mouse-clicked cash into the present by pushing a continuous stream of global threats that act as systemic scapegoats. On the other hand, they know that this criminal rationale leads to a "dollar inflation uncertainty nightmare," as recently acknowledged by technocrats at the Federal Reserve.[8] The alternative to inflating the currency is running Wall Street (and ancillary financial markets) to the ground through sustained rate hikes. This scenario would be deflationary, but only as a devastating depression pulverizing capitals across the board, triggering further swathes of job losses, business closures, rioting, and looting. If liquidity does dry up, contagion will spread like wildfire and the globally interconnected financial sector will crash, with catastrophic "collateral damage" facing us all. Of course, this scenario could happen as a controlled accident, but only if reliable countermeasures against sudden immiseration and social unrest were already in place.

The most likely outcome is that central bankers will explicitly return to the policy of cheap money and large-scale asset purchases known as quantitative easing. Despite Jerome Powell's "higher-for-longer" policy (higher interest rates for a long period, starting in March 2022), central bankers know that the debt monster can only be tamed by oceans of inflationary liquidity, which in turn needs global alibis. However absurd, the debt crisis will continue to be fought by the issuance of more debt. For if the money supply curve declines or even flattens, the financial sector locks up and the entire economy shuts down. A brief look at the United States' skyrocketing national debt—currently beyond $34 trillion (up 1 trillion over the past 100 days),[9] approximately 122% of GDP and projected to reach 566% by 2097[10]—tells us that debt servicing alone is unsustainable without returning to the money presses.

The choice is between killing the currency to save the system and killing the system to save the currency. While either option would be disastrous for most of the world's populations, protecting the financial markets by doing "whatever it takes" would seem to be the only option available to the elites moving forward. This is contingent upon securing a continuous supply of credit while also managing the scaling down of society. In short, for the credit chains to keep stretching into the future, the financial aristocracy must preside over the gradual demolition of consumer demand, both to keep inflation in check and to harness mass discontent. In this "new normal," the combination of mass poverty and revolt is met with media manipulation, behavioral conditioning, and social engineering. The endgame begins with a seemingly endless flow of global emergencies, whose function is to (1) shift the blame for systemic implosion onto external "evil agents"; (2) justify monetary expansion (lower interest rates and injections of easy money, as occurred during the "pandemic"); and (3) potentially usher in a novel social-credit system based on CBDCs (Central Bank Digital Currencies), which are already being tested in more than 100 countries.[11]

A key component of this sinister rationale is the dismantling of the implosive economic infrastructure as it still exists today. The "great reset" plan is to replace the latter with a new monetary ecosystem: a centralized, programmable, tokenized,[12] cross-border infrastructure of digital currencies. This is no longer a secret. A quick look at the 2022 Annual Economic Report by the Bank of International Settlements—the section "The Future Monetary System" in particular[13]—confirms that we are moving, in the name of innovation, efficiency, inclusion, and sustainability, toward a centralized monetary and socioeconomic dystopia. The faster the economy decays, the closer we get to the inauguration of the new hegemonic system whose criminal ambition is to make sure that capital survives despite the incurable disease of its mode of production, to the detriment of entire populations.

Terminal sickness

A world so fanatically set on denying its own implosion has many more shocks in store for us. I begin this book by expanding on the argument that I have developed since 2020: Covid-19 was not the Bubonic plague of the new millennium but, essentially, a financial *coup* enabled by one of the largest brainwashing operations ever visited upon humankind. It was a purely performative "pandemic," a hegemonic discourse with little correspondence to real experience. As such, it served to hide the fact that *the system* was infected by terminal sickness. Data from the New York Federal Reserve reveal that an astronomical $48 trillion in term-adjusted cheap loans was handed to distressed megabanks (the Fed's "primary dealers")[14] between the last quarter of 2019 and the first quarter of 2020 alone, when the "pandemic shield" had already been raised.[15]

It should not surprise that nearly all world authorities, reading from the same script, immediately applied the rhetoric of a "war against the virus." Nor should it surprise that the epidemiological war was replaced after two years by military war, first in Ukraine and then in Gaza and the Middle East. Let us not forget that modern wars are, first and foremost, a means of credit creation and technological investment. The advancement of the military industry has been essential for the development of modernity since the fifteenth century, playing a crucial role—alongside the original accumulation through land expropriation described by Marx—in the emergence of both the state and capitalism itself.[16] Since then, the military sector has driven technological research and development through massive state investment (deficit spending) that no private company could ever sustain. The two world wars of the twentieth century had already exposed both the state's dependence on capital and capital's dependence on credit, which the state could mobilize. Similarly, the "war on Covid"—which many professional fearmongers labelled World War III—switched off most economic activity (as well as people's brains) to allow for the injection of colossal amounts of electronic cash into a debt-fueled system, which in 2019 had once again reached its breaking point. And today, when its global supremacy is under pressure, the US continues to rely on the military-industrial complex as the backbone of its currency and GDP. Expanding the debt for Ukraine or Israel allows the US to finance its mammoth army at home and abroad, which keeps faith in the dollar as world reserve currency alive. In this respect, the expansion of credit, the financing of the US military—including via proxy wars—and the propping up of US debt (Treasury securities) are perversely interconnected phenomena. It is assumed that no endeavor on planet Earth creates a more urgent need for borrowed dollars than war.

As I write this introduction (January 2024), the world economy continues its freefall. The rise in global debt is unstoppable, and most government deficits are spiraling out of control. Credit cards are exploding; car and mortgage delinquencies are surging; bankruptcy filings are breaking new records; savings are evaporating;

homelessness is skyrocketing. Still, Gaza reminds us that the worst is yet to come. If the unfolding genocide is normalized in the West through sickening hypocrisy, its brutality is reminiscent of the darkest years of the twentieth century. For the racist West, the lives of Palestinians are worth nothing. We are not supposed to care about the ethnic cleansing of the poor and the oppressed. The wealthy oppressors, on the other hand, are invited by our liberal media to illustrate the rationale for their slaughtering tactics. After turning woke victimhood into a dogma, the same media are now keen to interview criminals who, armed to the teeth by the West (mostly the United States and Germany),[17] justify the carpet-bombing of thousands of Palestinian women and children. While Gaza's pulverization was becoming the worst civilian massacre in recent times, an eight-year-old in London was suspended from school for wearing a Palestinian badge to commemorate relatives who died under Israeli bombs.[18] Does this episode alone (only one among many) not prove that we live in perverse times? That we are sleepwalking back into the worst nightmares of modern history, pretending that things are just fine? Perversion is a form of denial. The causal link between the debt hyperbubble, the financialized economy, and a continuous stream of wars and emergencies is right in front of us, hidden in plain sight. And yet, we prefer to ignore it.

A sin against the Holy Spirit

Our world is held hostage to the needs of financial markets, which are global society's center of gravity, the place where we can safely assume all major events begin. On December 13, 2023, Jerome Powell, chairman of the world's most powerful central bank (the Federal Reserve), announced that interest rate hikes would be paused. He also signaled that three rate cuts would take place in 2024. Combined with the US military machine "owning" geopolitical conflicts in Ukraine and the Middle East, Powell's announcement pushed Wall Street to spectacular heights, since the promise of looser monetary policy creates an obvious market tailwind. Powell's pivot toward rate cuts worked as a lifeline thrown to the credit-addicted financial sector riddled with myriad zombie enterprises facing frightening debt rollovers in 2024 and 2025. The pivot was therefore meant to prevent a market bloodbath as well as a sovereign bond trap. Without cheaper borrowing, in other words, current IOUs will crush not only companies and ordinary folks but also broke governments. It is crucial to reiterate that the illusion of speculative wealth is kept alive by the artificial suppression of bond yields (the cost of servicing, or paying interest on, one's debt). Marx already presented a formidable critique of "the modern doctrine that a nation becomes the richer the more deeply it is in debt." As he explains, "Public credit becomes the *credo* of capital. And with the rise of national debt-making, lack of faith in the national debt takes the place of the sin against the Holy Ghost, for which there is no forgiveness."[19] It is in respect of this lack of faith that *war works wonders*. Even the threat of escalation makes cash flow into bond markets, which keeps yields suppressed and opens the door for liquidity to inflate stocks and derivatives. In short, our rulers have missiles in one hand and derivatives in the other. It is because they manage the latter that they decide who shoots first.

Cheap liquidity is the only option going forward since it buys time. If the Fed (and ancillary central banks) fails to create more (and cheaper) electronic cash, financial assets will tank, bringing down the whole "house of cards" and the economy with it. However, the attempt to save the system by "pumping it silly" will further damage the purchasing power of fiat currencies, fueling another inflationary wave, the brunt of which will be borne by the hoi polloi. Conversely, letting inflation rip also means that the real value of the debt burden, especially for governments, is conveniently reduced, or "inflated away," through negative real rates.

The powers that be are now pushing the narrative that inflation is under control, which allows the Fed to stoke a bull market in Wall Street's echo chamber (by hinting at rate cuts). In truth, however, we have experienced in the past few years only the initial symptoms of a structural inflationary disease that continues to spread under the veil of misinformation and will necessarily explode in a second wave of calamitous monetary devaluation. All economic value will therefore be squeezed beyond belief, and everyone will wonder how we got to the stage where fiat currencies cannot keep up with prices as goods begin to disappear from the shelves.

Geopolitics of recession

In this highly manipulated economic context, it should be easy to see how geopolitical hotspots play a crucial strategic role. We must acknowledge that our "leaders" have succeeded in setting up the ideal polycrisis scenario. They can now play on multiple tables, with several red buttons available on their touchscreens. The latest one is the "geopolitics of recession" linked to the escalation of the Gaza war, which was always meant to be "a new 9/11." When Yemen's Houthi rebels began disrupting world trade by attacking cargo ships in the Red Sea—in solidarity with the Palestinian cause—the United States set up an international coalition to protect commercial shipping vessels headed toward the Suez Canal. But what if the aim of "Operation Prosperity Guardian" was the opposite of what it said on the tin: not to *protect* global trade but to test the concrete possibility of triggering a widespread recession through controlled incidents followed by more military interventions and a faster pivot to rate cuts and mouse-clicked liquidity? The disruption of one of the world's key trade routes causes shipping and insurance costs to rise sharply as companies send their goods via longer sea routes. Let us not lose sight of the central issue—today's financial casino desperately seeks scapegoats for its credit addiction. As with Covid, geopolitical crises and liquidity creation go hand in hand; they belong to the same playbook. That is to say, the inevitable recession must be pinned on external "agents of chaos" so that the money spigots can stay turned on.

In the foreseeable future, the gap between the economy and market capitalization will continue to widen, which makes it legitimate to assume that the endgame is approaching. But what do we mean by "endgame"? Firstly, that at some point the "everything bubble" will pop; and secondly, that a regime of explicit physical control over the people should by then be in place, since the money-control infrastructure and attendant flip-flopping monetary policy will no longer work. The Covid operation was the first decisive step in this direction, among other things *testing* the extent to which chaos and instability can be brought under control. As expectations that fear shuts down critical thinking were emphatically confirmed, we can be sure that panic mongering will come in handy again. A short break is enough for most people to forget and take the same bait again.

Finally, I want to return to the root cause of the mess we are in, which is missed by those who personalize guilt and focus solely on the greed of the ruling classes. Wealth creation through financial transaction is, at heart, a systemic compensatory response to the secular crisis of real accumulation, which stems from the replacement of value-creating labor with technology. This insurmountable internal barrier within contemporary capitalism can only be counteracted, in the short term, with the supply of mouse-clicked liquidity, while its disastrous consequences are already with us. For many years now, artificial money creation for fictitious financial wealth has far outstripped any real economic growth. It is vital to acknowledge that the social narrative of "organic growth" through labor-intensive economic activity is already dead and buried—and we should not miss it. Yet, we are faced with a stubborn reluctance, especially noticeable among those on the left, to develop a serious reflection on the destructive nature of crisis capitalism. For our "radical" intelligentsia, it appears more convenient to acquiesce to propaganda or succumb to oversimplified moral judgments than to engage in the critique of political economy, which is the critique of capital as an impersonal totality that permeates each one of us. The least we can do is acknowledge that there is no turning back from *this* path to collective catastrophe. No nostalgic pining for healthier forms of capitalism will save us. As in the buildup to the 2007–8 global financial crisis, things today are already much worse under the surface than the psychopaths in the control room are letting on, with the crucial difference that bailouts and monetary policy acrobatics will just not cut it this time. Steering does not work after you have driven off the cliff.

Each of the seven chapters in this book revisits the basic conceptual foundations of my argument on emergency capitalism by linking them to key contemporary events. It is hoped that the gradual refining of the argument will help to paint a clear picture of the currently unfolding implosion and its causes.

1.
Systemic Collapse and Pandemic Simulation

> Precisely because of their mental capacities, human beings are not only enslaved, but turned into willing slaves of capital.
>
> —Jacques Camatte[1]

IN 2020, THE RULERS OF THE WORLD decided to freeze the global economy in the face of a pathogen that targeted the unproductive (those over 80) almost exclusively. The discrepancy between the actual epidemiological danger and the measures taken was staggering from the beginning. But because most of humanity increasingly struggles to grasp—both emotionally and intellectually—the criminal nature of today's power relations, entire populations (well-educated, reasonable, and enlightened) fell straight into the trap that was laid before them. Most people sheepishly complied with the global emergency blackmail, accepting the top-down decision to lock down society and believing (or, worse, pretending to believe) that grotesque restrictions of all kinds were mandated out of *compassion*. The modern masses' gullibility vis-à-vis power is the result of decades of soft ideological manipulation and intellectual debilitation, both relying on the fact that power—real power—remains invisible, operating from behind a smokescreen of inconsequential political gibberish. But the more invisible it is, the stronger its hold over the people can be.

The great freeze

In the 1960s, Jacques Lacan argued that capitalist power works by vanishing, by making itself undetectable, dissimulating not only its authority but especially its impotence (two sides of the same coin). Everything seems to function spontaneously in capitalism, as if no one is giving or obeying orders but just following their free and natural desires: "What is striking, and what no one seems to see, is that by virtue of the fact that the clouds of impotence have been aired, the master signifier only appears even more unassailable [...] Where is it? How can it be named? How can it be located—other than through its murderous effects, of course."[2] As demonstrated by the Covid fraud, the late capitalist master loves to hide behind a smokescreen of humanitarian benevolence. If it appears repressive at times, this is only to protect you. For instance, today's stakeholder capitalism (capital *for* and *with* the state; Big Society) wants to safeguard your liberties—which include the freedom to select your pronouns, your choice of "vaccine," and whether you will die of destitution or under some bombs. While the traditional master relied on symbolic authority, the capitalist master is, in principle, *against* authority. Or rather, it delegates authority to the intangible objectivity of its modus operandi—the economic dogma naturalized in the social relation. Recently, the "neoliberal turn" buried the dirty ideologies of the past under the ecumenical sense of responsibility shouldered by our leaders, whose role is to serve communities by "solving problems," or in other words, by making sure that nobody disturbs the smooth functioning of capital. And Lacan's point, which the pseudopandemic has emphatically demonstrated, is that the elementary stratagem of global capitalist power (making itself invisible, "decolonizing" itself) opens the space for more insidious forms of control and domestication—which become especially vicious at a time of systemic implosion.

Guy Debord expanded on the above as a key feature of totalitarianism:

> The ruling totalitarian-ideological class is the ruler of a world turned upside down. The more powerful the class, the more it claims not to exist, and its power is employed above all to enforce this claim. It is modest only on this one point, however, because this officially nonexistent bureaucracy simultaneously attributes the crowning achievements of history to its own infallible leadership. Though its existence is everywhere in evidence, the bureaucracy must be invisible as a class. As a result, all social life becomes insane.[3]

Among other things, Covid served to strengthen trust in the insane world of "global cooperation" guided by the sorcery of financial capitalism. In 2020, the political elites (especially those in the West) sought to regain the illusion of the leadership they had long since lost. They succeeded, albeit briefly, by fostering an unparalleled wave of panic among populations worldwide and by associating themselves with what they termed "real science." Yet, those very same political leaders could not hide their miserable subalternity for long, since their only real purpose is to serve the interest of financial power, which is where true mastery lies. But what matters is that we have now entered an age of widespread socioeconomic anemia, whereby the global capitalist vampire requires ever larger blood transfusions to stay alive—in both a literal and a metaphorical sense.

Today's world system improvises a life it does not have thanks to continuous injections of cheap liquidity. Capitalism is no longer even a free-market regime guided by the criteria of fair value, price discovery, business risk and other similarly outdated dynamics. Rather, it has turned into a huge community of junkies, all desperately enslaved by the only pusher capable of feeding the addiction: the central bank. Global capitalism now survives only through Monopoly money distributed by central bank ATMs. As soon as the money is disbursed, it turns into a liability to be managed through new credit injections. In 2019, this feedback loop threatened to break, to the extent that a Lehman-2 type of event was deemed necessary. In the last months of the pre-Covid era, the world (economy) was already crammed with terminally ill (financial) patients attached to (liquidity) ventilators.

As I will cover in greater detail below, in September 2019, the global economy suffered a potentially lethal heart attack. The culprit was not a virus but the "repocalypse,"[4] an event that, while largely obscured by the media, brought back memories of 2008 for many financial operators. The repo loan market is the virtual place where financial institutions lend each other money, to the tune of trillions of dollars per day. It is the financial equivalent of our cardiovascular system, and its interest rate can be regarded as the beating heart of the global economy. In mid-September 2019, the Fed's daily interventions began to keep the repo market on artificial life support while repo rates spiked, until the "miraculous" arrival of Virus—a godsend that, as we shall see, allowed for mouth-to-mouth resuscitation. Here, one needs to realize that although the risk of systemic lock up is dramatically real, the eschatological fantasy of the end-times is opportunistically exploited.[5] The "pandemic" revealed this exploitation by moving the apocalyptic goalposts from the economic to the microbiological context.

In Autumn 2019, most of us failed to realize that we were perched at the edge of a volcano poised to erupt. Mass distraction in the age of information overload is central to the functioning of power. Populations must be entertained and distracted by all sorts of trivial matters and irrelevant "cultural conflicts." They must turn their heads toward horizons of meaning that are immaterial compared to what is truly at stake. They must remain comfortably numb within their cultural bubbles, at a distance from the epicenter of real risk. They must be lobotomized by political correctness. Thus, amid various distracting narratives, very few realized that the Fed was stealthily trying to rescue the financial system through hefty daily repo auctions. At the same time, insiders at major corporations were selling shares by the cartload, for they knew that the Great Pandemic Reset was coming.

It is essential to emphasize that contemporary capitalism faces a specific paradox. The entire financial infrastructure is now *too big to fail*; it cannot avoid being saved, for if it did fail, the outcome would be the disintegration of our "way of life." On the other hand, it is also *too big not to fail*; the burden of hyperfinancialized capitalism can no longer be sustained without devastating consequences. In the meantime, the old political categories have dissolved. The proletariat—in the Marxian sense of a socioeconomic group endowed with class consciousness and capable of action—has been reduced to an inert, gullible, and easily exploitable *Lumpenproleriat* ("rabble"); an amorphous and uprooted social class engaged in desperate competition with migrants. The world is already split between a small minority of superrich owners and the immiserated, largely depoliticized masses, which must be managed "creatively."

Let us not forget that before deploying the Covid artillery, the capitalist matrix was already parasitizing on a series of manipulated emergencies. In 2019, the world was a pressure cooker, replete with low-intensity geopolitical conflicts, from Afghanistan to Yemen, Syria, Egypt, Iraq, Libya, and sub-Saharan Africa (especially Nigeria, Somalia, Burkina Faso, Mali, South Sudan, Cameroon, Democratic Republic of Congo); the hostilities between Turkey and the Kurds, Israel and Palestine, India and Pakistan; and destabilization in Lebanon, Chile, and Hong Kong. Yet the stock markets showed no signs of slowing down. In addition, the year 2019 witnessed a significant surge in nationalism, populism, and protectionism (tariff wars). Few, however, realized that the rise of nationalism was a card played by the very system that had faltered in 2008: it represented a false alternative aimed at relaunching globalism itself. There was, in other words, a concerted effort to persuade the public that reliance on the transnational establishment was indispensable for countering the surge of predominantly right-wing national sovereignty ideologies. The good (globalist) cop was working in complete harmony with the bad (nationalist) cop—and it still does. We must stop believing that the financial markets are a simple reflection of what takes place in the real world—the exact opposite is now true: the real world, including its politics, reflects the needs and "aspirations" of financial markets, driven by their algorithms. In fact, the financial galaxy imposes an enormous cost in terms of human lives and social devastation. With the increase in leveraging and a structural debt-chasing-debt mechanism in place (paying off loans with new loans), destabilization becomes a key strategic component of the financialized economy. If during the Cold War the "strategy of tension" (managed chaos) served to maintain a stable opposition between the two blocs, it is deployed today to keep global capital flows artificially alive—whatever it takes. Covid-19 was the perfect example of this perverse logic.

While by the end of 2019 the Fed was dealing with a highly contagious crisis in the repo market, China, the world's "global factory" and second largest economy, was dealing with its own demons. On January 20, 2020, Chinese authorities acknowledged person-to-person transmission of the novel coronavirus.[6] Prior to that day, China's top leaders and media outlets had not regarded containment of the epidemic as a high priority. Thereafter, however, they began taking aggressive measures to control its spread. That was only a week after it had been certified that the 2019 Chinese GDP had fallen to its lowest level in 29 years.[7] By then, the alibi of a trade war with Washington had also vanished. In fact, it had been replaced by a "Phase One" Economic and Trade Agreement signed by the US and China on January 15, 2020.[8] The timing of that deal is significant, as the "pandemic" was about to officially be crowned global enemy number one. Arguably, China also needed an invisible external foe to blame for worsening living conditions and the changing role of its central bank (the People's Bank of China), which until then had limited itself to small interventions on bank reserve requirements. The whole world, including China, was now forced onto the emergency freight train.

Follow the magic money!

In pre-Covid times, the world economy was on the verge of another colossal meltdown. Eleven years after the Global Financial Crisis (GFC), another intervention in the mechanics of the monetary system was needed. This time, however, it was going to be much more shocking. Here is a brief chronicle of how the pressure mounted in 2019:

June 2019: In its *Annual Economic Report*,[9] the Swiss-based Bank of International Settlements (BIS), the "central bank of all central banks," sets the global alarm bells ringing. The document highlights "overheating [...] in the leveraged loan market," where "credit standards have been deteriorating" and "collateralized loan obligations (CLOs) have surged—reminiscent of the steep rise in collateralized debt obligations [CDOs] that amplified the subprime crisis [in 2008]." Simply stated, the financial industry's underbelly is once again full of junk.

August 9, 2019: The BIS issues a working paper calling for "unconventional monetary policy measures" to "*insulate the real economy* from further deterioration in financial conditions."[10] The paper indicates that, by offering "direct credit to the economy" during a crisis, central bank lending "can replace commercial banks in providing loans to firms."

August 15, 2019: BlackRock, the world's most powerful investment fund (with more than $11 trillion in assets currently under management), issues a white paper entitled "Dealing with the next downturn."[11] Essentially, it confirms the BIS vision, suggesting that the US Federal Reserve inject liquidity *directly* into the financial system to prevent "a dramatic downturn." The message is again unequivocal: "An unprecedented response is needed when monetary policy is exhausted and fiscal policy alone is not enough. That response will likely involve 'going direct,'" which means "the central bank finding ways to get central bank money directly in the hands of public and private sector spenders." In short, a direct version of quantitative easing, but with an eye to potential hyperinflation: "Examples include the Weimar Republic in the 1920s as well as Argentina and Zimbabwe more recently." BlackRock therefore proposes "an unusual coordination of fiscal and monetary policy that is limited to an unusual situation—a liquidity trap—with a predefined exit point and an explicit inflation objective." The aim is to eventually "get the inflation genie back in the bottle."

August 22–24, 2019: G7 central bankers meet in Jackson Hole, Wyoming, to discuss BlackRock's paper along with urgent measures to prevent the looming meltdown. In the prescient words of James Bullard,[12] president of the St Louis Federal Reserve: "We just have to stop thinking that next year things are going to be normal."

September 15–16, 2019: The downturn is officially inaugurated by a sudden spike in repo rates (from 2% to 10%). "Repo" is shorthand for "repurchase agreement," a contract through which banks borrow money against collateral assets (normally, debt securities). At the time of the exchange, financial operators (banks) undertake to buy the assets back at a higher price, typically overnight. In a nutshell, repos are short-term collateralized loans. They are the main source of funding for traders in most markets, especially the derivatives galaxy. A liquidity freeze in the repo markets can have devastating domino effects for all major financial sectors.

September 17, 2019: The Fed begins the emergency monetary program, pumping hundreds of billions of dollars per week into Wall Street, effectively executing BlackRock's "going direct" plan. (Unsurprisingly, in March 2020, the Fed will hire BlackRock, also known as "the fourth branch of government,"[13] to manage the bailout packages in response to the Covid-19 crisis.)[14]

September 19, 2019: Donald Trump signs Executive Order 13887,[15] establishing a *National Influenza Vaccine Task Force* whose aim is to develop a "5-year national plan (Plan) to promote the use of more agile and scalable vaccine manufacturing technologies and to accelerate development of vaccines that protect against many or all influenza viruses." This is to counteract "an influenza pandemic," which, "unlike seasonal influenza […] has the potential to spread rapidly around the globe, infect higher numbers of people, and cause high rates of illness and death in populations that lack prior immunity." At the time—more precisely, on November 21, 2019—Claudia Stauber predicted the "pandemic" in a video recording for her blog Cabin Talk (Vermont),[16] which was subsequently removed by the algorithm for "violating YouTube's community guidelines," as is increasingly the case with any questioning of the propaganda. Here's what Stauber recorded in September 2019, after learning of Trump's Executive Order 13887:

> They are planning a pandemic… First of all, Bill Gates said, "there will be a pandemic and at least 30 million people will die." Boom. Then, just now Trump signed

> an executive order for a new task force to make a better and faster flu vaccine because, in case there is a pandemic, we're not prepared enough… how much more clear can it get that we have mandatory vaccines just around the corner… and if there is a pandemic anywhere, it will be global… all the countries will say, "Oh we have to rally together, because the virus can travel so fast we'll all globally have to implement the same laws."

Claudia Stauber's main bone of contention was the mandatory vaccinations and, more generally, the authoritarian climate rapidly spreading in the US. While she seemed unaware of the deep economic causality behind the "pandemic," she foresaw that it would be a planned event. All she needed to do was read the text of Trump's executive order, as the "pandemic" already features in that text as a *fait accompli*. Remember that we are in mid-September 2019—exactly the time when the repo-rate accident called for the Fed's emergency interventions.

October 18, 2019: In New York, a global zoonotic pandemic is simulated during *Event 201*,[17] a strategic exercise coordinated by the Johns Hopkins Biosecurity Center and the Bill and Melinda Gates Foundation.

January 15, 2020: The United States and China sign a Phase One agreement that ends the "trade war." President Trump says that relations between the two countries are the "best ever."

January 21–24, 2020: The annual meeting of the World Economic Forum (WEF) takes place in Davos, Switzerland, under the auspicious title "Stakeholders for a Cohesive and Sustainable World." There, global world leaders young and old not only discuss the usual topics, including climate emergency, tech investment, reskilling, responsible AI, poverty in Africa, and so on, but also the imminent pandemic.[18] The "novel coronavirus, the Wuhan virus," is introduced by WEF's Young Global Leader Juliana Chan,[19] as is the necessity for lockdowns, social restrictions, and "inflexible vaccinations." "We have this good you want to participate in, public education; this [mandatory vaccination] is the price you have to pay for it"—as Lisa Sanders (a US physician) aptly put it.[20]

January 23, 2020: China locks down Wuhan and other cities of the Hubei province.

March 11, 2020: The World Health Organization's director general calls Covid-19 a global pandemic. The rest is history.

Joining the dots

As most of us learned as kids, joining the dots is a simple and fun exercise. It allows a well-defined figure to form, which in our case can be read as follows: "pandemic" lockdowns and the global suspension of economic transactions were intended to (1) allow the Fed to flood the ailing financial markets and global economy with tons of freshly printed money and (2) escalate a global control system as the blueprint for a neo-techno-feudal regime of capitalist profiteering. As we shall see, the two aims merge into one, since operation Covid was designed to allow the ruling elites to accelerate their cynical response to systemic implosion. In 2019, the global economy was plagued by the same sickness that had caused the 2008 credit crunch, but at a much more advanced stage. Essentially, it was suffocating under an unsustainable amount of debt. While state economies were increasingly burdened by deficits, most companies could not generate enough profits to cover interest payments on their liabilities and stayed afloat only by taking on new loans. "Zombie companies" (with low year-over-year profitability, falling turnover, squeezed margins, limited cashflow, and highly leveraged balance sheets) were spreading everywhere.[21] To understand the repo market crisis of mid-September 2019, we must place it within the context of a very fragile constellation.

When the air is saturated with flammable material, a single spark can cause an explosion. And in the magical world of finance, everything is connected: one flap of a butterfly's wings in a given sector can send the entire house of cards tumbling. In financial markets powered by cheap loans, any increase in interest rates is potentially cataclysmic for banks, hedge funds, pension funds and the entire government bond market, because the cost of borrowing increases and liquidity quickly dries up. This is what happened with the "repocalypse" of September 2019, when interest rates spiked to around 10% in a matter of hours and panic broke out affecting not only money markets but also futures, options, currencies, and other markets where traders bet by borrowing from repos. The only way to defuse the contagion was by throwing unlimited liquidity into the system—like helicopters dropping thousands of gallons of water on a wildfire. This is what the Fed did when it bolted into action on September 17, beginning the execution of what now appears to be a long-prepared strategy.

Between 2007 and 2010, during the GFC, the Fed had already secretly funneled a whopping $29 trillion in cheap revolving loans (below 1% interest) to Wall Street megabanks (and their foreign counterparts), who were flirting with insolvency at the time.[22] Banks like Citigroup had been made to look healthy prior to late 2008 but were in fact accumulating massive losses due to high levels of leverage and risk-taking. While Lehman Brothers was conveniently scapegoated, in truth it was the whole system that was rotten. And when the system was bailed out, the Wall Street banks under the Fed's generous credit diet continued to charge double-digit interest rates on credit cards while foreclosing on millions of homes, profiting from shorting their own collapsing mortgage bonds, and using public funds to pay themselves billions of dollars in bonuses.

So, why should anyone be surprised when the same situation presented itself again in 2019? After all, since November 2008, the Fed's balance sheet had ballooned to unprecedented levels through consecutive rounds of quantitative easing, to the extent that the strategy of unlimited purchasing of Treasury bonds and mortgage-based securities came to be known as "QE infinity."[23] By late October 2014, the Fed (the lender and buyer of last resort) had accumulated $4.5 trillion in assets. It was already crystal clear at that point that the economy (and therefore the reproduction of entire societies) was *ontologically* dependent on monumental credit creation programs, which should now be regarded as the financial counterpart to the endless release of diabolical states of emergency.

It is worth keeping in mind that rather than being "public," central banks like the Federal Reserve are controlled by private megabanks. For instance, the largest shareowners of the New York Fed (the most powerful money-creating machine among 12 regional Fed banks) are Citibank, JP Morgan Chase, Goldman Sachs, Morgan Stanley, and Bank of New York Mellon. These institutions effectively control the Fed's magic money spigot and, as primary dealers, *are also among its main beneficiaries*. Each of the 12 regional Fed banks has 9 board members, 6 of which are elected by the member banks. The blatantly incestuous nature of such financial liaison is further aggravated by the role played by the US Treasury, which can formally veto the Fed but operates in practice as a revolving door between the supposedly "public" central bank and the private bankers. To provide just a few examples, Janet Yellen, current secretary of US Treasury, was chair of the Federal Reserve between 2014 and 2018; Jerome Powell, current chair of the Federal Reserve, worked for Carlyle Group, one of the world's largest private equity firms (and in 2005 founded Severn Capital Partners, another private investment firm); Alan Greenspan, Fed chairman from 1987 to 2006, worked as corporate director for JP Morgan, Mobil, and other private corporations. These incestuous connections are replicated at other central banks. Mario Draghi, president of the European Central Bank (ECB) between 2011 and 2019, was vice chairman and managing director of Goldman Sachs between 2002 and 2005. The swindle is right in front of our eyes, and yet we choose not to see it.

As anticipated, the Fed began its repo loan operations in the last quarter of 2019. The monetary avalanche set in motion at that point had nothing to do with the virus and everything to do with the critical condition of the financial sector. The mainstream narrative should therefore be reversed: in March 2020, the stock market did not collapse because lockdowns had to be imposed; rather, lockdowns had to be imposed because financial markets were already collapsing. With lockdowns came the suspension of business transactions, which drained the demand for credit and stopped the contagion. In other words, restructuring the financial architecture through extraordinary monetary policy *was contingent on the economy's engine being turned off*, which in turned required a major *casus belli*.

In short, in 2020 we were confronted with another bailout, but this time under the cover of a virus. As economist Ellen Brown put it, "In September 2019 and again in March 2020, Wall Street banks were quietly bailed out from a liquidity crisis in the repo market that could otherwise have bankrupted them. There was no bail-in of private funds, no heated congressional debate, and no public vote. It was all done unilaterally by unelected bureaucrats at the Federal Reserve." Brown's analysis is worth quoting at length:

> After 2008, banks were afraid to lend to each other for fear the borrowing banks might be insolvent and might not pay the loans back. Instead, the lenders turned to the repo market, where loans were supposedly secured

with collateral. The problem was that the collateral could be "rehypothecated," or used for several loans at once; and by September 2019, the borrower side of the repo market had been taken over by hedge funds, which were notorious for risky rehypothecation. Many large institutional lenders therefore pulled out, driving the cost of borrowing at one point from 2% to 10%. Rather than letting the banks fail and forcing a bail-in of private creditors' funds, the Fed quietly stepped in and saved the banks by becoming the "repo lender of last resort." But the liquidity crunch did not abate, and by March the Fed was making $1 trillion per day available in overnight loans. The central bank was backstopping the whole repo market, including the hedge funds, an untenable situation. In March 2020, under cover of a national crisis, the Fed therefore flung the doors open to its discount window, where only banks could borrow. Previously, banks were reluctant to apply there because the interest was at a penalty rate and carried a stigma, signaling that the bank must be in distress. But that concern was eliminated when the Fed announced in a March 15 press release that the interest rate had been dropped to 0.25% (virtually zero). The reserve requirement was also eliminated, the capital requirement was relaxed, and all banks in good standing were offered loans of up to 90 days, "renewable on a daily basis." The loans could be continually rolled over.[24]

Faced with the prospect of a chain reaction of insolvencies and defaults, the Fed executed BlackRock's "going direct" playbook. And only an *induced economic coma* could provide the Fed with the necessary space and rationale to defuse the time bomb ticking away in the repo market and, more widely, the financial sector.

Screened by mass hysteria, the US central bank plugged the holes in the shadow banking system. However, the "going direct" blueprint should also be framed as a *desperate* measure, for it only managed to prolong the agony of a mechanism set to implode.

At the heart of our predicament lies an insurmountable structural impasse. Debt-leveraged financialization is contemporary capitalism's *only* line of flight, the inevitable forward escape route for a reproductive model that has reached its historical limit. Capitals head for financial markets because the labor-based economy is increasingly unprofitable. How did we get to this? The answer can be summarized as follows:

1. The economy's mission to generate surplus value is both the drive to *exploit* the workforce and to *expel* it from production. This is what Marx called capital's "moving contradiction."[25] While it constitutes the quintessence of our mode of production, this contradiction today backfires, turning the mode of production into a mode of permanent devastation.

2. The basic reason for this change of fortune is the *objective* failure of the labor-capital dialectic. The unprecedented acceleration in technological automation since the 1970s causes more labor power to be ejected from production than to be (re)absorbed. The contraction of the volume of capital invested in productive labor ultimately means that the purchasing power of a growing part of the world population is falling, with debt and immiseration the inevitable consequences.

3. As less economic value is extracted from commodity-producing labor, capital seeks immediate returns in the debt-leveraged financial sector rather than in the real economy (or by investing in socially constructive sectors like education, research, and public services).

4. Today's financial elites are not merely the functionaries of capital but also, increasingly, the *functional manipulator* of a socioeconomic system in freefall. The events of 2001 (the World Trade Center attack), 2008 (the Great Financial Crisis), and 2020 (the Covid pandemic) should be understood as the main acts (so far) of a global theater of mass deception whose basic function is to delay the collapse of a world-system that could only, since its official inauguration in 1989 (the fall of the Berlin Wall), embark on a downward journey.

The bottom line is that the paradigm shift underway is the necessary condition for the *totalitarian* survival of capitalism, which is no longer able to reproduce its own social form through mass wage labor and the attendant consumerist utopia. The pandemic agenda was ultimately dictated by the specter of systemic implosion, which, at present, could threaten a drastic reconfiguration of the existing power relations that the elites are not willing to face. The deep causality that produced the Covid fraud, however, originates in the global profitability downturn of a mode of production that rampant automation is making obsolete. For this *immanent* reason, capitalism is increasingly unstable and aggressive, since it must rely on continuous extensions of fictitious capital, the financial centralization of wealth and power, and the unleashing of a near-permanent state of emergency.

If we follow the money, we should be able to see that the results achieved by the economic blockade deviously justified by the "pandemic" are far from negligible, not only in terms of social engineering (preparing the masses for increasing doses of authoritarianism) but also financial predation. I will quickly highlight three of them: (1) as anticipated, it has allowed the Fed to momentarily rebalance the banks' books by printing grotesque amounts of cash out of thin air; (2) it has accelerated the extinction of small and medium-sized companies and the lower middle-classes, allowing major groups to monopolize trade flows and wealth creation; (3) it has enabled the growth of e-commerce, the explosion of Big Tech, and the proliferation of the pharma-dollar. In 2020 alone, the wealth of the planet's roughly 2,200 billionaires grew by $1.9 trillion,[26] an increase without historical precedent. All thanks to a pathogen so lethal that, according to official data, only 99.8% of the infected survive,[27] most of whom without experiencing any serious symptoms. In this respect, I must add that the debate on the actual existence or origin of the pathogen holds secondary significance for my analysis. What matters, rather, is to highlight how the Covid shutdown was a *fabricated* global emergency that facilitated the acceleration of totalitarian capitalism as the only line of flight for a fatally sick socioeconomic model.

Doing capitalism differently?

The economic motif of the Covid deception must be placed within a broader context of social transformation. If we merely scratch the surface of the official narrative, a neofeudal scenario begins to take form. Masses of increasingly unproductive consumers are being regimented and cast aside, or exterminated, simply because Mr. Global no longer knows what to do with them. Together with the underemployed and the excluded, the impoverished middle classes are now a problem to be handled with the stick of lockdowns, curfews, mass vaccination, propaganda, the technological militarization of society, "divide and conquer" narratives, and eugenics, rather than with the carrot of work, consumption, participatory democracy, and social rights (replaced in the collective imaginary by the civil rights of minorities).

It is therefore delusional to believe that the purpose of lockdowns was therapeutic and humanitarian. *When has capital ever cared for the people?* Indifference and misanthropy are the typical traits of both capital and its managers, whose only passion is profit and the power that comes with it. As previously noted, capitalist power can be broadly associated with the names of the three biggest investment funds in the world: BlackRock, Vanguard, and State Street Global Advisors. These giants, sitting at the center of a huge cluster of financial entities, oversee a mass of assets whose value is nearly half the global GDP, and they are major shareholders in around 90% of listed companies. Around them gravitate transnational institutions like the International Monetary Fund, the World Bank, the World Economic Forum, the Trilateral Commission, and the Bank for International Settlements, whose function is to coordinate consensus within the financial constellation and beyond. We can safely assume that all key strategic decisions—economic, political, and military—are made by or with the approval of these elites. Or do we really believe that Virus took them by surprise? Rather, Covid is the name of a special weapon of psychological warfare that was deployed precisely when it was deemed most needed.

Why should we trust the World Health Organization, a mega pharmaceutical cartel that is *not* in charge of public health but rather of marketing private products worldwide at the most profitable rates possible? In the hands of Big Pharma, medicine tends to destroy natural defenses and to replace them with artificial (often toxic) ones. Public health problems stem from abysmal working conditions, poor nutrition, air, water, and food pollution, and above all from *rampant poverty*, yet none of these "pathogens" are on the WHO's list of humanitarian concerns. The immense conflicts of interest among the predators of the pharmaceutical industry, national and supranational medical agencies, and cynical political enforcers is an open secret.

If the military industry needs wars, the pharmaceutical industry needs diseases. It is no coincidence that "public health" is by far the most profitable sector of the world economy, to the extent that Big Pharma spends roughly three times as much as Big Oil and roughly twice as much as Big Tech on lobbying.[28] The potentially endless demand for experimental gene concoctions, pills, drugs, and any other "treatments" offers pharmaceutical cartels the prospect of nearly unlimited profit streams, especially when guaranteed by mass vaccination programs subsidized by public money (i.e., more debt that will fall on our heads). Why have all "alternative" Covid treatments been banned or sabotaged? Probably because, as the FDA candidly admits, the use of emergency vaccines is only possible if "there are no adequate, approved and available alternatives."[29]

The staging of the Covid pantomime succeeded through an unprecedented manipulation of public opinion. Every "public debate" was shamelessly *privatized*, or rather monopolized, by technical-scientific committees bankrolled by the financial elites. Every "free discussion" was legitimized by adherence to pseudoscientific protocols carefully purged from the socioeconomic context. One "followed the science" while pretending not to know that "science follows the money." Karl Popper's famous assertion that "real science" can only thrive within the framework of liberal capitalism, which he referred to as "the open society," now comes true in the globalist narrative that endorses organizations such as George Soros's Open Society Foundations. The combination of "real science" and "open and inclusive society" made the Covid consensus nearly impossible to challenge. Let us not forget that the privatized discourse on public health has long been a means of social engineering as well as economic leverage. Indeed, it has replaced religion as the ideological vanguard of capitalist imperialism—as clearly understood by philanthropist Frederick T. Gates, chief business adviser to the great oil industrialist John Rockefeller. In 1901, Gates persuaded Rockefeller to create a research facility for experimental medicine against infectious diseases, the Rockefeller Institute for Medical Research (later renamed Rockefeller University). Nothing new on the Western front.

For Covid-19, then, we could imagine the following agenda. A fictitious narrative is prepared based on an epidemic risk presented in such a way as to promote fear and submissive behavior. All that is needed is an epidemiologically ambiguous pathogen on which to build an aggressive marketing campaign,[30] a tale of contagion relatable to geographical areas where the impact of respiratory or vascular diseases in the elderly and immunocompromised population is high—perhaps with the aggravating factor of heavy pollution. There is no need to make much up, given that intensive care units in "advanced" societies had already collapsed in the years preceding Covid's arrival,[31] and were thereby ready for the pandemic script.

But this time there is method in madness. A state of emergency is declared, which triggers panic, causing the clogging of hospitals and care homes at high risk of sepsis, the application of nefarious protocols, and the suspension of medical care. *Et voilà*, the killer virus becomes a self-fulfilling prophecy. The deafening propaganda raging across the main centers of financial power (especially North America and Europe) is essential to maintain widespread submission. Entire populations exposed to heavy media bombardment surrender through self-discipline, adhering with grotesque enthusiasm to forms of "civic responsibility" where coercion is sold as altruism. The world is suddenly at war against Virus.

And yet, we should never lose sight of the economic motif. As noted, several trillions in newly printed cash were created by central banks with a few mouse clicks and injected in the financial system and the retail economy. The primary aim of the printing spree was to plug liquidity gaps. The newly created money is *insubstantial* in real capitalist terms, but it has the power to profoundly destabilize the system. This is what Marx called "fictitious capital," a virtual outgrowth that continues to expand today in an orbital loop almost independent of economic activity on the ground. The bottom line is that this inordinate amount of cash cannot be allowed to flood the real economy, for the latter would overheat and trigger a hyperinflationary nightmare. As Robert Kurz put it in 1995, "Should the entire mountain of fictitious commercial values be set into motion as real effective demand, this would lead to an immediate situation of hyperinflation even in the West."[32] And this is where Virus came in handy. If it initially served to "insulate the real economy" (to quote again from the BIS paper), it later legitimized a very *tentative* reopening, characterized by submission to the vaccination dogma and other methods of mass regimentation, which might soon include "climate lockdowns."[33] Remember how we were told that only vaccines would give us back our "freedom"? All too predictably, we then discovered that not only were "vaccines" useless (in the best-case scenario) but that the road to freedom was littered with "variants" and "subvariants," which is to say, iterations of Virus whose purpose was to prolong the emergency pantomime while shepherding us deeper into a new variety of toxic capitalism equipped with specific inflation targets.

While the Covid crime was far from perfect, the orchestrators of the global *coup* must nevertheless be credited with sadistic brilliance, for their sleight of hand succeeded, perhaps even beyond expectations. However, there is still hope, for any power that aims at totalization is destined to fail, and this also applies to the high priests of the Covid religion and the institutional puppets they have mobilized to roll out the psyop. Power deludes itself about its omnipotence. Those sitting in the control room fail to realize the extent to which their dominance is inherently uncertain. What they do not see is that their mastery is hostage to a "higher mission" to which they are at least partly blind, namely the *anonymous self-reproduction* of the capitalist matrix. Today's real power lies within the profit-making machine whose only purpose is to continue its reckless journey, potentially leading to the premature extinction of Homo sapiens. The elites who have conned the world into Covid obedience are the anthropomorphic manifestation of the *capitalist automaton*, whose invisibility is as cunning as that of Virus itself. And the novelty of our era is that the "locked-down society" is the model that best guarantees the reproducibility of the capitalist matrix, irrespective of its dystopian destination.

2.
A Self-Fulfilling Prophecy

Sheep spend their entire lives being afraid of the wolf but end up eaten by the shepherd.

—African proverb

ESSENTIALLY, COVID WAS A SYMPTOM of financial capital running amok. More broadly, it was a symptom of a world that is no longer able to reproduce itself by profiting from human labor, thus relying by necessity (as well as greed of course, which is a central component of capital as such) on a compensatory logic of *perpetual monetary injections*. While the structural shrinking of the work-based economy inflates the financial sector, the latter's volatility can only be contained through global emergencies, mass propaganda, and biopolitical tyranny. How can we break out of this vicious cycle? This will no doubt be *the* question for the years to come.

The Covid symptom

In chapter 1, I highlighted how automated capitalism has, since the advent of microelectronics, been busy abolishing its own substance in wage labor. We have now passed the point of no return.[1] Due to escalating technological advance, capital is increasingly impotent vis-à-vis its mission to squeeze surplus value out of labor power. With the unleashing of artificial intelligence, this truly becomes mission impossible—*game over*. This means that the foundations of our world no longer reside in the *socially necessary* labor contained in commodities such as cars, telephones, or toothpaste. Rather, they reside in highly flammable debt-leveraged speculation on financial assets like stocks, bonds, and especially derivatives, whose value is securitized indefinitely. Only the religious belief that the mass of these assets creates value prevents us from taking cognizance of the yawning abyss beneath our feet. And when our faith dwindles, divine providence intervenes by sending us into collective hypnosis through apocalyptic tales and attendant narratives of salvation.

Yet, reality is stubborn, and it keeps knocking on our door. With the financial tumor spreading through the social body, capital opted to release its leviathan doppelganger: a vampire that feeds on global chaos and business models anchored in digital technology with the potential to securitize the entirety of life on earth. The writing is on the wall; a "soft dictatorship" is already on our doorstep. Today, resisting the tide means first of all defending the elementary and inviolable dimension of human freedom, a nonnegotiable starting point for the construction of an alternative social project. There is still time, but we need collective awakening, critical awareness, and the courage to embrace real change.

Let us surmise that our future will be characterized by the following events: (1) central banks will continue to create inordinate amounts of electronic money, mostly destined for financial markets; (2) the "global emergency" model of governance will continue to distract and hypnotize entire populations; (3) liberal democracies will be stealthily dismantled and eventually replaced by regimes based on what we might refer to as a "digitized panopticon," a metaverse of control technologies legitimized by deafening, metaemergency noise. This is essentially a future with no future: "As contemporary finance enables a monetization of the future by means of a *reductio ad certum* of prospective value, it effectively negates the radical alterity inherent to the future. And it does so, literally, in the name of money."[2]

Is this too dark a prediction? Not if we consider that the 2020–22 health crisis rollercoaster (lockdowns followed by partial openings alternating with new closures caused by mini waves of contagion) functioned as a global role-play in which institutional actors made sure the bio-emergency ghost would continue to circulate. The simple reason for this is that without Virus to justify sustained monetary stimulus, the debt-leveraged financial sector would have collapsed. At the same time, however, rising inflation coupled with supply-chain bottlenecks threatened a recession. This catch-22 appeared difficult to overcome, which is why the elites did not let go of the Covid narrative. The introduction of digital health passports such as the "Green Pass" (which were prior to 2021 still ridiculed as conspiracy theory) represented a critical juncture. The tagging of the masses (just like the tagging of cattle)[3] is crucial if the elites are to gain our trust in an increasingly centralized power structure. We are moving toward the zootechnical management of the immiserated and superfluous masses. Having crossed the digital-ID Rubicon, the crackdown is likely to continue smoothly and gradually, as in Noam Chomsky's famous anecdote:[4] if we throw a frog into a pot of boiling water, it will jump out with a prodigious leap; if, on the other hand, we immerse it in lukewarm water and slowly raise the temperature, the frog will not notice, even enjoying the warmth; until the fatal point when, weakened and unable to react, it will boil to death. It is no surprise, then, that a digital network for health certification is now a staple of global partnerships, such as the one between the WHO and the EU.[5]

The above prediction does, however, need to be contextualized within a conflictual and deeply uncertain scenario. It is worth reiterating that the conundrum—management of extreme financial volatility, retention of capitals and ruling class privileges, and avoidance of destabilizing depressions followed by civil wars—is of a fundamentally socioeconomic nature. Our social lives are literally insured by a financial system that increasingly resembles a gigantic Ponzi scheme. In the absence of any alternative to capitalism, the sad truth is that if those who run our decaying system were to lose control of liquidity creation, the ensuing explosion would nuke the entire socioeconomic fabric beneath it. Simultaneously, such an event would also deprive politicians of any remaining credibility. This is why the only strategy available to the elites seems to reside in synchronizing the planned demolition of the current economic model with the rolling out of an interoperative digital infrastructure for technocratic takeover. Timing, as always in life, is of the essence. The system's inherent complexity, and the number of entities participating in it, makes controlled demolition a job requiring the greatest balancing skills. Just like with the popular game of Jenga, the system is now being dismantled block by block. The skills of the players can prolong the duration of the game, but sooner or later the Jenga tower topples.

Back in 2021, Italian financial analyst Mauro Bottarelli summarized the perverse logic of the "pandemic economy" as follows: "A state of semipermanent health emergency is preferable to a vertical market crash that would make 2008 seem like a walk in the park."[6] The "pandemic" was indeed a lifeboat for a drowning system driven by the dogma of profit making. Strictly speaking, it was a *monetary event* that aimed to extend the lifecycle of a grotesquely financialized mode of production. In the wake of the repo market crash of September 2019, the Federal Reserve printed too much money too quickly in an attempt to save a credit-addicted system that had for decades operated precisely via money printing and cheap loans. In this respect, Covid was the perfect cover for continuing to perpetrate the metafraud that contemporary capitalism has become. We must understand that the social relation (the labor-based society) is no longer a priority in systemic terms. In fact, it has become "collateral damage" in the elites' mission to protect their wealth within the current power structure.

As we have seen, the September 2019 bailout of the financial sector—which was, after eleven blissful years of quantitative easing, once again on the verge of another nervous breakdown—involved an unprecedented expansion of monetary stimulus. The injection of this inordinate amount of money required the freezing of society. From the perspective of the short-sighted capitalist mole, there was no alternative. Computer money created as digital bytes cannot be allowed to cascade onto economic cycles on the ground, as this would cause a devaluation tsunami à la 1920s Weimar, only much more catastrophic for a stagnant and globally interconnected economy. Saving the repo market—where, in 2020, transactions amounted to $1.0–2.2 trillion per day and kept the financial system afloat—also meant saving hedge funds, pension funds, and in fact the entirety of the interconnected economy. Slogans like "everything will be fine,"[7] which unsuspecting citizens repeated in Italy and elsewhere, meant that everything would be fine (temporarily at least) for a rotten system whose racketeering logic required the orchestrated dismantling of the economy by forcing everyone into house arrest.

Inevitably, while Virus was still "top of the pops" and the money supply had vastly increased, the cautious reopening of society caused inflation to rise, triggering further impoverishment. The purchasing power of salaries were severely dented, as were revenues and savings. It is important to stress that commercial banks are positioned at the interface between the magical world of central banks and the emergency-swept wasteland where most mortals live. Thus, any wild or protracted expansion of central bank reserves triggers price inflation as commercial banks leak cash (i.e., debt) into society. The point here is that the "pandemic" accelerated the effect created by the preexisting macrotrend of monetary expansion. Mirroring the actions of the Federal Reserve, the world's central bankers created oceans of liquidity, thus further devaluing their currencies to the detriment of populations.

While this took place, transnational turbo-capital kept expanding in the financial hemisphere, destroying and absorbing small- and medium-sized businesses.

One tool that prevents liquidity from reaching the real economy is the Federal Reserve's Overnight Reverse Repo facility (RRP). While financial markets are flooded with freshly printed money, reverse repos allow the Fed to mop up any excess of the very cash it pumps into Wall Street. It is effectively a zero-sum game of give and take. At night, financial operators deposit their excess liquidity with the Federal Reserve, which delivers as collateral the same Treasuries and mortgage-backed securities it drains from the market during the day through its purchases. In August 2021, the Fed's usage of RRPs topped $1 trillion per day,[8] which led the Federal Open Market Committee (FOMC) to double the RRP counterparty limit to $160 billion[9] as of September 23, 2021.

The twisted logic of this monetary mechanism confirms both that the solipsistic "mad dance" of financial capital has spun out of control well beyond its customary madness and that the day of reckoning looms. A recession and subsequent depression can be momentarily avoided only through the gradual destruction of real demand. In fact, no crime against humanity can be ruled out when systemic implosion is in full swing and yet so stubbornly denied. The external shocks the world experiences on a daily basis are, for the most part, meant to take care of the potentially cataclysmic financial exposure to toxic risk. Financial acrobatics of the current magnitude only work under a metaemergency cover: blockades, lockdowns, restrictions, curfews, etc. The purpose of false flags and cover-ups is thus twofold: (1) to conceal the sinking of the finance-driven "work society" and (2) to coordinate the implementation of a colossal monetary reset that attempts to normalize economic crisis and a sharp decline in living standards.

Biopolitics on steroids

The consequences of emergency capitalism are emphatically biopolitical.[10] They concern the administration of a human surplus that is growing superfluous for a largely automated, highly financialized, and implosive reproductive model. This is why *virus, vaccine* and *Covid pass* became the Holy Trinity of social engineering in 2020. "Virus passports" were meant to train the multitudes in the use of electronic wallets controlling access to public services and personal livelihood. The dispossessed and redundant masses, together with the noncompliant, are the first in line to be disciplined by digitalized poverty management systems directly overseen by globally interconnected capital managers. Simply put, the plan is to tokenize humanity and place it on blockchain ledgers supervised by algorithms. And the spreading of global fear is the perfect ideological stick to herd us toward this outcome.

As public debates are increasingly silenced by censorship and intimidation, and a "trickle down fascism" is already with us, we are being escorted to a bio-techno-capitalist dystopia whose hellish character is likely to manifest fully with the next global downturn. This would justify the rolling out of Central Bank Digital Currencies, which, in the words of Agustín Carstens (general manager of the Bank for International Settlements), will grant "absolute control on the rules and regulations that will determine the use of that Central Bank liability [i.e., money], and we will have the technology to enforce that."[11] Digital cash linked to digital identity is shorthand for high-tech monetary serfdom, which will likely first be extended to the unemployed (e.g., recipients of Universal Basic Income) and then to most of us. In 2011, Larry Fink (BlackRock CEO) stated that "markets prefer totalitarian governments to democracies"[12]—we had better believe him.

Separating the population on the basis of vaccination status is an epoch-making achievement typical of totalitarian regimes. The next step is a compulsory digital ID to record the "virtuousness" of our behavior and regulate our access to society. *Covid was the ideal Trojan horse for this breakthrough.* A global system of digital identification based on blockchain technology has long been planned by the ID2020 Alliance,[13] backed by such giants as Accenture, Microsoft, the Rockefeller Foundation, MasterCard, IBM, Facebook, and Bill Gates' ubiquitous GAVI. From here, the transition to monetary control is likely to be relatively smooth. CBDCs would allow central bankers not only to track every transaction but especially to turn off access to liquidity for any reason deemed legitimate. The "digitization of life" project also includes an Internet passport which, subject to periodic review, would exclude from the web anyone considered undeserving. Should one's social credit score fall below a certain level, finding a job, traveling, and obtaining loans would depend on willing subjection to "rehabilitation programs." Presumably, there will be a black market for the outcasts.

A cornerstone of historical fascism was industry controlled by government while remaining privately owned. It is quite astonishing that, despite the overwhelming evidence of revolving doors between the public and private sectors, most public intellectuals have not yet realized that this is where we are heading. Italian writer Ennio Flaiano once said that the fascist movement is made of two groups: the fascists and the antifascists.[14] Today, when most self-proclaimed antifascists are quietly or enthusiastically supporting the authoritarian turn, this paradox is more relevant than ever. We are witnessing the accelerating dissolution of liberal capitalism, which is now obsolete. Technological productivity and finance, as well as the reorganization of power in supranational centers such as NATO, the IMF, the Fed, the ECB, the UN, the BIS, etc., have made the masses redundant as producers, consumers, and voters—these are the same people who prior to a few decades ago were still indispensable if oligarchs were to preserve and expand their power and revenues. The outlook is objectively depressing. Global financial and geopolitical interests will be secured by mass data harvesting, blockchain ledgers, and slavery by digital apps peddled as empowering innovation. At the heart of our predicament lies the ruthless evolutionary logic of a socioeconomic system that, to survive, is ready to sacrifice what is left of its democratic facade and embrace a control regime bolstered by corporate-owned science and technology, media propaganda, and disaster narratives accompanied by nauseating pseudohumanitarian philanthro-capitalism.[15] This sounds the death knell for so-called liberal democracies, which were always only the protective filter for the iron laws of market economies. To put it in Guy Debord's terms, we now live in a *fully integrated* "society of spectacle." The strange fusion of formal democracy and a real structure of control is what defines our dark age.

History tells us that biopolitical control is inscribed in the operative logic of modern technologies of power. The obvious reference here is Niccolò Macchiavelli's *The Prince* (1532), where we find *ante litteram* descriptions of recipes for how to traumatize populations with real, fabricated, or fake threats in order to crush their critical capacity and manipulate them into accepting prearranged responses. Today, the dominant class controls more than 90% of global media (primarily news agencies, newspapers, and televisions) and uses it to convey only the information it chooses to release, filtering and eliminating from the start what it deems not functional for its own interests. Yet one is left to wonder whether such forms of media control are actually necessary. Despite perceiving themselves as enlightened individuals, the cynical subjects of modern capitalist societies are, in fact, willing to endure nearly anything, accepting the most absurd demands with a mixture of empty fatalism and smug opportunism. Having long been incapacitated as critical thinkers, they can no longer differentiate between right and wrong and must rely on expert analyses and statistical data to determine whether they are sick or are being harmed. In 2020, many countries imposed the use of face masks, not only in hospitals, workplaces, and public spaces, but even outdoors. While completely useless if not harmful, face masks retain a profound symbolic meaning. If in the past similar devices were associated with servitude, today they mark the arrival of new forms of conformity and subjugation.

From conspiracy theory to successful paranoia

Today's fashionable "conspiracy theory" watchdogs conveniently disregard not only that conspiring is a fact of history common to all societies but especially that the power of the social machine of capital is ipso facto conspiratorial. Lies and propaganda are embedded in the modus operandi of a system that functions precisely by pretending to relinquish any form of mastery. Modern history as capitalist history is a priori inscribed in a reified social narrative programmed to recreate its own conditions of possibility, *whatever it takes*. Hegel famously wrote that "world-history [...] is self-caused and self-realized reason."[16] But this self-causative process—which capital embodies to perfection as the "self-valorization of value"—would not take place without the covert steering of the ruling classes, no matter how dull, delusional, botched, or even counterproductive their actions might turn out to be. Today, the steering in question corresponds to the need to prop up and eventually reboot the system's financial and monetary presuppositions. In this respect, the subjective agency of capitalism's functional elites becomes indistinguishable from systemic objectivity, just as emergency capitalism is indistinguishable from its sociopathic planners. Thus, the current war on "conspiracy theories" bears an uncanny resemblance to the war on "heresies" in medieval Europe.[17] Its main ideological purpose is to discredit and silence what is left of critical thinking, stigmatizing any question or belief that conflicts with the official narrative.

In fact, the epistemology of conspiracy theory drives much of today's propaganda as a rhetoric of exclusion. The a priori rejection of "paranoid thinking" leaves the official narrative as the sole bearer of truth, irrespective of empirical verification. Therefore, as argued by Ole Bjerg, "The real pathology emerges on the side of the mainstream reactions to so-called conspiracy theorists [...] in the form of an epistemic state of exception, which threatens to undermine the functioning of public debate and intellectual critique."[18] In other words, paranoia qualifies the position of those modern-day Torquemadas whose inquisition tribunals aim to silence any heretical thought that dares to depart from the dogmas of emergency capitalism. The blanket accusation levelled at "paranoid Covid-deniers" and "antivaxxers," for example, is symptomatic not only of the dissolution of the democratic bond but especially of a top-down contagion of ideological sickness never before experienced on such a global scale.

Just like our corporate-owned mainstream media, much of today's "academic left" loves to ridicule "conspiracy theorists" (as evidenced by the myriad journal articles and monographs on the subject currently being churned out). I am particularly aware of the responses to the "Covid emergency" voiced by colleagues who, like me, share a research interest in critical theory and ideology critique. For instance, a typical way of refuting "conspiracy theorists" involves brandishing some of Jacques Lacan's mottos, like "there is no such thing as a big Other" (the Other—the controlling agency—is radically inconsistent and therefore ultimately powerless) or "les non-dupes errent" (those who believe they are "nobody's fool" are in the wrong). However, when stripped of their historical context, these maxims turn hopelessly abstract and begin to sound like the worst kind of postmodern gibberish. They can, in other words, be utilized as a conservative justification for political acquiescence and intellectual relativism. An example of this attitude is Slavoj Žižek's argument in favor of vaccine mandates. Since, he argued, "we are all manipulated" (manipulation and alienation being regarded as the formal condition of any kind of socialization), "sometimes, naivety is our best weapon against deception."[19] The obvious problem with this stance is that, based as it is on an abstract/formal principle, it provides a theoretical justification for oppression. Moreover, it is articulated as a defense of a specific "mode of enjoyment"—that of the liberal (bourgeois) neurotic subject of the market society, who ultimately finds it more convenient to be duped by the capitalist Other.

While it may seem theoretically astute (since we are all alienated in/by the Other, be it language or power), Žižek's view is deeply ideological since it circumvents critical examination of the specific strategies of coercion employed by power and instead asserts, from a metahistorical perspective, the ontological inevitability of alienating power structures. These, however, are two separate issues requiring different sets of analytical tools. Just imagine a philosopher of the early 1940s who, upon hearing that millions of Jews were being led to gas chambers under the pretense of disinfection, upheld Žižek's view that, ultimately, "we are all manipulated," and "sometimes, naivety is our best weapon against deception." The universal principle of ontological deception—the "necessity of illusions"—should not be misused against the analysis of concrete instances of mass manipulation. To do so is intellectually disingenuous and politically reactionary.

Commenting on my reading of Covid as a monetary event, Žižek claimed that "it comes dangerously close" to a "paranoiac construct," adding that "there is no need to invent pandemics and weather catastrophes, since the system produces them by itself."[20] Typically, the charge of paranoia here hides a self-indulgent type of conservatism corroborated by the misuse of abstract theoretical formulas. Specifically, Žižek overlooks the obvious fact that a particular power structure functions precisely by occupying the inconsistency of what Lacan calls the big Other (the presupposition of a symbolic order of sense) and does so by manipulating it in its favor. While the place of the Other remains ontologically inconsistent, the political issue Žižek conveniently brushes aside is that the power structure operates precisely by occupying such inconsistency. We can put this in psychoanalytic terms: if there is an unconscious qua locus of radical alterity, conspiracy and manipulation are inevitable. The success of the power structure (especially under global capitalist rule) depends on its ability to weaponize the symbolic order's lack of foundation against the neurotic masses. Žižek knows this well, and yet, as demonstrated by his response to the Covid hoax, he continues to hide behind ahistorical formulas, which provide a philosophical and political cover for today's universal market society and its criminal strategies of crisis management.

The rhetoric of exclusion that animated the public discourse on Covid (real science versus conspiracy theory) can be described through what Lacan, borrowing from Freud, named "successful paranoia," which "might just as well seem to constitute the closure of science."[21] Essentially, "closure" refers to the positivistic belief in scientific objectivity, which is built on the rejection (foreclosure) of the subject of the unconscious as a source of questioning, doubt, and error. In the context of Lacan's discourse theory, successful paranoia aligns with a hyperefficient belief system secured by what he called the "curious copulation between capitalism and science."[22] The power of what is today unilaterally promoted as "real science" (so real that it bans doubt, prohibits debate, and promotes censorship) is akin to the power of a dogmatic religion, as Lacan cautioned in 1974: "Science is in the process of substituting itself for religion, and it is even more despotic, obtuse and obscurantist."[23] And capitalism banks on science and technology just as it capitalizes on health, which is with war the most profitable business that exists. To paraphrase Adorno and Horkheimer, the progress of science and technology has not diminished the power of myth; instead, it has amplified myth's capacity to deceive.[24]

It should be a no-brainer that the "science" we were ordered to follow was hijacked by the financial elites and their political cronies, thus working as a barrier against any critical inquiry into the reasons why a "pandemic" was declared. At a systemic and existential level, blind faith in "Covid science" betrayed a desperate desire to hang on to our fading socioeconomic illusion, inclusive of its authoritarian mutation. So, to argue that the tyrannical measures were necessary because the health situation was objectively desperate (as Žižek, Chomsky, and other prominent leftist thinkers did) is to confuse cause with effect. Furthermore, the history of scientific progress shows that science is, fundamentally, a discourse emphatically centered on what it lacks. All major scientific advances are based on a principle of insufficiency: the awareness that truth as cause of knowledge is lacking. Or, to quote Lacan, "Il n'y a de cause que de ce qui cloche" (There is cause only in what doesn't work).[25]

While the system's driving presupposition (the value-creating dialectic between capital and labor) has stopped working, the Covid decoy allowed capitalism to once again suspend any serious inquiry into its structural sickness and ongoing transformation. The clinic of neurosis shows us the extent to which the average neurotic wants a master, whose role is to reassure the neurotic that their world lies on solid foundations. Thus, the more our identities are weakened (cultural fragmentation, desocialization, fluidity, hyperrelativism, relentless destabilization of the self), the more we end up accepting the status quo as the sole guarantor of the social bond. Neurotics are often so desperately attached to their power structure, or universe of sense, that they turn into perverts to secure its functioning—like a masochist eagerly handing the whip to the dominatrix.

Ultimately, there is nothing transgressive in perversion, since its unconscious aim is to solicit and bring into existence a punishing type of power. For instance, today's common manifestations of narcissistic exhibitionism betray the unconscious desire to surrender to the gaze of the Other. The aim is both to conjure up the Other and to consequently safeguard the ego ("they look at me, therefore I exist"). Offering oneself up to the (authority of the) Other is, for an incapacitated subject beleaguered by anxiety, the most direct way of guaranteeing a degree of self-consistency. Given their existential confusion and psychological enervation, which are increasingly marketed as progressive traits by the education system and the culture industry, contemporary subjects (particularly those among the youngest generations) tend to submit to the mechanics of capitalist power naturally and willingly in a bid to retain a modicum of self-identification through the Other. We are therefore witnessing the accelerated transformation of the human toward a one-dimensional anthropology that enables the painless amputation of any prospect of change. Unfortunately, the conservative structures of neurosis and perversion are increasingly supported by the "progressive intelligentsia" (including liberal and radical leftists). As stated by psychoanalyst Timothy Lachin, "For all of human history, the idea of moral goodness has been used as a hypnotic weapon against the people. Control the definition of what is good using mechanisms of shame and guilt, and you control the behavior of every neurotic who wants to be good. It's the oldest trick in the book."[26]

The morality ruse

"La conjuration des imbéciles"[27] is the title of a short essay penned by Jean Baudrillard and published in *Libération* on May 7, 1997. Reflecting on the political success of Jean-Marie Le Pen's *Front National*, Baudrillard lashes out against the moralistic conformism of the left. Two questions from that text strike at the heart of our present: "Is it possible today to utter anything unusual, insolent, heterodox or paradoxical without being labelled a far-right extremist?"; and "Why has everything that is moral, compliant and conformist, which was traditionally on the right, now moved to the left?" Baudrillard argues that the left, "by stripping itself of all political energy," has become "a purely moral jurisdiction, the embodiment of universal values, champion of the kingdom of Virtue and guardian of museum values of the Good and of Truth; a jurisdiction that can hold everyone accountable without having to answer to anyone." Given this depressing context, "repressed political energy necessarily crystallizes elsewhere—in the enemy's camp. The left, therefore, by embodying the reign of Virtue, which is also the reign of the greatest hypocrisy, can only feed Evil."

While it could be added that most of the hysterical left has now abandoned even the hypocritical ambition to embody the reign of Virtue, Baudrillard's argument nevertheless proves useful to understand our epoch's ideological obsession with evil. Essentially, the narratives of evil that fill our collective imaginary serve to consolidate the illusion that globalized capitalism is morally grounded. This illusion is increasingly necessary for a world that eliminates all external referents. A global economic system approaching the point of maximum saturation cannot stand on its own feet. The more capitalism perseveres in liquidating anything that refuses to comply with its laws, the more it implodes—and the more it develops a perverse form of hubris based on the promotion of "ferocious enemies" that are desperate to annihilate us. As Baudrillard put it apropos the aftermath of 9/11, "Evil is now everywhere and it must be eradicated. Every extreme phenomenon is Evil. It is the perfect alibi for the totalitarian extension of the Good."[28]

One of the most fashionable manifestations of today's evil is the vulgar populist mob, that infamous "basket of deplorables" once evoked by the warmonger Hillary Clinton. But what really makes a difference is the promotion—by our marketing, advertising, and media PR sectors—of individual figureheads who embody unadulterated wickedness. Over the past two decades or so, we have been shocked by the unspeakable crimes of brutes like Saddam Hussein, Osama bin Laden, Muammar Gaddafi, Kim Jong Un, Vladimir Putin and others—some of whom the collective West has already punished. The liberal and democratic forces of the planet fight evil by drawing on the inexhaustible repertoire of Hollywood binaries, where the good invariably triumphs. However, today's moralizers conveniently ignore the fact that the humanity they want to save has already been plundered and crushed precisely by the knights of the liberal apocalypse.

There is a simple claim in Baudrillard's text that perfectly captures the hypocrisy I am referring to: "Le Pen is criticized for rejecting and excluding immigrants, *but this is nothing compared to the processes of social exclusion that take place everywhere.*" Why limit yourself to fighting the racism of those who reject immigrants when racism and social discrimination are systemic in the form of exclusion, ghettoization, enslavement, ethnic cleansing, and so on? For instance, the genocide in the Gaza Strip following the Hamas attacks of October 7, 2023, typifies the systemic violence that the US-led collective West has enacted since the inception of the neoliberal era. An unrestrained capitalist system is bound to revert to a permanent state of emergency reminiscent of its initial industrial expansion, wherein the state rapidly regresses to its violent essence. In Jacques Camatte's words, "the State becomes an enterprise or racket that mediates between the different gangs of capital."[29]

Furthermore, as shown by the late Domenico Losurdo, among others, the civil conquests of liberal ideology were established in symbiosis with the modern tragedies of slavery, deportation, and genocide.[30] These tragedies returned in the diabolical project of globalization under the guise of "just wars" against enemies that the West requires in order to prop up its own failing economic model. The paradox that guides the moralistic mission of today's "good politics" was indeed perfectly summarized by Baudrillard: "If Le Pen did not exist, he would have to be invented. It is he who frees us from the evil side of ourselves, from the quintessence of all that is worst in us. For this, he is cursed. But woe to us if he disappears, because his disappearance would trigger our racist, sexist and nationalist viruses (we have all of them) or, simply, the homicidal negativity of social being." Le Pen is a stand-in here for all the representatives of evil that the global West has actively promoted inside, and especially outside, its operational center. This colorful carousel of monsters is the lever that supports processes of socioeconomic devastation that push millions into misery, despair and the fratricidal struggle for survival. Today's ideology sustains itself not only through what Goethe called "active ignorance"[31]—equivalent to what in psychoanalysis is known as "fetishistic disavowal" (where knowing subjects act as if they are unaware of a given truth)—but also through a duplicitous kind of moralism that immunizes those who promote it.

Drawing on Roberto Esposito's key philosophical theme, the obsession with vaccination during the Covid "pandemic" should be read as an immunological metaphor that accurately depicts our *zeitgeist*. While mass vaccination is firmly tied to Big Pharma's profiteering machine, it also captures, at a metaphorical level, the functioning of a global power apparatus that self-inoculates evil pathogens in order to stimulate the production of allegedly virtuous antibodies. From Le Pen to Trump, from Saddam Hussein's weapons of mass destruction to Islamic terrorism, from the Covid narrative to Iran's nuclear program, we are looking at a long series of *immunological operations* through which a blatantly (self-)destructive socioeconomic model seeks legitimacy via the displacement of its murderous madness onto "flavor-of-the-month" enemies. A global governance fatally addicted to emergency narratives determines by itself what constitutes a democracy and, especially, what should be classified as dictatorship and terrorism. But as with the character of Colonel Kurtz (Marlon Brando) in Francis Ford Coppola's *Apocalypse Now* (1979), evil eventually emerges as a byproduct of "the good" and must be eliminated precisely to hide this embarrassing truth. In this respect, Max Horkheimer's immortal admonition should always be borne in mind: "Whoever is not willing to talk about capitalism should also keep quiet about fascism. [...] The totalitarian order differs from its bourgeois predecessor only in that it has lost its inhibitions."[32]

In the meantime, the philanthropic web of the so-called great reset, which is defined as a fairer, safer, more resilient world, is being woven. At a digital meeting modestly titled "Pioneers of Change,"[33] which took place on November 16–20, 2020 (with the "pandemic" in full swing), the World Economic Forum (WEF) discussed the "future of work," arguing for a "platform economy" capable of "unlocking prosperity for billions of workers" while also urging for the commitment of "*corporate activists*: companies that take concrete action on the most prominent challenges that we are facing," i.e., "the climate crisis, the increasing disconnection of urban and rural communities, or even the current global pandemic."[34] It is worth noting that these corporate pioneers of change are also encouraged to reinvent faith, which is why they rely on decidedly Franciscan (as in St Francis of Assisi) slogans like "Believe in something, even if it means sacrificing everything."[35]

In 2016, the WEF published a short piece by Ida Auken (onetime Danish minister for the environment and now a member of the Danish Social Liberal Party) titled "Welcome to 2030. I own nothing, have no privacy, and life has never been better."[36] Auken essentially described for us the type of "communism" in the making. In the near future, we will live in model cities wherein we can say, "I don't own a car. I don't own a house. I don't own any appliances or any clothes." Our private property will truly be abolished.

Yet, we will be happy, because in the city of digitized services, freed from traffic and pollution, "we have access to transportation, accommodation, food and all the things we need in our daily lives." There will be no need to "pay the rent," because when we are out cycling or picking daisies, "someone else is using our free space." Shopping will be a distant memory, as "the algorithm will do it" for us, since by now it "knows [our] taste better than [we] do." With robotics in full swing, work will have morphed into the pleasant activity of "thinking-time, creation-time and development-time."

But it gets better. Although Auken is genuinely concerned about the people "who do not live in our city," "those we lost on the way," who have perhaps "formed little self-supplying communities," or "stayed in the empty and abandoned houses in small nineteenth century villages"; and although she acknowledges that "Once in a while I get annoyed about the fact that I have no real privacy," since "somewhere, everything I do, think and dream of is recorded"—despite these small complications, life will nevertheless be "much better," since we will have defeated "all these terrible things happening: lifestyle diseases, climate change, the refugee crisis, environmental degradation, completely congested cities, water pollution, air pollution, social unrest and unemployment."

It requires little effort for the imagination to see that this utopian fairy tale is actually a techno-dystopian nightmare, for the simple reason that if we no longer possess anything, the world's elites will truly own everything. This is no doubt the vision of our enlightened technocrats, a perverse plan that says nothing about relations of power. If everything is a service, who is providing it? If artificial intelligence takes over work and algorithms make decisions for us, who designs, applies, maintains, and controls these technologies? Regarding AI, Jean Baudrillard wrote, "The sad thing about artificial intelligence is that it lacks artifice and therefore intelligence."[37] In other words, we should be wary of turning the inherent stupidity of AI into one of the four horsemen of the apocalypse. If anything, the problem is that human intelligence in general is rapidly approximating the stupidity of AI. The decay of humanity's social and cognitive capacity—the ability to access the symbolic and metaphorical level of communication—suggests that more and more people are already losing what distinguishes them from machines.

Of course, there is a good chance that the elites will destroy everything in an effort to save "the system" and their own privileges. Military wars will continue to be waged on behalf of economic wars. Typically, the scheme is enforced downwards while the benefits accrue upwards. As Daniel Guérin wrote in 1936, "When the economic crisis becomes acute, when the rate of profit sinks toward zero, the bourgeoisie can see only one way to restore its profits: it empties the pockets of the people down to the last *centime*."[38] Guérin's final message, like Horkheimer's, was clear: "Any antifascism is a frail illusion if it confines itself to defensive measures and does not aim at smashing capitalism itself."[39] How can we fail to see that at the heart of today's great reset there is none other than a new "fascism of big capital," to paraphrase the title of Guérin's book? The endgame is the gradual destruction of what remains of the real economy, and thus of the social bond. This would lead to the stipulation of a new social contract in which our own survival depends upon the "charitable" role of supranational governmental, and especially monetary, institutions.

The new normal is the reshaping of humanity so that it accepts Capitalism 4.0, based on the fourth industrial revolution. Global governance in the field of biosecurity is today the most evident manifestation of such despotism, which finds its perfect economic expression in so-called stakeholder capitalism: while gobbling up huge stock market profits, managers and shareholders of large multinationals also control a powerful political and media-friendly front driven by philanthropic sensitivity. This is the greatest paradox of our time. The 0.1%—the winners of globalization, the most predatory class in the history of humankind (from Bill Gates and Warren Buffett to Bill Clinton, Mark Zuckerberg, George Soros et al.)—are also socially committed to supporting noble causes such as health and the fight against world hunger. Thanks to their donations, these philanthropic prophets exercise a despotic influence on governments and their fragile (debt-soaked) institutions. The interlacing of money, power and lobbying alliances deprives politics of the last crumbs of autonomy, to the point that democracies all over the planet now welcome our philanthropic predators with open arms, without asking questions. Moral blackmail works, which also means that capitalist implosion is not necessarily *explosive*: it does not automatically produce revolutionary contradictions, as many deluded Marxists still believe. Rather, in its current phase, the implosion of capitalism once again generates its own fascistic *deterrence*. To focus our energy on fighting anything else is, perhaps, the most dangerous mistake. Yet, all is not lost. Despite the increasing repression of dissent, our "successfully paranoid" universe will fail to totalize itself.

3.
Quo Vadis, Homo Pandemicus?

> An epidemic of panic is spreading throughout the circuits of the social brain. An epidemic of depression is following the outbreak of panic.
> —Franco "Bifo" Berardi[1]

WHEN THE COVID CRISIS ERUPTED, some commentators noted that it provided us with an increasingly rare object: a *time* at least partially freed from the conformist hyperactivity that binds us to our commodity-producing system. For most of us it was possible, if not unavoidable, to escape some of the alienating imperatives that regulate our lives. The fixity of the "house arrests" was offset by a temporality somewhat liberated from the ideological regimes of postindustrial turbo-capitalism. Whether we liked it or not, we were forced to stop and listen to the silence of a world that no longer seemed to belong to us.

The absent cause

The substantial blockage of the immense assembly line of globalized capitalism opened a small hole in the ideological blanket that makes us all complicit in a reproductive mechanism grown toxic. The regime of self-isolation showed us how passive we were, not so much in our forced seclusion but in our feverish participation in a socioeconomic narrative that many already perceived to be weakening. In other words, the coronavirus crisis conjured up a fantasy of emancipation from *the obligation to enjoy*, which in our world is always *the obligation to enjoy on behalf of capital*—i.e., to perform as hamsters (or guinea pigs) in the great capitalist wheel. The trauma of lockdown, no matter how sadistically it was inflicted upon us, allowed some to imagine, if only in vain, a life detached from those compulsive regimes of enjoyment that tie us to the dogmas of productivism and consumerism. We seemed to have an unprecedented window of opportunity to envisage a more humane future *beyond* the logic of profit.

Contra Marx, Walter Benjamin wrote that revolutions are not necessarily "the locomotive of world history." Rather, they are "an attempt by the passengers on this train—namely, the human race—to activate the emergency brake."[2] While the "pandemic" was always baked into the implosive capitalist cake—and therefore not meant for a second as an emergency break—it temporarily relieved us from the superegoic pressure to participate at all costs. In what follows, I attempt to correlate this state of "ontological suspension" with the logic of a mode of production that is accelerating toward the precipice. Virus arguably revealed both the sinister trajectory of financialized capitalism and the void around which the increasingly worn-out conveyor belt of capital spins.

The implosion of global capital is desocializing the world, dissolving its social moorings, and imposing a generalized state of exception where the existence of the superrich depends on the exclusion of the immiserated and disposable plebs. However, it is a mistake to think that neoliberalism, as it affirmed itself over the past forty years, is merely the aberration of a fundamentally efficient mode of production. Rather, the violent wave of privatization and financialization that occurred during the "neoliberal revolution" was capital's *stricto sensu* necessary response to the valorization crisis that had been undermining the foundations of the real economy since the 1970s—and which today, at the dawn of the fourth industrial revolution, is irreversible. To understand the reasons for the disproportionate expansion of the financial industry, we must place it within the fold of the original mode of production. Paraphrasing Marx's reading of Darwin,[3] we would say that the anatomy of finance is the key to understanding the anatomy of the real economy. In its manifestly asocial character, in other words, financial capitalism reveals the elementary mechanism through which the real economy acquires social effectiveness in the modern world. Its sleight of hand (money that turns into more money without the mediation of labor) replicates at a basic level the ruse of capitalism as such. Let us see how.

Capital is not an empirical object (money, market, banks, individual companies, etc.), and therefore it can only be grasped as capital*ism*, a historical formation that socializes the buyers and sellers of labor power. As a social bond, capitalism entails the institutionalized mediation of money that buys labor power to create more money, part of which is reinvested in labor power to produce further value, in a theoretically infinite spiral. This dialectical process has now (in postindustrial times) been aggressively eroded and simultaneously taken over by the financial markets, which sidestep value-productive human labor. Let us briefly focus on its historical origins.

The capitalist narrative was established through a structural transition concerning the role of money. We can summarize this transition via Marx's quotation of Aristotle:[4] it is the passage from a precapitalist economy, where money acts as a mediator of trade, to *chrematistics* (or the art of moneymaking), where money becomes narcissistically infatuated with itself, activating the drive to self-expansion we call *capital*, which hinges on the "rational" mediation of that unique commodity we call *labor power*. The latter is the special ingredient that makes money rise into the capital-cake. In philosophical terms, we would say that capitalism is a logical and dialectical totality in which capital and labor represent two antagonistic sides of the same coin. With respect to this correlation, we must go back to interrogating the role of work. Relying on Hegel's speculative dialectics, without which we would not have Marx's *Grundrisse* and *Capital*, we could say that work is retroactively "seduced" by money on its journey to become capital. But Marx ends up neglecting, to an extent, the constitutive role of money capital in *retroactively* subsuming labor power. That is to say, he underestimates what Hegel calls *Setzung der Voraussetzungen*, the dialectical figure of "positing the presuppositions." In order to assert itself as a social form, capital must posit labor as a presupposition, or condition of possibility, for capital's own self-expansive deployment.

Think of the opening montage in Charlie Chaplin's *Modern Times* (1936). The film begins with the image of a huge clock filling the entire screen, marking the passage of time. This is followed by a shot, from above, of a flock of sheep running neatly in the same direction, which dissolves into the frame of a crowd of workers overflowing from an underground station and hurrying toward the factory gates. Modernity is captured by Chaplin as a specific mode of regimentation characterized by the temporal measurement of work. This means that work counts (for capital) only when it can be counted via the dehumanizing cult of labor time, from which surplus labor is extracted, in turn feeding into surplus value and, eventually, crystallizing as profit. In capitalist modernity, whatever exceeds labor time is basically a *waste of time*.

But going back to Marx, to what extent is it true that labor is the "substance of value," as maintained in his labor theory of value? The law of value shows how profit is generated solely through the extraction of surplus value from living labor. While this is the basis of capitalism as a social relation, a speculative approach reveals a deeper level of complexity. Let us think of "abstract labor" as the epochal invention through which money posits itself as its own externalized substance in order to be able to determine itself as capital. The term *invention* must be taken literally since it refers to the *autopoiesis* (self-creation) of capital: money ejected from the feudal mode of production becomes money capital as a *self-causing effect*. This is why history for Hegel is self-caused and self-realized reason (*Vernunft*). Civilizations emerge through the capacity of reason (or Spirit/*Geist*) to organize itself out of its own real inconsistency—an inconsistency which does not disappear but returns at a different level of notional mediation. This is what *Aufhebung* (sublation) means in Hegel: both to overcome and preserve the contradictory (negative) status of reality through reality's conceptual mediation. The more general implication is that we are able to affirm the existence of a *cause* for our actions only on the basis of the *absence of the cause*, the radical inconsistency of "all that is."

This counterintuitive perspective invites us to ponder the nature of any causal relationship between the critical dysfunctionality of a normative order and the birth of a new one. This is what we call "a revolution." What does a revolution revolve around? The short answer is—*nothing*. Without accessing the intrinsic impossibility, or self-contradictory status, of a particular social formation, we would not be able to reconfigure it. In fact, human existence, organized in a social bond, is always in a state of fragile equilibrium over its "groundless ground" or absent cause. Our relationship with the absent cause is therefore ontological, in the precise sense that without it, there would be no order of sense, no symbolic bond with fellow human beings, no social community. Put differently, the trauma of the inexistent cause is inherent in the social norm. Symbolic meanings, which support our existence, emerge out of their ontological inconsistency. Walking is the other side of falling, just like swimming is an effect of drowning, and life itself begins to make sense for us only in response to the sentiment of death. And the same goes for capitalism. To claim that capital is *causa sui* means that it is the effect of a cause (abstract labor, organized and exchanged as units of labor time) which it signifies *ex nihilo*. Only by creating its own symbolic presupposition in work as a *countable entity* exchangeable for a sum of money did capitalism manage to affirm itself as the hegemonic sociohistorical formation of modernity. Labor, then, is not merely "an eternal natural necessity" as "creator of use-values." Rather, precisely as expenditure of "brains, muscles, nerves, hands, etc.,"[5] it must be *signified* (assigned a socio-symbolic role) literally from nothing.

Obsolescence of valorization

To be clear, Marx was not mistaken in theorizing the universality of work as the organic metabolism between humankind and nature. Still, he did not take into full account the fact that work is a *negative* determination rather than the revolutionary hero of a teleological narrative culminating in the triumph of communism and the end of class struggle. In fact, turning labor power into a socio-ontological category is the elementary move through which capitalism asserted itself, as indeed did socialism as its rebel offspring. Put differently, the dogma of labor time is the modern form of alienation without which *Homo economicus* would lose its ontological compass, no longer knowing what to do with itself. In this respect, it is significant that Covid impacted our lives by depriving them, if only momentarily and illusorily, of their symbolic substance. But the argument I wish to pursue here is that this specific traumatism has been present for some time and that the "pandemic" merely brought it to the forefront.

The violent crisis of contemporary capitalism is, at heart, a crisis of surplus-value creation, which originates in the introduction of pervasive and unprecedented levels of technological automation. It is, essentially, the crisis of a blind and impersonal mechanism that employs human labor to "mine" from it a surplus of productivity, which functions in turn as the Holy Grail of the entire reproductive system. The initial and founding ruse is the one described by Marx: the socially necessary salary does not cover the extra labor that the worker therefore performs for free. In the context of this remainder of *gratis* labor, modern workers are still medieval serfs. But, as anticipated, in order to extract surplus labor and convert it into surplus value (and then profit), capital must first *signify* work. It must first "seduce" it to impress upon it the specific *social* character we call value. Marx, of course, was correct in denouncing the fact that the capitalist extracts from labor power a certain amount of surplus labor time without paying for it. This particular type of exploitation is indeed the centerpiece of capitalist civilization. However, hidden in Marx's denunciation is the risk of (unintentionally) endorsing capitalism's very conditions of possibility by authorizing a *positivistic* ontology of work as creator of use-values. Thus, the emancipatory categories of traditional Marxism (such as "use-value" and "concrete labor") can be seen to belong in the valorization narrative that serves the capitalist purpose.

There is no use-value outside the anthropological horizon of exchange-value. In other words, use-value is the alibi of the abstract logic of exchange-value. In a similar manner, the universal value of labor productivity, as upheld by Marxism, is actually a retroactive projection of the capitalist dialectic of forms. By positing the intrinsic generative power of labor (*Arbeitsvermögen*), as Marx does, one risks forgetting that such reproductive force is the crucial presupposition for capital's self-expansion. The Marxist notion of use-value, then, is overdetermined by that of exchange-value, and thus by the logic of valorization. Labor power is already "useful" for capital as its condition of possibility. As Robert Kurz argued, "Not only can the concrete side [of labor] not be separated from the abstract, but the former is subordinated to the latter. In other words: use-value is only a form of representation or appearance of abstract labor. Overarching both is the abstraction 'labor' as a real abstraction."[6]

The ontologization of labor has consistently led historical Marxism to dismiss the notion of an absolute internal limit to capital's expansion—a dismissal that essentially ensures the law of accumulation remains unquestioned. This is particularly evident in the assumption that over-exploitation for extraction of relative surplus value allows capital to continue expanding; as the cost of labor per worker diminishes, the relative surplus value extracted from each worker increases. However, what capital—and frequently its critics—fail to recognize is that this process of valorization enacted by individual capitals encompasses a tendency to inhibit the role of living productive labor, which is the sole source of *total* value creation. Such tendency today becomes openly self-destructive. In light of the current overwhelming reliance on technological automation, any increase in the rate of surplus value undermines the very object of exploitation: the generation of value through living labor. The paradox is that the competitive race for increased surplus value extraction through the scientification of production results in a decrease in the total amount of surplus value created, which in turn leads to an unstoppable decline in the rate of profit. Thus, if left under capitalist control, production ceases to be socially sustainable, fostering stagnation and causing societies to implode. The key political implication is that this inherent contradiction within the capitalist mode of production cannot be resolved by employing capital's own categories, because capital is at heart an asocial drive that remains blind to its own immanent logic based on the socialization of labor.

In terms of the capital-labor dialectic, we should think of its product, surplus value, as nothing other than the signifier of what the capitalist *lacks*—ultimately, it stands for the intrinsic impossibility for labor to produce any economic value whatsoever. We are dealing here with the manipulative elementary ruse of capitalism as a social bond, for the entire system of profit creation relies on a *minus* passed off as a *plus* (as in *surplus* value). Marx argued that profit stems from surplus value as the unpaid surplus of valorized labor power. This is no doubt correct, but only if we endorse the metanarrative of capitalist valorization, which relies on the dogmatic belief in labor as measurable in monetary terms. Seen from a more radical perspective, however, surplus value cannot fail to appear as the insubstantial trigger of the entire process of value formation. It is, in other words, a "negative remainder," a signifier of the impossibility of valorization itself (of the fact that what we call economic value is, ultimately, a matter of belief). In this respect, profit, too, bears the insignia of the negative magnitude of surplus value, as shown by the capitalist perception of it as *lacking*. The reproductive secret of capitalism lies precisely in *not* (and *never*) having enough of *it* (surplus value, profit)—in missing *it* as the object of desire; and this negative trigger is engendered by the original movement of the capitalist dialectic, in which money and labor "embrace" and signify each other. Surplus value is therefore a lacking, radically devalued signifier that, as an "impossible" object, supports the socioeconomic structure built around its quest. It is, in other words, the meaningless remainder of the capitalist narrative rather than a measurable quantity of labor power stolen from the laborer.

Precisely because it circles around a lacking object, capital has the structure of the Freudian drive. It is resolutely *beyond* the pleasure principle, enjoying its journey by missing the target. In the same way that smoking and gambling are compulsive, capital as a process valorizes itself by chasing a surplus of enjoyment (more profit!) as its absent cause. While Marx resolved the riddle of surplus value within the context of exploitation for profit making, he did not see that the answer to such a riddle is that *there is no positively quantifiable answer*: surplus value makes the world tick as a negative signifier, a logical impasse, an aporia. And my point here is that the Covid hoax revealed how financial capitalism—the con game that feeds on debts that accrue within states, banks, enterprises, and households—replicates the logic of "impossible redemption" that qualifies capital as such. Capital works precisely by endlessly postponing its redemption—it can never be made whole.

The ironic name Jacques Lacan gave to the negative magnitude of surplus value was *Mehrlust*, surplus *jouissance*.[7] While this may sound outlandish to Marxist exegesis, shifting the focus from value to *jouissance*—the paradoxical satisfaction of the (capitalist) drive through a compulsion to remain unsatisfied, to miss the object of desire—is probably the best way to make sense of not only capitalism as a mode of production propelled by the enjoyment of what it does not have but especially of its ferocious character, which is again being unleashed today on a global scale. Insofar as political economy continues to think of itself in positivistic terms, namely as an economic science concerned solely with quantifiable surface phenomena, it will fail to grasp capital's presuppositions and therefore its operative logic.

With respect to this deeper logic, Covid unwittingly told us the truth about labor and its value. By taking them away from us so abruptly, it brought to light their real inconsistency within a mode of production that must, in order to function, reduce every aspect of life to a measurable and exchangeable entity. The point, then, is not only to denounce the iniquities of capitalism as a system based upon labor exploitation. More crucially, we need to realize that the capitalist fiction as such is losing its socio-symbolic efficiency. The structural crisis of financial capitalism, which follows the crisis of labor valorization, reveals the central void around which our way of life has for centuries organized itself as a particular form of *social immunization*. The only way this social form can now survive is through unmitigated barbarism; that is to say, by violently denying the historical obsolescence of its founding categories. This also implies that the meaning of human work, as the increasingly *unproductive* foundation of capitalism, should now be radically re-signified. It should be given a new role within a social bond that must leave behind capital and its moribund narrative.

Panic consumption and the new narcissists

Precisely because it is imploding, capitalism relies on increasingly desperate forms of ideological manipulation. The coronavirus emergency should have prompted us to reflect on the power of ideology in an era that was too hastily defined as postideological. The fall of the Berlin Wall, *ça va sans dire*, did not free us from ideologies. Rather, stepping out of old divisions made us more vulnerable to the tyranny of one-dimensional thinking, which is calibrated on the anonymous brutality of economic computation. Through globalization and the emancipation from the grand narratives of the past, we have given ourselves over to increasingly subtle forms of coercion that co-opt us viscerally. The dissolution of old symbolic ties has thrown us into the flat and invisible jurisdiction of the economy, which defines how free we are. Yet this spurious freedom (truly a caricature of freedom) resolves itself in the obligation not only to produce and consume commodities but also, increasingly, to consent to official narratives and modes of collective manipulation, no matter how absurd they are. Hence the perception of a historical time that is both *irreversible* and *eternal*, in which all human experience folds back into a destiny where every event is posited and presupposed by the metaphysics of capital.

While cynical and disenchanted, the contemporary subject is in fact, as Walter Benjamin realized,[8] a fervent believer. The inflexibility of our faith manifests in a Pascalian way, that is, in the *practical act* rather than in the work of the spirit.[9] If our moral and spiritual life is now devoid of any meaningful sense of militancy, the active one devotes itself to a single cult: belief in the sacred cycles of capital. Elevated to a universal religion, capitalism continues to feed on the discipline of billions of believers who, crippled by the fear of the unknown, have long persuaded themselves that the meaning of life lies in the satisfaction of its purchasing power. For this reason, the subliminal order not to disturb the law of profit is by far the dominant ideological injunction of our time and continues, moreover, to be effective in our postgrowth and debt-based constellation.

Long before the onslaught of Covid panic, a ferocious type of mass conformity had imposed itself as the only way to achieve personal fulfilment. In colonizing the unconscious (our modes of enjoyment), the global commodity-producing society had already weakened our socio-symbolic bonds, consigning us to a solipsistic relationship with God-capital. It was always naive to think that, in the midst of the coronavirus crisis, *Homo pandemicus* could change its fate through class solidarity. When Covid erupted, Slavoj Žižek was quick to argue that the pandemic would deal a mortal blow to capitalism, "a kind of 'Five Point Palm Exploding Heart Technique' on the global capitalist system," as he put it in reference to Quentin Tarantino's *Kill Bill 2*.[10] However, just as that technique is part of the mythology of martial arts, Žižek's claim belongs to the mythology of leftist radicalism in its assumption that capitalist contradictions will (sooner or later) give birth to "some form" of communism. Žižek was quite explicit about this in *Pandemic! 2*: "If the last few weeks have demonstrated anything, it is that global capitalism cannot contain the Covid-19 crisis" and that therefore "something like a new form of communism will have to emerge precisely if we want to survive!"[11] In the meantime, however, Covid had already turned panic itself into a universal object of consumption, harmoniously inserted into the anthropological routines of *Homo economicus*. Consuming global panic became an irresistible new frontier in capitalist ideology, fulfilling the specific aim of mass brainwashing.

Marx's *Capital* begins with the famous line, "The wealth of the societies in which the capitalist mode of production prevails appears as an 'immense collection of commodities.'"[12] Today, the world dominated by commodities establishes not only a global governance dictated by competition between capitals but also a typically *obtuse* kind of self-congratulatory individualism that inhibits critical thinking and, at the same time, foments in the subject a delusion of "passive omnipotence." The latter can be regarded as a subtle variation on Nietzsche's immortal image of the last men (*Letzter Mensch*), the archetypal passive nihilists: "Alas! The day of the most despicable man is coming, of him who can no longer despise himself. [...] No shepherd and *one* herd! Everyone wants the same, everyone is the same: he who feels otherwise goes freely to the madhouse. [...] They have their little pleasures for the day and their little pleasures for the night: *but they revere their health*. 'We have discovered happiness'—the last men say, and blink."[13]

Narcissistic disorders, as well as the normalization of psychopathological behaviors of various kind, are consonant with the acquiescence required of the contemporary subject. The latest version of Nietzsche's last man is seen in today's hordes of self-victimizing narcissists. Even today's obsession with mental health—the fact that everyone seems to have discovered a right to embrace some form of mental disability—would seem to correspond to a devious form of narcissism cynically promoted by a "system" intent on desocializing society. The status of the newly atomized subject must be that of a passive and simultaneously egocentric victim, annoyed by the complexity of the world, incapacitated by the different levels of interpretation, and exasperated rather than fascinated by the metaphorical dimension of language and communication. The people must be one-dimensional like the "smart" machines they increasingly interact with, since intellectually ambitious subjects are no longer central to the system's reproduction. In other words, it is in the interest of financialized capitalism to turn the value-producing subjects of yesteryear—including the increasingly obsolete middle-classes—into docile, fluid, anemic narcissists who are so caught-up in their own "difference" that they grow blind to the "undifferentiated" herd status they are reduced to. The fight for gender equality, for instance, increasingly takes place against the background of equal (truly "gender neutral") dispossession.

Ultimately, this "cultural shift" serves a diabolical strategy of domestication within a new ideology of mass poverty management. In a world dominated by the libidinal economy of leverage, where the future is abolished by the suffocating presentism of monetary debt, the subject must be turned into a victim of misfortune so that they remain blind to socioeconomic causality. In this respect, Covid accelerated the individual's passive submission to financialized capitalism's asocial, virtualized mode of wealth reproduction. Arguably, the subject who is eager to be placed on the spectrum of mental health disorders is unwittingly enslaving themselves to a pervasively manipulative socioeconomic agenda. This applies particularly to the new generations (so-called Z and Alpha, the demographic cohorts born between 1995 and 2009 and since 2010, respectively); the more they narcissistically identify with their incapacitation, the more controllable they become and the more they disavow the socioeconomic cause of their atomization. Behind today's mass conformity there lies the "mad rationality" of an implosive mode of production whose sadistic dream is to achieve absolute control over materially impoverished and psychologically overwhelmed "superfluous masses."

Contemporary subjects willingly abolish their singularity. The Cartesian distance between *res cogitans* and *res extensa* evaporates, as thinking subjects (*cogitans*) flatten into the empty objectuality (*extensa*) of the increasingly virtualized prison they inhabit. Today, people find themselves not only immiserated and deprived of fundamental rights (home, food, health) but also *reified*, reproduced serially as passive and superfluous extensions of the finance-driven capitalist apparatus. The economic mechanism that until a few decades ago still managed to create the semblance of a social bond now instigates the slow decomposition of the human community. As Ralf Dahrendorf wrote in the 1980s, "The work-centered society is dead, but we don't know how to bury it."[14] We should now add that the stench is becoming unbearable. Yet, no matter how unproductive, depressed, and atomized it may be, the globalized subject is still dominated by capital and its categories. In fact, never before has the fetishistic theology of capital asserted itself with such totalizing violence, extending to all areas of life, including education and (mental) health.

Prey to a socioeconomic compulsion perceived as destiny, *Homo pandemicus* withdraws into its fragile shell when it faces a deviously overblown health scare. No longer able to face its own transience (which is the only way to live intensely and imagine a real process of transformation), *Homo pandemicus* relies on apotropaic rituals like wearing a face mask, finding in mute terror its only comfort and basis for belonging. Thus, ideological panic expresses the people's will to continue to be defined by capitalist inertia, despite the real-time collapse of the "society of opulence." Ultimately, the successful consumption of the panic-commodity relies on the stubborn denial of death as the only "thing" capable of giving meaning to life. The enthusiasm of living, the love of life, can only arise from the perception that one day we will no longer be here, and from the real practices (desires, aspirations, affects) that such perception determines in the subject.

It is no coincidence that philosophers, sociologists, and anthropologists have for decades told us that our age of material wealth *represses* death.[15] It is quite clear that this is an ideological type of repression, as it is functional to the imposition of the enchanted temporality of capital. Dissociating life from death characterizes all modern cultures, for it allows for the economic valorization of every fragment of our existence. The abolition of the symbolic link with death, still central in premodern societies, allows political economy to establish the repressive socialization of life based on dead labor (contained in commodities) and exchange-value. The only value that matters is the capitalist pseudovivification of life, where death is turned into a spectacle performed by "unfortunate" others and cynically exploited by the corporate media. The success of the Covid operation, particularly in the West, was predicated upon the return of the repressed, the sudden reactivation of the ghost of *our* mortality. The shock effect of this *memento mori* was not the solidarity of a human species aware of its own fragility and finitude but the intellectual *rigor mortis* of *Homo pandemicus*, already mortified by its numbing obsession with security. Confronted with their own potential demise at the hands of an invisible enemy, narcissistic consumers coddled by the cult of self-victimization could only turn speechless or mumble (under their masks, behind their screens, or inside their sarcophagus-like homes) a series of tragicomic clichés.

Ideology today

The media hype that surrounded the pandemic farce had an easy time inoculating the virus of panic in an increasingly anemic social body. Globalized capitalism long ago established the total commodification of the human being, who is as hyperactive as psychically empty, and therefore susceptible to manipulation. We are now sliding toward a new despotic order that replicates at a different level the old fascist objective of using the state to advance the interests of wealthy elites. Among other things, the coronavirus provided the managers of contemporary capitalism with the opportunity for colossal emotional blackmail: you are either with us (the "lifesavers") or with the ineffable microkillers and their conspiracy theorists. In the meantime, the usual suspects continued to casually accumulate wealth and power.[16] Mired in panic and seduced by the media fanfare, most people opted for blind faith instead of legitimate doubt. According to various world-renowned immunologists (including members of the WHO), the virus's mortality rate,[17] all variables considered, was likely to be between 0.1% and 0.2%; that is, at the level of a "strong seasonal influenza," as claimed by none other than Anthony Fauci back in March 2020.[18] This means that more than 99% of those who were infected could carry on with their lives with either normal flu-like symptoms or none at all. But even numbers can do precious little if they are not part of the winning narrative.

Apart from the rise of censorship, the most common media strategy during the days of Virus can be described with what Vladimiro Giacché named "false synecdoche,"[19] a rhetorical figure that describes how a fragment of a factual occurrence—often an insignificant detail—is inordinately amplified to spread terror and justify draconian measures. This is now at the heart of capital's self-reproduction. The capitalist mode of production normally survives its own contradictions through violent internal technological-managerial revolutions, which Joseph Schumpeter famously described as the "gale of creative destruction."[20] What the Covid crisis made clear is that the inertial movement of the mode of production, inclusive of its creative destruction, is now powerless vis-à-vis its dogma of internal expansion. The pandemic experiment showed us that the capitalist order seeks ways of preserving the power structure while no longer expanding. It showed us what the future will increasingly resemble under "net-zero growth": only an illiberal, totalitarian model of society can preserve a structurally stagnant capitalist regime.

It is worth considering that the ideological management of the socioeconomic trend toward stagnation began long before the lockdowns. Even in prepandemic times, for instance, death had been reduced to a private and purely biological fact, and there was no hesitation to let the sick die anonymously in hospitals and let the elderly die in care homes. Similarly, (a-)social distancing had already been established by the addiction to (a-)social networks. Yet, the acceleration of ideological coercion since 2020 is perhaps the most original aspect of emergency capitalism, especially when justified as a humanitarian act. Theodor Adorno's famous aphorism from *Negative Dialectics*, "No universal history leads from savagery to humanitarianism, but there is one leading from the slingshot to the megaton bomb,"[21] comes to mind here. Clearly, years of "humanitarian warmongering" have failed to persuade us that behind every desire to save humanity there is a desire to dominate it. It is no coincidence that in the last twenty years, beginning with the 9/11 attack on the World Trade Center, the political discourse accompanying the crisis of globalization has employed the oldest ideological weapon: the spreading of terror vis-à-vis external enemies, from Isis to Putin, portrayed as being desperate to penetrate and destroy "our world." The ideological effectiveness of the "us versus terror" rhetoric, however, depends on its ability to innovate itself creatively. For this reason, the ancestral nightmare of heads severed by hordes of hooded jihadists, which hypnotized the West's collective imagination until the 2010s, was replaced by a new and updated model of what Naomi Klein famously called "shock therapy."[22] The "pandemic" evoked a scenario more apocalyptic than anything that preceded it. One of its aims was to prevent us from realizing how our epochal crisis—which reduces millions of humans to destitution and destroys societies despite the enormous technical potential available—has nothing to do with the nature of a virus and everything to do with the nature of capitalism.

As is often pointed out, the narrative of a deadly pathogen had already been trialed in 2009 when the H1N1 ("swine flu") pandemic was declared. However, that attempt (a test bed?) gained limited traction and turned out to be something of an anticlimax. In 2020, panic instead spread like wildfire, so much so that, to quote Alan Cassels, it made us all feel *pre-sick*.[23] In other words, we willingly consigned ourselves to the tracing and tracking statistics, having become what could be described, paraphrasing Ivan Illich,[24] as *algorithms* of a health system that frames us within probabilistic calculations. In this sense, the daily "war bulletins" activated a preexisting identification mechanism that turns us—anonymous populations at the mercy of anonymous abstractions—into subjects of medical control (as Michel Foucault understood long ago). In 2020, however, a unique situation arose whereby, for the first time in the history of humanity, it was not the sick who sought medical attention but rather the medical professionals who actively sought out those who were presumed to be sick. This assault on the subject is deeply ideological, displacing the problem of the End—of our lives, of our civilization, of a derelict model of social reproduction—onto the trauma carried by an invisible enemy embodying absolute evil, against which we can only "fight together," cost what it may.

Denkverbot and faceless humanity

The rhetoric of a "world war against the virus," popularized with perfect timing by Bill Gates and his philanthropic foundations,[25] meant that the only goal was to win the war, regardless of who paid for it, who benefitted from it, and what happened next. A war scenario primarily requires *obedience*. Not only are civil liberties limited but a regime of *Denkverbot* prohibits critical thinking. When airing dissenting opinions, one is immediately accused of conspiracy theory by the useful idiots who do not know (or pretend not to know) that *power has always conspired*. It is almost trivial to observe how capital today, in its dominant financial manifestation, holds in its grip entire populations, shaping their actions and exercising absolute power over our increasingly naked form of life. This occurs while politics, reduced to an accounting exercise (even when rekindled by ancient passions), continues to genuflect to economic diktats.

The financial industry's hegemony over the real economy sanctions the defeat of a social model based on the exploitation of human labor. This is regardless of the fact that labor exploitation continues, both in criminal forms of underemployment and through the creation of what the late David Graeber referred to with ingenious simplicity as "bullshit jobs."[26] Stated more clearly, Wall Street has now achieved near-complete independence from Main Street. Markets are manipulated and are no longer a reflection of what takes place in the labor-based society, to the point that, as Graeber claims, the system is forced to invent useless and unproductive jobs to maintain a semblance of structural consistency. But the wealth created in sectors that do not produce any value (such as the financial, retail, commercial, and property sectors) cannot be decoupled, without serious consequences, from the rate of profit in the value-creating sectors.

In both *Grundrisse* and the third volume of *Capital*, Marx had predicted, albeit with various disclaimers, the tendency of the rate of profit to fall in relation to an increase in organic capital, calculated as the ratio between *constant* capital (machines) and *variable* capital (living labor). Today, Marx's intuition has achieved the status of a verdict:[27] the more that investment in high-tech increases, the more the profitability of capital falls in absolute terms, since the shedding of human labor can no longer be offset by productive employment. For good or for ill, this internal contradiction of political economy marks the end of the modern anthropology of labor that characterizes the reproductive model of capitalism. In Baudrillard's words, "The *scenario* of work is there to conceal the fact that the work-real, the production-real, has disappeared."[28] From a "work society," our world is inexorably mutating into a "society without work," or at least into a "society of shitty work" (to repeat Graeber), and it is for this reason that it delivers itself to financial alchemy. Although work continues to define us, the fate of mass wage labor is to continue morphing into more or less explicit forms of slavery. We are faced with a quasi-deterministic mechanism that undermines the foundations of society. If debt-leveraged capitalism depends on constant injections of liquidity, it by the same token liquidates the foundations of our world.

It is precisely the "faceless" (anonymous, rarefied, algorithmic) but omnipotent power of financial capital that compels us to a final reflection on the symbol of the fight against Covid-19: the face mask. There is something vicious and at the same time comical in the use of such a "stupid" object. The obligation to wear a face mask recalls Beckett's and Ionesco's theater of the absurd, which captures the essence of corona ideology—namely, the "facelessness" of capitalist power. In its deepest meaning, the apotropaic ritual of masking, which mummifies contemporary humans as it did slaves in antiquity, is an attempt to force us into compliance with the criminal anonymity of financialized capitalism. The desocializing nature of the latter requires anonymous (isolated, depressed, impotent, confused, passive, distracted, and "liquid") subjects.

As an expression of "voluntary servitude,"[29] the face mask reflects the acceleration of a process of *soft dehumanization* that has been with us for quite some time. It does so by depriving us of our singularity, to be understood as a *"lack* to ourselves", a gap between *what we are not* and *what we believe we are.* Only by acknowledging this lack and putting it to work are we open to the hypothesis of an alternative future. But humans who gag themselves due to a perceived risk that they may infect or be infected by their neighbors are already heavily coerced and therefore unable to exercise critical thought. In its miserable banality, the face mask is a symbol of reactionary *Denkverbot*. Critical awareness instead arises as the intellectual capacity of the thinking subject to simultaneously acknowledge and resist its definition by external conditions. If individuals do not acquire *self*-distance, if they do not think *against* their own identity insofar as it is mediated by the Other (that is, by their language, ideology, privileges, power relations, etc.), there can be no critical conscience and no real drive toward change.

In short, the mask of *Homo pandemicus* hides the cynical and obtuse grin of *Homo economicus*. Without becoming aware of what emergency capitalism means for us today, we will soon wake up in a neofeudal, fully digitized dystopia. Repeating Gramsci, we can say that a long "interregnum" awaits us, where "the old is dying and the new cannot be born" and "a great variety of morbid symptoms appear."[30] Covid aside, our problem remains our real susceptibility to the capitalist virus, for which a vaccine—the only one we urgently need—has yet to be invented.

4.
When All Else Fails, They Take You to War

The rules are simple: they lie to us, we know they're lying, they know we know they're lying, but they keep lying to us, and we keep pretending to believe them.
—Elena Gorokhova[1]

Post-Covid inflation began to spike in mid-to-late 2021, as the world was leaving lockdowns behind. By devaluing money (the purchasing power of fiat currencies), inflation pushes more and more people into debt, poverty, and despair. As such, it marks the later stages of crisis capitalism. To make it appear as if it fell from the sky, inflation was labelled "the cost of living" crisis, and, to add insult to injury, "experts" began to warn about "inflation inequality."[2] But what is inflation? As is well known, bourgeois economic science (especially following the emergence of marginal utility theory) overlooks the connection between labor, value, and money—the fact that money, in capitalism, represents objectified, "dead" human labor as the *substance* of its value. Instead, it superficially equates value with realizable prices, thereby ignoring the inner logic of labor mediation. Within the context of this shift to a subjectivist understanding of value, economic science distinguishes between demand-pull inflation (where aggregate consumer demand for goods and services exceeds their supply) and cost-push inflation (where the aggregate supply of goods and services decreases due to a surge in production costs). Both theories correlate with the market law of supply and demand, and as such they miss the objective dimension of capital as a totality built on the labor-fetish (the reduction of human work to a quantifiable and exchangeable commodity). In truth, then, today's inflation emerges as the epochal outcome of the separation of money from its basis in labor valorization. In other words, it derives from years of expansive monetary policy, where demand is increasingly sustained by money created out of "economic nothingness," resulting in the inevitable devaluation of the money medium. In what follows, I retrace the latest stages of the causal connection between "warmongering" and "fictitious capital," which is the underlying phenomenon of our time. The "collective West"—i.e., the United States and its subservient allies—sees war as the key economic activity that might be able to protect its hegemonic status based upon debt, finance and currency control. The West is now a gigantic "rentier economy" that, as such, lives off the new value created by economies like China, which are however also slowing down or shrinking.

Monetary variants

As I argue throughout this book, the deep function of the war against Covid can only be grasped if situated in its macro context, namely the *terminal* crisis of the capitalist mode of production. The causal sequence to bear in mind when reflecting back upon the 2020–22 period is economic implosion—pandemic simulation—military offensive. Should it come to full fruition, this paradigm shift would culminate in the establishment of a *totalitarian model of implosive capitalism*, perhaps still nominally democratic but in truth characterized by the despotic management of global geo-biopolitical crises that are either *grotesquely disproportionate* to any actual threat or that preemptively aim to generate planned reactions. As shown by the "Covid vaccine" indoctrination campaigns and the attendant "antivaxx" scapegoating, the totalitarian potential of mass propaganda is virtually limitless. For the first time in history, the blame for a treatment that did not and does not work (at least not in the way we were promised) was placed on those who did not use it.

We must be mindful that today's ideological pressure is a reaction to a looming socioeconomic collapse whose magnitude has never before been experienced. The first substantial shock came with the 2007 credit crunch and subsequent global recession. At that time, the bailing out of the financial sector led to the European debt crisis (2010–11), which turned QE into the "mother of all monetary policies." Since 2008, routine central bank distortion through QE injections has spawned an ultrafinancialized regime of capitalist accumulation contingent upon the creation of asset bubbles, whose volatility resurfaced in mid-September 2019 in the form of the liquidity trap in the repo loan market. This, in turn, cleared the way for Virus and the perverse logic of "pandemic capitalism," which allowed the top 0.1% to increase its wealth at record speed.[3]

Countermeasures for the impending meltdown were planned months in advance. As I argued in chapter 1, official documents indicate that financial elites were fully aware that the post-2008 artificial expansion of the money supply was becoming unmanageable, not least because it was accompanied by a global economic contraction that had pushed Germany, Italy and Japan to the verge of recession in 2019 while Britain, China, and other advanced economies also struggled.[4] Rather than risk a sudden and catastrophic collapse, the elites arguably opted to *control the accident* while, as it were, dialing 911 in advance. As we have seen, when the Wall Street repo market froze up in mid-September 2019, the Fed swiftly prescribed a higher dose of the old medicine in the form of an unprecedented monetary expansion in repo loans. But this time it did so under protection of a pandemic shield. For two years, the "Covid emergency" worked like Linus's blanket for a global economy that was sinking under mountains of unsustainable deficits and unserviceable debts.

What matters here is not only the *quantitative* character but especially the *qualitative* character of the Fed's monetary maneuver. In the Federal Reserve's entire history (which begins in 1913), there had never been a *direct correlation* between central bank reserve creation and monetary supply in the retail banking circuit. However, as of September 2019, the new reserves created by the Fed began to be replicated *dollar for dollar* as deposits within what were then 4,336 US commercial banks. In other words, the expansion of the Fed's balance sheet came to correspond directly with the overall money supply in the economy, exactly the monetary remedy prescribed by BlackRock. What needs to be reiterated is that the financial house of cards was already on the verge of collapsing in 2019 and that Virus arrived *at the right time* to enable the monetary deluge and related paradigm change.

This strategy, orchestrated by the world's most powerful central bank in partnership with the world's most powerful asset manager, has three immediate, interconnected, and irreversible *social* consequences: (1) more debt (credit creation programs); (2) more fiat currency devaluation; and (3) more geopolitical conflict (and related global emergencies). What does our macroeconomic and financial environment look like today? Its basic features can be summarized as follows:

- Global debt of more than $313 trillion, growing exponentially
- Rapidly increasing deficits in most advanced and developing economies
- Colossal bubbles in the stock, bond (debt), and real estate markets
- An astronomical bubble in the derivatives market
- Secular inflation (with risk of hyperinflation)

- Stagnant or recessionary economies

Within this implosive context, both the war against Covid and the real military conflicts that followed (from Ukraine to the Middle East) function primarily as magnets with which to attract cash in the present, thereby attempting to conceal the system's bankruptcy—the fact that profits no longer predominantly derive from value-productive sectors of the economy. However counterintuitive it may seem, prolonging the lifespan of hyperindebted "rentier capitalism" entails the *controlled demolition* of both its economy and liberal-democratic infrastructure. It requires, in other words, a violent paradigm change. While the speculative industry is consecrated as the absolute center of fictitious wealth production (*not* contributing to social wealth), the work society winds up immiserated. This is ultimately what emergency capitalism is about. For the financial elites, navigating unavoidable economic depression via a crisis-to-crisis mechanism of controlled demolition is more convenient than accounting for socioeconomic downfall of biblical proportions. The global health psyop of 2020 showed us that the system's puppet masters are ready to do "whatever it takes" (as Mario Draghi put it back in 2012)[5] to postpone the *redde rationem*.

During the Covid lockdowns, what is obvious in hindsight began to become apparent: the best virologists operate on Wall Street. I am referring, for instance, to those so-called insider traders who, a month prior to the emergence of the Omicron variant (at the end of 2021), already knew that the Covid pantomime would be extended. A glance at the pricing of stocks in the so-called Stay at Home basket (from Zoom to Peloton and Roku) proved incomparably more helpful than the opinion of any medical "expert." Even more blatantly than its predecessors, Omicron had nothing pandemic-like about it. The grotesque discrepancy between the impact of "Covid variants" and the repressive measures taken on their behalf can only be explained in economic terms: these variants acted as yet another tool of financial leverage. Furthermore, their immediate role was to control the inflationary spike in the short term, since the renewed fear campaigns sapped spending, preventing the money supply pumped into the financial sector from circulating as real demand.

In conditions of at least minimally functional capitalism, inflation is fought by raising the cost of money (interest rates). But in a hyperindebted context like ours, where capital is mostly profitable in nonproductive sectors, this can only be allowed to happen partially and superficially, because financial markets kept in a state of perpetual excitement by easy money would suffer devastating consequences if rates were increased beyond a given threshold. On the one hand, then, liquidity must continue to flow into the debt and stock markets; on the other hand, however, the resulting price inflation must be managed with care. "Covid variants" worked as a deflationary gauge designed to extend into the future the loose monetary policies of central banks and postpone the implementation of gradual interest rate hikes. The latter kicked off in March 2022, when the Fed raised its federal funds benchmark rate by 25 basis points to the range of 0.25–0.50% (the first hike since 2018). Keeping societies half closed and consumption suppressed by evoking life-threatening variants was relatively painless compared to a sudden increase in the cost of money, which would have destroyed both the balance sheets of most financial institutions and the debt servicing costs of governments with skyrocketing deficit ratios.

The debt's unstoppable flight forward

Government debt and speculative money capital are closely intertwined. A dramatic devaluation of the financial superstructure would undermine the state's ability to finance its operations. This was confirmed when countries like Italy and Greece promptly adopted the most draconian measures with respect to the Omicron variant so they could plead for further monetary support, from the extension of state aid and PEPP (the ECB's Pandemic Emergency Purchase Programme) to the possible revising of the European Stability and Growth Pact. But since there are no free meals in capitalism, the insane flight forward of debt translates into more poverty and tighter control for (nearly) everyone, with the middle classes indebting themselves to the teeth in a desperate bid to retain their status. It is in this context that variants were deployed to manage an epochal shift to what increasingly resembles a neo-feudal type of senescent capitalism ruled by monetary seigniorage. By the end of 2021, Virus was still weaponized against inflation, which had in the meantime turned so real that even chairman Powell was forced to drop the narrative of its transitory character.[6] In December 2021, the US saw inflation reach 6.8% on an annual basis, the highest level since 1982. And if housing prices were to be added while avoiding cheap wizardry like the artificial lowering of CPI (consumer price inflation) through calculating data from 2019–20,[7] the rate would easily have reached double digits.

That inflation surge was a record high not only in the US but also in Great Britain (+5.1% in November 2021), and it caused the fastest spike in the history of the Euro.[8] Insofar as central banks were snookered regarding monetary policy, the management of inflation via Covid variants was their only realistic way forward. What the prolonged Covid crisis made manifest is that currency depreciation is a feature, not a bug, of central banking. In the grand scheme of things, fiat currency devaluation is inevitable. At the same time, it can also be exploited to manage the transition to a two-tier global society in which oligarchs control (or fight for control of) the money supply while entire populations are subjugated through poverty, control, fear, and a permanent state of warmongering. This, in a nutshell, is the criminal trajectory of contemporary capitalism. The surreal protraction of the "pandemic" throughout 2021 confirmed that entire societies were hostage to the reproduction of fictitious chains of value in the financial sector. Perpetually bullish markets required Covid variants, quarterly vaccination programs, wave after wave of media terror, and a whole panoply of Kafkaesque emergency regulations that aimed to (1) keep the money printer switched on while depressing the real economy; (2) acclimate us to subjugation by *force majeure*; and (3) distract us from what takes place in Mount Olympus, where the real game is played.

Like all war campaigns, the "war on Covid" justified money printing and low rates, which exacerbated currency devaluation. This depressing logic can only resolve itself today in the centralization of the money supply. In capitalist terms, there is no other way out. This is because the erosion of purchasing power results inevitably from the secular oversupply of fictitious money (coming from nonproductive sectors), which is now snowballing with the destructive force of an Alpine avalanche. Because of ongoing currency destruction and economic "bad news," the controllers must train us to live in fear and guilt, forcing us to internalize the new normal condition of permanent chaos, precariousness, and destabilization. What matters in a closely intertwined system is the big picture, which in our case is characterized by the automatic reproduction of *unproductive* capital, meaning wealth that is increasingly *asocial*, detached from the productive sectors of the economy.

The problem here is that our civilization will never be able to return to the growth standards necessary for its social reproduction. Because of this internal limit within the mode of production, the ongoing paradigm shift requires the gradual dismantling of the social bonds. The dominant emergencies of our time—infectious disease outbreaks, climate change, Russia's invasion of Ukraine, military conflict, etc.—are highly manipulated narratives that stem from a single overarching cause: the slow-motion collapse of the capitalist system, which nobody wants to face. For years, the dominant capitalist center—essentially, the United States—has nourished and globally imposed a false economy rooted in deficit spending backed by the central bank's low interest rates and purchasing of assets. This has nothing to do with real growth, which is in fact quickly evaporating throughout planet Earth. The reason for implosion is therefore immanent and has to do with the historical trajectory of the mode of production. Over the past half-century, value-productive (living) labor has been steadily crushed by unproductive capital in its holy alliance with science and technology, dictated by competition. This self-inflicted impairment, which the proponents of emergency capitalism refuse to acknowledge, first manifested in all its destructive capacity during the global financial crisis of 2007–8. However, its potential for devastation remains unresolved, having, in fact, intensified.

Societal decomposition

Because of what John Maynard Keynes called the era of "technological unemployment,"[9] capital with increasingly higher rates of "organic composition" (which, in Marxian terms, means the ratio of materials and fixed production costs to the cost of labor power) is unable to squeeze sufficient surplus value (both relative and absolute) out of wage labor, which is the main reason why it throws itself headlong into the magical world of finance. As is well-known, Marx had anticipated this outcome in his theory of the "tendency of the rate of profit to fall" (TRPF), outlined in the third volume of *Capital*. However, he could not foresee the effects of the exponential increase in automation (and therefore in the organic composition of capital), which now determines the pathological addiction to mountains of fictitious money destined for ruinous devaluation. Financial collapse is most likely to happen through a meltdown of the bond markets, which are the drivers of the entire "fake economy." Today, this outcome is postponed by cynical emergency deception. As we have seen, the acceleration in monetary control since September 2019 was enabled by the freezing of the real economy. By hypnotizing the populations and by placing them under house arrest while waiting for the miracle serum, our political rulers, directed by their financial bosses, allowed central banks to replenish the speculative sector.

After the failures of neo-Keynesian (public spending) and neoliberal (austerity and market deregulation) policies, in 2020 we experienced the first iteration of "lockdown capitalism"—a significant acceleration toward a postliberal world. In capitalist terms, financial hubris is the inescapable consequence of capital's ever-diminishing ability to generate new surplus value. But the proliferation of disaster narratives will not save us from economic collapse. The latter might hit us as a sudden lockup of the system, including as a controlled accident; or, perhaps more likely, we may continue in slow-motion mode. Whatever the case, the least we can do is prepare ourselves, by, for instance, building autonomous networks and communities that are not dependent on the currently disintegrating model. While this will not save us from a collapsing economy, it will generate circuits of resistance and cooperation that could function as the seeds of a future postcapitalist society. Politics, as we have it today, is completely enslaved to the economic dogma and thus deprived of emancipatory potential. Specifically, as summarized by Franco "Bifo" Berardi, the "political left" can only offer false perspectives: "There is no political way out of the apocalypse. For thirty years, the left has been the main political instrument of the ultracapitalist offensive, and whoever invests their hopes in the left is an imbecile who deserves to be betrayed, since betrayal is the only activity that the left is capable of performing competently."[10] Bifo is right. The "leftists" in power keep touting, with increasingly nauseating hypocrisy, their egalitarian principles, but in truth it is precisely through the blackmail of such egalitarian posturing that they have long since become the most zealous servants of global capital and its criminal agenda.

If we want to protect what remains of our critical independence and human dignity, and especially the hope of a better future for our children, we must free ourselves, at least mentally, from this idiotic subjection to the logic of emergency capitalism. At the same time, we must rehabilitate a political critique of capital as *Weltanschauung*; that is to say, as a worldview incarnated in the dialectical relationship between money and labor aimed at the creation of commodities for profit. Whether we like it or not, this capitalist worldview is irredeemably obsolete in the age of accelerated technological automation. If we are to avoid the tsunami of barbarism heading our way, we will need, sometime soon, to redefine the relationship between work, community, and social wealth beyond its capitalist meaning.

The Putin virus

In February 2022, like a textbook example of continuity editing in film, the de-escalation of the "war on Covid" transitioned seamlessly into the escalation of the Ukraine war, with Vladimir Putin replacing Virus as public enemy number one. If the emergency changeover was predictable, its timing was impeccable. When Jean Baudrillard wrote that "The Gulf War did not take place,"[11] he meant that its violence was overwritten as a media spectacle (simulacrum) that turned it into *hyperreality*, something so unequivocally and overwhelmingly real that it suspends any question, doubt, or disbelief regarding the intrinsic opacity of the referent. "Covid" and "the Russian invasion" are emphatic explosions of hyperreality. As such, they have replaced the complexity of the real with a prepackaged model of false binary oppositions (healthy/sick, true/false, good/evil) where rational discussion is ousted by emotional blackmail. How else could we explain the decision by

Meta Platforms to allow Facebook and Instagram users to call for violence against Russians (apparently a temporary change to their hate speech policy)?[12] Or the suspension of a university course on Fyodor Dostoevsky *because he was Russian*?[13] In other words, Covid and Ukraine mobilized the same divide & conquer strategy. "Putin's war" was the ideal continuation of the "war on Covid," and the emergency loop is the macroevent of our time. Let us explore this claim further.

Two sets of questions were immediately excluded from the representation of "Putin's war." First, the (obvious) geopolitical one: Ukraine was a ticking time bomb waiting to go off. NATO's eastward expansion had culminated in the orchestration of Ukrainian regime change of 2014, which, as US political scientist John Mearsheimer put it laconically, "overthrew a pro-Russian leader and installed a pro-American leader" as part of a plan to "turn Ukraine into a western bulwark on Russia's border."[14] In plain language, it was a *coup*, with sickening repercussions like the Odessa massacre of May 2, 2014. For those who still need confirmation of US involvement in Ukraine's regime change, the recording of the (now infamous) February 2014 Nuland-Pyatt phone conversation will help.[15] It reveals the US State Department under the Obama administration planning the composition of a new Ukrainian government just days before the Maidan uprising that triggered the downfall of the Yanukovych government.

Despite petitions to stop the arming of Ukrainian neo-Nazis,[16] NATO had intensified its militarization of the country in recent years[17] while the Donbas Republics and Roma minorities were under continuous attack by Ukraine's ultranationalist militias, causing thousands of civilian victims. The role of Ukrainian neo-Nazis is far from marginal in a country whose parliament voted in 2018 to commemorate the 110th birthday of Nazi collaborator Stepan Bandera. NATO acted in full knowledge that its deal with Ukraine would, for Russia, be equivalent to a declaration of war—as Putin stressed in his speech at the Munich Conference on Security Policy of February 11, 2007.[18] NATO troops and military bases equipped with defensive antiballistic missiles (convertible into offensive nuclear weapons) have mushroomed in various regions of Eastern Europe. Here, then, comes the rhetorical question: if Russia had such weaponry deployed near a US border (in, say, Mexico), would Joe Biden (or anyone else in his place) tolerate it? This is why, after decades of provocations, the Ukraine bomb was ready to detonate.

The second set of issues concerns the economic agenda, whose mode of appearance is that of financial warfare. Draconian sanctions by tough-talking Western leaders—mostly asset freezes and the exclusion of Russian banks from the SWIFT global payment system—were supposed to hurt Putin and Russia. However, it was immediately obvious that this objective was neither achievable nor desirable, at least for European countries. The sanctions that the US implemented elsewhere (for example, against North Korea and Iran) were far harder than those against Russia, as they also targeted third countries that traded with the "evil regimes." Instead, despite what Joe Biden called "the largest sanctions regime ever imposed on any country in history,"[19] Russia continues to sell oil to India and China (at a discount, and they then exported it to Europe at a premium), and even uranium to the US (for nuclear power).[20] Conversely, throughout 2023 Russia continued to import large volumes of "war technology" from the West.[21] Moreover, Russia is the world's largest producer of nearly all raw materials, and with inflation levels rising across the globe, it seems impossible, or suicidal, to do without such supplies. Corporate media, of course, were quick to predict that sanctions would destroy the Russian economy, causing the end of Putin's reign. Reality, however, turned out to be quite different. By the end of 2023, Russian energy revenues continued to grow, which in turn allowed Putin to decrease Russia's budget deficit and increase defense spending.[22] So, perhaps a different question should be posed: what if the "sanctions from hell" were a decoy?

Like Covid, the Ukraine affair can be regarded as a "geopolitical derivative" of the financial markets. The reason for this is that a protracted conflict legitimizes more liquidity being pulled into the present while blame is apportioned to the latest reincarnation of Dr. Strangelove. With his military offensive, "Mad Vlad" essentially allowed the Federal Reserve (and other major central banks) to once again postpone the day of reckoning. This is because fighting a debt crisis by adding more debt to it is the only way forward for a bankrupt system. In a world in which the demand for financial assets is sustained by the demand for debt securities (e.g., bonds), wars and global conflicts play a vital role in clearing the way for more borrowing. Massive amounts of cash are created out of thin air and deployed as financial leverage, as well as to boost ailing GDPs through deficit spending for the military industry. Global emergencies are the main catalyst for artificial monetary expansion, which in turn provides a means of escape from the valorization crisis that has plagued our mode of production since the implosion of the Bretton Woods system in the 1970s. It is therefore reasonable to surmise that all major geopolitical events either originate in or are heavily conditioned by what occurs in the financial sector. The "Putin pandemic" was driven by the same ruse that drove the "Covid pandemic": giving central banks free rein to extend their monumental printing sprees, which boost stocks and bonds while putting the world economy under further pressure. This is the one-way street of contemporary capitalism. It is no coincidence that the US, as the global capitalist hub, specializes in the two key sectors of finance and war. From its perspective, war is necessary because the monopoly on violence determines the monopoly on financial capital.

We should always keep the big picture firmly in mind. Since 2009, all major central banks have been on an unprecedented money-creation binge, for which there is no end in sight. Churning out cheap liquidity works as a compensatory mechanism for a freefalling economy increasingly dependent on an "everything bubble" of grotesque proportions. We have now entered a new age of stagflation that recalls the 1970s but without the leeway to repeat what was done at that time to avoid collapse. Only by placing them against this background can we understand what the current "global shocks" are for. All wars sponsored by the West are today a desperate attempt to extend the life expectancy of unproductive, rentier capitalism. They allow the bond markets to stabilize as yields fall (bond markets act as "canaries in the coalmine" for a potential market crash). This is why the Ukraine crisis is the geopolitical mode of appearance for the debt crisis. What the latter requires is a perennial QE regime (whether explicit or implicit) calibrated through a cyclical succession of global shocks: pandemics, terrorist campaigns, nuclear threats, trade wars, military conflicts, cyberattacks or even, *why not?*, an alien landing. Chaos needs to be invoked at every given opportunity, and with it, ideally, the figure of a brutal, bloodthirsty enemy. Whether it takes place in the media or in reality, it is the *emergency loop* that matters because it forces the liquidity tap open. Capital is a blind process that abhors stagnation: it must be in constant motion, even when motion means accruing ever-larger amounts of unsustainable debt.

The tangled web we weave

Soaring inflation facilitates the management of socioeconomic decay through the erosion of purchasing power. We have seen how saving financial markets today also means depressing real demand. And with the unique privilege to create dollars out of nothing, the Federal Reserve is always at least one step ahead of the game. As previously discussed, the Fed's balance sheet began ballooning again in September 2019, when massive amounts of mouse-clicked cash were pumped into the ailing financial sector. After two years of relentless fearmongering, however, the Covid narrative had grown stale and increasingly difficult to sustain—as evidenced by the Canadian trucker protests that began in early 2022, for example. The economy suddenly needed a new horror story to exploit, a new blanket of hyperreality to drop on the world.

In 2022, NATO engaged in asymmetric war with Russia over the Donbas region. Above all, this proxy war hit defenseless populations and economies already affected by two years of pandemic-induced economic contraction. Gas bills and commodity prices rose, especially for European economies dependent on cheap Russian gas. But is this not what the great reset requires, as the neoliberal fantasy of the "end of history" dissolves? The roaming specter of energy- and food-related crises caused by a recognizable villain shifts responsibility away from the unmanageable capitalist contradiction. Furthermore, it justifies further oppressive policies—including, if necessary, the rule of martial law, as experimented with in democratic Canada under the Emergency Act in February 2022, which led to the freezing of ("antivaxxer") protesters' bank accounts. The first thing we must acknowledge is that the geopolitical chessboard is the playing field of the capitalist elites.

Global conflicts today are the key symptom of a collapsing socioeconomic order wherein simulated wealth creation has supplanted real productivity. Geopolitical divisions are thus the effect of the underlying economic cause. In a context dominated by the pursuits of finance, capital as fetish emerges in all its empty and destructive glory. As already recognized by Marx, capital appears to financial managers as an object that has broken its tie with its substance.

> In interest-bearing capital, therefore, this automatic fetish is elaborated into its pure form, self-valorizing value, money breeding money, and in this form it no longer bears any marks of its origin. The social relation

> is consummated in the relationship of a thing, money, to itself. Instead of the actual transformation of money into capital, we have here only the form of this devoid of content.[23]

Today, capital's near-total dissociation from its origin in value-productive labor makes the violence of its self-serving causality increasingly visible. Circling the globe in quadrillions of dollars, fictitious money capital literally dictates how life must be lived—from "pandemic" lockdowns and "immunizations" to "debt discipline" and the dispossession of land, resources, and livelihoods (especially in the Global South). The *dictatorship of finance*, enabled by an unholy alliance of corrupt domestic officials, multinational corporations, and transnational institutions, could be framed as the highest stage of capitalist imperialism. While it represents what is strictly speaking a *necessary* outcome of the historical trajectory of capitalist accumulation, its destructive, desocializing, and highly manipulative characteristics must be confronted head-on rather than dismissed as just another chapter in the epic poem of capital. If the current use of emergencies is perverse and utilitarian in nature, psychotic episodes with apocalyptic potential are increasingly likely. Strategically, however, what matters most is the proliferation of geopolitical hotspots to be stoked when needed. This manipulative rationale requires false flags and credible actors, along with a global audience willing to be shocked, or at least to acquiesce.

The sad truth is that, when it comes to military conflicts, nothing is to be ruled out if the aim is to extend the life of a terminally broken socioeconomic mechanism. Here is a paradox that should make us think: on the day Vladimir Putin invaded Ukraine and was officially crowned the new Hitler, financial markets registered the biggest intraday rebound since March 2020, when anti-Covid QE programs were launched to save the world. By the end of 2023, the European Union had adopted 12 rounds of sanctions against Russia. In the meantime, all peacekeeping attempts were sabotaged while the West inundated Ukraine with hundreds of billions in "aid packages." At the start of February 2024, when the EU arranged its latest €50-billion deal, it should have been clear that the issue at stake is not Ukraine's freedom but a proxy war that must be prolonged indefinitely to comply with the greatest strategy of financial manipulation and economic-industrial destabilization since World War II—in which Europe is once again the principal theater of devastation while the US call the shots from a distance.

Cynical warfare pragmatism on the part of the US should not surprise us. Some will recall the Project for a New American Century (PNAC), a neoconservative think tank founded in 1997 that included influential characters like Dick Cheney, Donald Rumsfeld, and Paul Wolfowitz. In September 2000, PNAC released "Rebuilding America's Defenses,"[24] a secret report that promoted "the belief that America should seek to preserve and extend its position of global leadership by maintaining the preeminence of US military forces." The report called for an aggressive shift in US foreign policy that would commit Washington to "fight and decisively win multiple, simultaneous major theater wars." The blueprint also states that "advanced forms of biological warfare that can 'target' specific genotypes may transform biological warfare from the realm of terror to a politically useful tool." To create a new American century, a massive rearmament of the United States and a much more aggressive transformation of its leadership in foreign policy were envisaged as necessary. Such a process would take a long time, unless accelerated by "some catastrophic and catalyzing event—like a new Pearl Harbor," which indeed arrived promptly on September 11, 2001.

That project is ongoing today. It keeps functioning as the armed wing of financial policy. What is at stake for the US is the global supremacy of a financial model based on the control of fiat money (the US dollar as global reserve currency), energy (the petrodollar), and debt (the US bond market). Given this context, drawn-out geopolitical crises "owned" by the US play two interrelated economic roles: they convey the perception that US debt is one of the safest havens for investors (which allows for more deficit spending and internal consumption), and they boosts the GDP of a largely unproductive economy (unsurprisingly, 2023 was a record year for US military exports, up more than 50% from 2022).[25] But the "military/defense spending" model, which the EU is now opportunistically embracing on the back of its anti-Russian rhetoric,[26] is a last-ditch (not to mention intrinsically nefarious) attempt to manage the unmanageable.

The tragic strategy of "when all else fails, go to war" will not stop systemic failure. The first criminal implication is more military damage inflicted upon helpless populations caught in the middle of the capitalist charade. The new arms race and an increase in geopolitical disruption will also cause further currency devaluation through unlimited debt issuance (fiat currencies are already returning to their intrinsic value, which is zero). Combined with an increase in the mass migration of cheap labor, the strategy will provoke a faster deterioration of socioeconomic conditions, with civil wars and the introduction of martial law being realistic prospects. We should also expect more false flags and relentless disinformation campaigns, more bank failures, and possibly the return of pandemic threats that support ongoing endeavors to globalize "vaccine passports" and the digitalization of life. As the failure of capitalist civilization deepens, all the pieces seem to fall into place to create the conditions for a global conflict whose magnitude could be much greater than both world wars combined.

Hyperreality and forever wars

Even if almost no one wants to admit it, our "system" is obsolete, and for this reason it is now morphing into a "closed system"—totalitarian in nature. It is equally clear that the few who continue to benefit materially from it (the 0.1%) are willing to do anything to prolong its obsolete existence. At its root, contemporary capitalism works in a simple way: debt is issued from one door and purchased from another via the issuance of new debt in a depressive loop from which most of the destructive phenomena of our time originate.

The facilitators of the "debt-chasing-debt" mechanism are a class of profiteering technocrats whose main psychological trait is psychopathy. They are so devoted to the mechanism that they have become its *extensions*—like automatons, they work tirelessly for the mechanism, without any remorse for the devastation of human life it dispenses. However, the psychopathic dimension (uninhibited, manipulative, and criminally antisocial) is not the exclusive prerogative of the transnational financial clique, since it extends to both the political-institutional caste (from heads of government to local administrators) and the so-called intelligentsia (experts, journalists, scholars, philosophers, artists, etc.). In other words, the institutional mediation of reality is now *entirely mediated* by the mechanism itself. Whoever enters the system must accept its rules while also, *ipso facto*, assuming its psychopathological traits. Thus, blind capitalist objectivity (the drive for profit making) becomes indistinguishable from the subjects representing it.

Because of their personality disorder, the technocrats in the control room tend to overestimate their ability to enforce a closed system that might conceal the decline of capitalist socialization. The tragic pandemic farce, and now the cold wind of permanent warfare, put the average citizen's unconditional trust in their representative institutions to the test. If it was relatively easy to silence doubt and dissent with "humanitarian lockdowns" and emergency rule—which allowed a most opportunistic political class to briefly regain some clout—complicity in the Gaza genocide coupled with the neo-McCarthyistic construction of a "democratic front against the Russian monster" and the related arms race have begun to undermine the old certainties of the silent majority.

In the new totalitarian normal, reality does not quite make it to the newsfeeds and television screens. What we get instead is the hyperreal as theorized by Jean Baudrillard, which is neither real nor fiction but instead the narrative container that has replaced both. Thus, the brutal ethnic cleansing of Gaza continues at full speed along with bleeding-heart humanitarian concern for civilians, telegenic campaigns against all forms of extremism, and cynical warnings of rampant antisemitism. At the same time, we are reminded 24/7 that the Russians (who else?) are preparing to launch a nuclear cyberattack from space and invade Europe. Without even realizing it, the conspiracy theory ghostbusters turn into the very thing they love to hate. The resulting maelstrom of infotainment induces a state of collective hypnosis which proves to be more effective than traditional censorship since it eliminates *ex ante* the request for a real referent, in all its radical ambiguity.

The hypermediation of the world aims to become the only available world. The events narrated by corporate media are no longer thought of as something *other* than their narration, since, in the hyperreal reversal, it is the narration itself that thinks the subject. Our saturated infosphere exists in the form of an infinitely malleable self-referential spectacle that a priori sterilizes all critical thought. The official debate on Gaza and on Ukraine, for example, is continuously reframed as *a debate on the debate itself,* strictly demarcated by morally preformatted binary codes (democracy/terrorism, etc.). This tendency to liquidate the referent must be understood in its etymological sense as a tendency to "make it liquid." More crucially, we must realize that this tendency established itself, historically, as the consequence of a process of economic virtualization based on the replacement of the profitability of wage labor with the simulated profitability of speculative capital.

We live in a world where the stock markets of Western countries reach record highs as their economies slip into recession, while the United States manages to stay afloat courtesy of a monstrous deficit guaranteed by monetary and military hegemony. Regardless of the cyclical corrections and potential crash in the making, the ongoing financial market party (with very few invitees) is inextricably connected with the euphoria of war. Why? First, military production for "long-term security commitments" now constitutes essential support for increasingly sagging real growth as measured in GDP. For example, 64% of the $60.7 billion allocated to Ukraine in one of the latest aid packages is absorbed by the US military industry. The source here is not Putin's TASS but the *Wall Street Journal*,[27] which also admits that US industrial production in the defense sector has increased by 17.5% since the beginning of the Ukraine conflict. At the end of August 2024, we were informed that "top defence contractors [are] set to rake in record cash after orders soar."[28] The *Financial Times* piece unashamedly reports,

> Five top US defence contractors are forecast to generate cash flow of $26bn by the end of 2026, more than double the amount in 2021. [...] In Europe, national champions BAE Systems, Rheinmetall and Sweden's Saab, which have benefited from new contracts for ammunition and missiles, are expected to see combined cash flow jump by more than 40 per cent. The industry is benefiting from a sharp increase in military spending as governments increase their budgets in response to Russia's full-scale invasion of Ukraine and escalating tensions in the Middle East and Asia. In the US, recent aid bills for Ukraine, Taiwan and Israel allocated nearly

$13bn for weapons production at America's five biggest defence groups — Lockheed Martin, RTX, Northrop Grumman, Boeing and General Dynamics — and their suppliers. In the UK, the Ministry of Defence has committed £7.6bn for military aid to Ukraine over the past three years, including for stockpile replenishment.

It is important to highlight that this sickening, utterly manipulated military fervor continues to function as a tailwind for a hyperinflated financial sector now in thrall to AI mania. The current S&P 500 bubble results from the hysterical overvaluation of a handful of tech corporations, the so-called Magnificent Seven (Alphabet, Amazon, Apple, Meta, Microsoft, Nvidia and Tesla, which today are actually down to a Magnificent Two: Nvidia and Meta). The pronounced imbalance closely resembles the dot-com tech bubble of the late 1990s, when excitement about the internet led to the overvaluation of Microsoft, Cisco, Amazon, eBay, Qualcomm, etc. While these companies managed to save their own skins, many start-ups were wiped out by the bursting of the bubble. *Ergo*, a sensational market moved by the lever of war-driven artificial intelligence ought to brace itself for an equally sensational fall.

Let us remind ourselves that financial risk is immensely higher today than it was twenty-five years ago. Over the past two decades, the system has been supported by the creation of liquidity out of thin air (and related scapegoats), whose purpose is to refinance the mass of outstanding debt which supports state deficits as well as speculative bubbles populated by heaps of zombie companies. A stock market collapse of around 80%, like that of the dot-com burst at the end of 2000, would now be equivalent to a barrage of atomic explosions—metaphorically and literally. This is because the warmongering psychopathy is, ultimately, *an extension of financial psychopathy*: the real outcome of out-of-control speculative risk. This explains why, in February 2024, a technocratic superstar like Ursula von der Leyen,[29] president of the European Commission, called for the production of "weapons like Covid vaccines"—inadvertently spilling the beans about the real purpose of both.

The armament industry is the Cerberus-like guardian of financialized capitalism, which has in its traditional version—the fantastic world of full employment, hedonistic mass consumption, endless growth, and democratic progress—been dead and buried for quite some time. Hence, the undeclared objective of the US and its vassal states: to maintain military hegemony, both as the backbone of monetary hegemony (the dollar as global reserve) and to protect what is already a virtually unsustainable mass of toxic debt. It is no surprise that, also in February 2024, the Estonian Prime Minister, Kaja Kallas, recommended the same monetary strategy implemented for the EU during Covid: the issuance of €100 billion in Eurobonds (€750 billion in Coronabonds was mobilized in 2020) to relaunch the EU's military industry whilst awaiting the new barbarian invasions. The use of borrowing to deal with Putin and other "apocalyptic emergencies" duly packaged by the media is the last-ditch economic model for crisis capitalism. The internal limit (collapse of the mode of production) is denied through its external projection, embodied by providential enemies who are thirsty for democratic blood. "War bond" as fiscal bulwark; this is how the liberal, progressive, and morally superior West faces its own implosion.

The war dividend

In 2024, the arms race began nearly everywhere in the West. In Great Britain, General Patrick Sanders, head of the British Army, proposed the mass recruitment of citizens to send to the (obviously, Russian) front,[30] while new Defence Minister Grant Schapps could not even be bothered to conceal the economic opportunism of the call to arms:

> *The era of the peace dividend is over.* In five years' time we could be looking at multiple theatres involving Russia, China, Iran and North Korea. [...] Firstly, we must make our industry more resilient to empower us to re-arm, re-supply and innovate far faster than our opponents. *There's a huge opportunity here for British industry.* The UK has long been a by-word for pioneering technologies. We gave the world radar, the jet-engine and the world wide web. We've not lost that spark of creativity. On the contrary, today the UK is one of only three $1 trillion tech economies. But just imagine what we could do if we managed to better harness that latent inspiration, ingenuity and invention for the Defence of our nation?[31]

Similarly, EU technocrats suddenly took to reading from the same script as they did during the Covid-19 crisis, preparing European populations for decades of war against Russia. Above all, this means that we are entering an era of growing military indebtedness for the (supposed) monopoly on violence in multiple theaters of war that, precisely because they are financially motivated, must never disappear from sight. As Julian Assange put it in 2011 in reference to Afghanistan, "The goal is an endless war, not a successful war."[32] This scenario comes with socioeconomic and cultural decadence, the repression of dissent, and the domestication of impoverished plebs—who are also forced to applaud the performance of a former comedian turned "leader of the resistance," who travels the world demanding weapons and money in order to send generations of Ukrainians to the slaughterhouse. But it would be delusional to believe that the narrative of the West's "noble military commitment" is merely the latest episode of a Netflix show we can afford to watch from the safe distance of our sofas, perhaps cleansing our consciences with generic pacifist slogans. Because the more the model of financial capitalism falters, the more those who continue to profit from it will not hesitate to sacrifice under "democratic bombs" not only the "wretched of the earth" of which Franz Fanon wrote (populations which have, like the Palestinians, long been abandoned to conditions of subhuman misery and abuse) but also the placid dwellers of the "affluent world," who are as highly considered by the elites as a herd of grazing cattle with smartphones glued to their noses.

The now permanent call to arms (against Virus, Putin, Hamas, the Houthis, Iran, China, and all the villains to come) functions as a cover both desperate and criminal for the failing economic logic at the mercy of its financial degeneration. The emergency drama must be stoked without interruption, or else the balloon that carries the "civilization of profit" will burst. As the monetary methadone guaranteed by the psycho-pandemic runs out, liquidity issues once again come to a head. During 2024, central bankers' monetary policy of higher interest rates was at risk of flopping as the balance of the Federal Reserve's reverse repo facility (which acts as a primary indicator of bank reserves by draining liquidity) continued to nosedive[33] and the BTFP (Bank Term Funding Program,[34] the emergency loan program created by the US central bank in March 2023 to deal with the crisis triggered by the bankruptcy of Silicon Valley Bank) came to an end. In a repeat of September 2019, the ominously named "March madness" heightened the risk of a bloodbath in the debt markets. Here it is important to note that loans from traditional banks to the shadow banking system (the poorly regulated financial sphere populated by pension funds, insurance companies, hedge funds, asset managers, etc.) has recently exceeded 1 trillion dollars.[35] The recipients of these loans—highly leveraged nonbank financial companies—package and invest them as debt for increasingly risky subjects.

Such an increase in leverage, which was also at the heart of the 2008 crisis, is an obvious indicator of growing systemic volatility. According to data from the Financial Stability Board (US Supervisory Authority), shadow banking assets amounted to 218 trillion dollars at the end of 2023,[36] approximately 50% of global financial assets. These are mostly highly leveraged securitizations and repurchase agreements (repos), which constitute the essence of today's financial system: debt structured into more debt; a forward flight of debt-based speculation without real underlying value. The fragility of this mechanism is intrinsic, since the insolvency of a single player would cause the entire pyramid to collapse, subsequently triggering large-scale economic contagion. For this reason, the financial sector is perpetually thirsty for liquidity. It is therefore fairly easy to predict what comes next: in a setting dominated by a QT policy (reduction of the central bank's balance sheet) that is essentially bogus—since it is offset by fixed-term emergency programs like BTFT—the Fed (and its associates) will soon need the lever of new major emergencies to justify cutting interest rates and inject freshly minted liquidity into the system.

It is interesting to observe how Western political and economic institutions, even when harshly criticized, are depicted by the media as if in a painting from the early Middle Ages: without context. They exist *eo ipso* courtesy of a self-referential metaphysical aura that insulates them from any relationship with their real environs. Individually, of course, politicians and technocrats are regularly reprimanded and ridiculed. Their governing institutions, however, which are in principle responsible for carrying out tasks of public interest, remain untouchable, since they supposedly embody the highest point in the scale of "best possible worlds." Yet it has become increasingly clear that the quasi-sacred character of liberal-democratic governance hides its total dependence on the movements of financial capital. The moral pillars on which liberal power is built are, more obviously than ever, an extension of the amoral drive of capitalist profitability.

The Western middle classes are prisoners of their past, convinced that postwar liberal-democratic capitalism is, as a model of social organization, not only fundamentally just but also eternal and unquestionable. This optical illusion, which has until now allowed for nearly unconditional trust in our institutions (even when harshly criticized), is understandable: the Western middle classes have for years been the object of big capital's most loving attention, in the context of a profitable social contract organized around mass wage labor and growing consumption habits. Capital, in other words, has simultaneously shaped and exploited a work society modelled on the "ideal standard" of the worker-consumer satisfied by the dream of upward social mobility. But this stems from the bygone era of the baby boomers, who still delude themselves by thinking they are ontologically relevant when, in truth, they were always opportunistically engineered by a postwar economic boom that, incidentally, resulted from the "creative destruction" of two world wars. And the point is that such a "world" lasted, in the capitalist center, for about thirty years, which is like a flutter of the hummingbird's wings when compared to the centuries-old history of a mode of production that, in Marx's words, comes into the world "dripping from head to foot, from every pore, with blood and dirt."[37]

The fog of war, in which we are now lost once again, obscures the real object of contention: not the enemy to be fought but our toxic dependence on the mother of all modern illusions—the illusion, that is, that capital spontaneously generates a civilizing social bond. The civilization I am referring to is the same one that today justifies the shameless extermination of the Palestinians. Such extermination is more atrocious the more it conforms to the racist matrix of a "development model" of society that, as a rule, imposes its values by crushing those who do not conform to them—including millions of the destitute and the oppressed who testify, with their painful diversity, to the very failure of capitalist socialization.

Our Zone of Interest: The noise of permanent warfare

The string of geopolitical conflicts we are experiencing (predicted, as a rule, by corporate media and either launched or escalated when financial markets are closed) are neither accidental nor arbitrary. They are symptoms of growing systemic fragility, inscribed in the dialectical deployment of the collapsing logic of capital. Such a depressive constellation is in no way unique in history, and yet it is symptomatic of the implosion of our civilization. The causal connection between socioeconomic downfall and relentless emergency may appear counterintuitive, but it is *the* existential requirement of global late-capitalist work society insofar as it is supported by the artificial creation of colossal and ever-increasing amounts of debt. We must appreciate the inverted logic at play here: wars at the peripheries of empire are not the reason for economic decline. Rather, the implosive economic environment activates military conflicts in a desperate bid to save appearances and postpone the moment of truth. Wars (especially when marketed as humanitarian, defensive, or "against terror") are, in essence, criminal means to "easy money," which is what keeps today's financial bubbles inflated to record-breaking highs while the actual economic conditions of millions of workers (or the "inactive workforce") crater at an equally record-breaking pace.

Let us zoom out a little further. The enormous mass of debt that has for decades been pumped into a labyrinthine financial architecture, requiring constant refinancing, is now the key driver of the eschatological narratives that have mushroomed all around us—from the planetary anthropogenic climate change catastrophe to the Covid "pandemic" and the revenant of the nuclear holocaust. The debt spiral we are in is a death spiral, literally. It can no longer be placed in any "productive" context. World debt is surging at an unprecedented pace while the real economy is contracting steadily, with no end in sight. In capitalist terms, more and more debt must be brought into existence to chase the debt that hangs over our heads like a sword of Damocles. Without this mechanism in place, the entire financial and socioeconomic system locks up. And it is easy to imagine what would ensue: mayhem in the streets, civil wars, and the sudden disintegration of the social bond. However, the immediate side effect of expanding debt perpetually in order to "finance emergencies" is currency devaluation—the epochal crisis of the money medium that is already sweeping the globe.

Perhaps it is a sign of the times that even the sharpest thinkers, historians and geopolitical commentators struggle to comprehend the existential nature of the liaison between our debt-based economic system and military escalation. In particular, they seem not to understand why the hyperindebted West keeps trying to pick a geopolitical fight, when the logic is very simple: today's emergencies are not independent variables but the destructive modus operandi of implosive capitalist reproduction. The sound of bombs in Ukraine, Gaza and the Middle East is the operatic accompaniment to the deadly dance of recession and inflation in the era of QE infinity, stagnating incomes, and structural debt monetization. The ineluctable realities of economic implosion need to drown in the deafening cacophony of war or the promotion of its threat. Psychopathic financial elites love the smell of napalm in the morning. The Maginot Line of their financial casino is under such severe pressure that only continuous geopolitical noise can preserve the illusion of systemic sustainability. This is how perverse the mechanism has become: global capital needs Covid, Ukraine, Gaza, the Houthis, Iran, and so on—ideally all at once, but also in alternation—so that the can is kicked a little further down the road.

The accelerating disintegration of the highly integrated socioeconomic system demands more social destruction and human blood so that the sacred profiteering mechanism can grind on. The economic function of the global industry of chaos and destabilization is, at heart, *aggressively self-defensive*, working as a Pavlovian trigger for (1) mass monetary injections into the bulimic body of financialized capitalism and (2) the turning of the authoritarian screw on immiserated populations. We should not be afraid to spell it out: the havoc wreaked on humanity by "crisis capitalism" feeds into the formation of a new dictatorial order, namely a techno-fascist, AI-driven, interoperable control infrastructure that draws its force from, among other things, infectious pseudoleftist rhetoric.

Whether it is identity politics, concern for public safety, or the new religion of net-zero green economy, such humanitarian rhetoric plays a powerful ideological role for two interconnected reasons: it responds to the need to manipulate and control increasingly destitute populations while also disabling any serious collective struggle against rampant poverty and the physical removal of the superfluous and unproductive. In a nutshell, the critique of political economy is preemptively disabled by faux-leftist conservatism serving the interests of the elites rather than the underprivileged and excluded. The result is that oppression has long since become anonymous. Any sense of class solidarity is lost, while the atomized masses fail to grasp that they have turned into objects of a socioeconomic process that they, in a bitter twist of irony, enthusiastically support.

Insofar as it works with corporations, bankers, and the invisible elites, the liberal left contributes significantly to the exacerbation of our systemic crisis. That today's "progressive" discourse is not only unable to reflect upon the economic cause of the emergency paradigm but also denounces it as conspiratorial is the definitive proof of its surrender to, or opportunistic participation in, the destructive logic of contemporary capitalism. It is the fashionable liberal left in particular that is now a pathetic force for status quo conservation, having therefore relocated to the right. *Any left deserving of its name should always begin from the beginning: the critique of political economy.* This task is particularly urgent at a historical moment when the discourse of political economy has achieved global dominance. Capital's criminal operations are in full view, and to turn a blind eye to them is equally criminal. The consequences we face will be nothing short of disastrous. In the best-case scenario, the steady devaluation of fiat currencies translates into unforgiving desocialization and the bleeding to death of the social link.

In 1968, at the dawn of the neoliberal class war, Theodor Adorno cautioned that

> the relations of production [between the capitalist owners and the workers] have not been revolutionized, and their power is greater than ever. However, at the same time, since they are objectively anachronistic, they are debilitated, damaged, and undermined. They no longer function autonomously. Economic intervention is not, as the older liberal school believed, an alien element grafted from the outside, but an intrinsic part of the system, the epitome of self-defense.[38]

This dismal picture has now rapidly degenerated. As I have argued, the "self-defense" of today's bankrupt brand of Western "advanced capitalism" necessitates *economic intervention* in the form of external monetary leverage (debt); which in turn requires *emergency intervention* in the form of geopolitical, epidemiological, etc. leverage; which in turn demands *ideological intervention* in the form of political and corporate media "narrative leverage" to both expedite the above constellation and take control of the resulting socioeconomic folding. The direction of travel for this leveraged mechanism was indeed predicted by the Frankfurt School of Critical Theory: the liberal democratic West, controlled by iron-clad economic laws that have reduced the political class to an obedient technocratic administrator of financial interests, is turning totalitarian. Political conditions are dictated by the automatic pilot of the financial algorithm while the old illusion of the invisible hand of the market has evaporated. Parliament is increasingly the expression of a political ideology whose purpose is to mask real socioeconomic contradictions. And because capitalism—as a social relation sustained by value-producing labor—is now in terminal agony, the political managers of the algorithm are enabling a permanent state of emergency that increasingly resembles a permanent state of barbarism.

This is why the "zone of interest" (*Interessengebiet*) depicted in the eponymous film directed by Jonathan Glazer should be read as both a metaphorical indictment of our moral and intellectual bankruptcy vis-à-vis the ongoing genocide in Palestine (as intimated by the director) and a powerful reminder of how barbarism is the inevitable outcome of capitalist denialism. Glazer's is a film on memory that speaks to present and future returns of the same (which is why it has no temporal narrative development). It deliberately presents Hannah Arendt's theme of the "banality of evil," embodied by Rudolf Höss (Auschwitz commandant) and other Nazi officers, as blind compliance with capitalist objectivity, including concern with surplus value extraction and productivity (e.g., in relation to the incineration of bodies), the ruthless individualistic pursuit of career moves, mindless bourgeois hyperactivity, and the professional planning of new "business models" for maximizing efficiency in concentration camps. Barbarism originates in this specific zone of dogmatic capitalist interest, which is so ingrained in the modern mind that it makes the disavowal of genocide possible. As Glazer put it, "The more fragments of information we uncovered about Rudolf and Hedwig Höss in the Auschwitz archives, the more I realized that they were working-class people who were upwardly mobile. They aspired to become a bourgeois family in the way that many of us do today. That was what was so grotesque and striking about them—how familiar they were to us."[39]

Contrary to Glazer's approach, the cultural operators of the West have always sought to place the atrocities of the Nazis (and others) in the extrahistorical and metapolitical realm of absolute evil, essentially replicating at the opposite end of the moral spectrum the central myth of Nazi mysticism: purification through annihilation.[40] A glaring example of this ideological ruse is in Steven Spielberg's *Schindler's List* (1993), which provides us with the figure of the redeemed Nazi as an enlightened industrialist (Oskar Schindler), thus propping up a wall between the free capitalist work society and Nazi totalitarianism. For Spielberg, work indeed makes you free. In the unexpected final scene of *The Zone of Interest*, this cliché is challenged in a subtle, thought-provoking way as Glazer cuts to the present-day Auschwitz-Birkenau Memorial and Museum, showing custodians (all women) dusting the exhibits and vacuum-cleaning the empty corridors after closing time. The camp, in other words, is still a workplace, deeply embedded within the capitalist mode of production. Far from amounting to a sentimental flash-forward, as some critics have claimed, this is probably the most weirdly obscene moment in the film, reminding us that the past, present and future atrocities of the modern world share a very precise common denominator.

The current deadlock shows that there is no progressive teleology in the history of modernity, as the conditions for barbarism resurface regularly. Capitalism as a "socially necessary illusion" is breaking at the seams, and yet it perseveres through a mixture of insidious manipulation and unadulterated violence. At the heart of this persistence lies another crucial achievement: the persuading of fragmented and impoverished workers that they are responsible for their own fates. They need to assume responsibility. They also need to sacrifice by adapting, reskilling, disqualifying and requalifying, all while being patronized by the media and the political class. Precisely because it no longer needs labor-intensive production, capital has successfully dismantled the working class, thus elevating its exploitation to new peaks. The new technologies eliminate much more labor power than capital can profitably reintegrate while also demanding of workers a dehumanizing degree of flexibility, speed, and cynical opportunism—the eye must be faster than the mind. This all confirms that today's emergency capitalism is of an administrative kind. Its project is to *manage* gargantuan profits for a small elite while the rest end up excluded. However, precisely due to the disabling of the old proletariat as the subject of value production and consumption, the new poor have nothing to lose. They will continue to constitute a latent threat that could explode at any moment.

Capital no longer knows what to do with millions of humans who vegetate in conditions of symbolic death, no longer having a role to play—not even as a Marxian "industrial reserve army"—in its grand narrative. Many in future generations will find themselves occupying the position of "human surplus" with respect to reckless profit-making dynamics. They are likely to end up locked into a system of control with respect to the capitalist zone of interest, or worse. But as "inoperable and disposable excess," they represent the negation (and potential rejection) of the system. In all probability, a socio-anthropological horizon of sense alternative to the capitalist one will need to be built by and for them from that position of radical exclusion.

5.
Perversions of Crisis Capitalism

> In recent days, scientists from the *School of Plant Sciences* at Tel Aviv University have announced that with special ultrasound-sensitive microphones they have recorded the screams of pain that plants emit when they are cut or when they lack water. In Gaza there are no microphones.
> —Giorgio Agamben[1]

THE BEST WAY TO GRASP the meaning of our new normal is to frame it as an irreversible paradigm shift toward crisis capitalism. The key macroeconomic implication here is that today's capitalism no longer needs crises to enhance its capacity for growth, instead requiring crises to hide its chronic impotence. What has changed is therefore the epistemic function of "crisis." While it was in the past a means for new economic cycles, crisis today (whether economic, geopolitical or otherwise) serves to facilitate the aggressive management of irreversible societal decay, since the boom-and-bust engine is flooded and Schumpeter's "creative destruction" creates only rubble. However counterintuitive it may seem, the credit addiction of ultrafinancialized capitalism thrives on the *contraction* of the real economy, which it brings to fruition through a continuous stream of global shocks—the job of today's "emergency industry." It is precisely because of its inherent entropy that crisis capitalism is not only politically authoritarian but also shamelessly perverse. Upon returning from leave in November 2003, reservist Joseph Darby asked a colleague at Abu Ghraib prison (Baghdad, Iraq) to brief him on what had happened during his absence. Specialist

Charles Graner handed him two CDs containing hundreds of digital photographs, many of which captured US Army officers and Secret Service agents torturing and abusing prisoners. The images depicted men and women being attacked by dogs; having electrodes applied to their legs, arms, and genitals while being hooded; being forced into humiliating poses while naked; and being sodomized with phosphorescent tubes and objects of various types, with some victims having been tortured to their deaths. In 2024, the same obscene images—including in the form of videos posted on social media by IDF soldiers, which exhibit torture and humiliation like a badge of honor[2]—have returned. These images continue to offer, as Slavoj Žižek put it long ago, "a direct insight into 'American values,' into the core of an obscene enjoyment that sustains the American way of life."[3]

Calculated crises and selective defaults

It is revealing that today's critical voices, whether conservative or progressive, share the same nostalgia for a world that is withering away: the liberal-democratic work society, which capital itself is making obsolete. Even those radical thinkers who insist on seeing emancipatory potential in the highly volatile present are more often than not liberals in denial, since the emancipation they invoke relies on the very values and categories that brought us to where we are. In other words, they fatally underestimate the totalitarian appetite of crisis capitalism. This is understandable, since the limits of capitalism are also the limits of our imagination. No problem can be fully solved from the same level of consciousness that brought it into existence. However, it is high time for us to question the actual sustainability of our existential comfort zone, for history tells us that humanity's descent into barbarism is, as a rule, expedited by political disavowal—the same stubborn disavowal that seems to unify conservatives, progressives, and much of the so-called radical left today. What today's critical voices tend to fail to consider is that capitalism is perfectly capable of reproducing its worn-out categories within a despotic framework, just as it is perfectly capable of faking a liberal façade while gradually suspending the social contract.

The main lesson of the Covid affair is that the manipulation of financial markets translates directly as the manipulation of reality. "Systematically distorted markets" equals "systematically distorted reality." The master discourse is no longer the labor-driven economy but the finance-driven ideological management of collective socioeconomic burnout, which the "pandemic" has introduced on a global scale. The decoupling of a work society in freefall from the financial stratosphere—where distortion across the spectrum of asset classes is the norm—confirms that a new capitalist era, one based not merely on surveillance but on prevarication and control in particular, has now begun.

The aim of central bank monetary policy is no longer the stabilization of prices but the stabilization of decline so that markets continue to flourish. For example, the Fed's rate-hike cycle that began in March 2022 was meant to fight inflation by tightening credit to the real world, especially to SMEs (small and midsize enterprises).[4] Stated differently, today's structural inflation can only be kept under control by depressing demand, which crushes the economic resilience of ordinary people. At the same time, interest rates cannot be kept "higher for longer," since such a prospect increases the potential for a devastating liquidity freeze in the bond and stock markets. It is therefore clear that central bankers are caught between a rock and a hard place. The crisis of regional US banks in March and April 2023 offers a particularly instructive example. The wreckage initiated with the collapse of Silicon Valley Bank (SVB) on March 10, 2023, can be read simultaneously as an inevitable consequence of "higher for longer" rates and as a step toward the centralized restructuring of the banking sector. A credit-addicted economy that has no way to reignite a labor-intensive cycle of real growth has no choice but to consolidate control of fiat currencies, thus thriving on calculated crises and selective defaults, which must of course be ascribed to external rather than systemic factors. An indebted system that piles risk needs a steady flow of not only liquidity but also scapegoats and alibis—including "regional bank failures." Let us see why.

As far as today's markets are concerned, financial actors know that any global alarm or geopolitical shock causes central banks to leap into action to support bonds, thus pushing risk assets higher and galvanizing the speculative sector as a whole. Everyone, from megabanks to investment funds and retail investors, has *at least* some intuitive awareness that the "fair value" mechanism of financial markets is rigged, and one might argue that this is precisely why they continue to have faith in it. In this context, sacrificial lambs like SVB trigger artificial rallies based on buy-the-dips, short squeezes, corporate buybacks, and other occurrences that are now factored into the "silent reward" agreement insured by the Fed's backstop programs.

It could be surmised that the collapsing of regional banks through rate hikes was (yet another) stroke of evil genius from our financial aristocracy, being predicated on the knowledge that Global Systemically Important Banks (G-SIBs) like JP Morgan Chase would not risk contagion, since they were still buffered by reserves from "pandemic QE." For example, JP Morgan ended up consolidating its position thanks to its cut-rate acquisition of insolvent First Republic Bank. Moreover, billions in deposits moved out of disgraced regional banks and into megabank coffers. At the same time, we should bear in mind that the banking crisis inaugurated by SVB originated in the failure of the underlying collateral, i.e., US debt securities. Essentially, SVB collapsed because it held a high volume of traditionally safe long-term Treasury bonds (US government bonds) that suddenly lost much of their value. As interest rates increased, the price of these bonds fell, making the bank's debt exposure untenable and causing bank runs. The overarching point is that despite being an opportunistic event, this banking crisis was at the same time a symptom of systemic breakdown. In 2023 alone, five regional US banks went bust in succession, like falling dominoes: Silicon Valley Bank, Signature Bank, First Republic Bank, Heartland Tri-State Bank, and Citizens Bank.

After that symptomatic collapse, banks at risk of failure were allowed to take full advantage of generous long-term loans from the previously mentioned BTFP facility (activated by the Fed in March 2023 following SVB's bankruptcy), which was further backstopped by £25 billion from the Exchange Stabilization Fund. The BTFP was essentially a bank bailout facility, providing a new source of liquidity for those banks (as well as savings associations and credit unions) who pledged as collateral US Treasuries, mortgage-backed securities, and similar assets, which were valued at "par" (i.e., at face value, irrespective of market value fluctuation). Furthermore, the Fed already provides banks with billions of dollars in short-term loans through its discount window. In short, the banking sector is leaking from all sides and needs continuous monetary support from the "last resort" central bank. It is worth noting that mid-January 2024 saw usage of the BTFP pass the $160 billion mark in weekly funding.[5] What banks did was borrow money from the BTFP at a discount and deposit it at the Fed to earn higher interest (the current interest on reserve balances), effectively receiving free money.

With SVB, a case could be made that by choosing a scapegoat in advance, the system once again kicked the can a little further down the road. Yet it is crucial to bear in mind that, should the insubstantial financial scaffolding built on free money and layers of derivative bets fall apart, it is not only banks but society as well—the whole world as we know it—that would suddenly crumble. A debt-shackled system like ours could be compared to a black hole that sucks all the cash thrown at it like spaghetti. The exposure of most banks to derivatives is already through the roof (in June 2023, Goldman Sachs alone was exposed to over $53 trillion in derivatives).[6] Because a liquidity freeze could happen at any time in our inflated environment, the Fed (in lockstep with other major central banks) must not only remain vigilant if it is to keep confidence levels high; it must also find ways to preempt potential collapse. How? For instance, by nudging the system to selective defaults through which to justify "rescue and consolidation" packages. Arguably, controlled demolition now means that even the fragile financial structure is being dismantled piece by piece, in preparation for the new, highly centralized and fully digitized monetary infrastructure. However, a substantial crisis will be required if the new system is to be implemented successfully. We will need to be traumatized so heavily that we not only accept our new digital chains but even beg for them.

"Safe and effective" digital shots

As the debt crisis turns into a banking crisis, it becomes increasingly clear that implosive capitalism needs some form of centralized mechanism for digital currency jurisdiction. The embryonic stage of this shift to top-down monetary control is what the BIS (the "central bank of all central banks") fittingly calls Project Icebreaker.[7] Its initial aim is for central banks to use digital transactions among themselves. In reality, however, we have good reason to suspect that this is only the "icebreaker," the significant first step toward creating the infrastructure that will "save us" from the next downturn. We should not forget that central banks have, since the dawn of the "pandemic," persistently announced Central Bank Digital Currencies as the future of monetary transactions. It is true that, as Yanis Varoufakis (among others) reminds us,[8] the state and the police already have the power to control our transactions, as was demonstrated with the freezing of truck drivers' bank accounts during the Canadian antivaccination protests of February 2022.

However, that disturbing intervention required the Emergency Act—a time-limited "state of exception"—which was always likely to be met with widespread popular resistance. The authorization of a centralized digital system of absolute monetary control is quite another kettle of fish. As a matter of fact, Varoufakis sees central bank digital technology as a democratic tool,[9] presumably because he projects it (whether romantically or disingenuously) onto a world that has somehow managed to rid itself of the capitalist relation: "Privacy could be better safeguarded if transactions were to be concentrated on the central bank ledger under the supervision of something like a *Monetary Supervision Jury* comprising randomly selected citizens and experts drawn from a wide range of professions." While this may tickle our utopian imagination, unfortunately we are still at the mercy of implosive capitalism, which suggests that any monetary supervision jury is likely to be supervised by the ultrarich oligarchy in a coordinated effort to keep rising poverty levels in check while retaining power and privileges.

This is not merely a question of political ingenuity, or desire, as the money issue is rooted in complex and unforgiving socioeconomic terrain. Varoufakis's proposal to cut out the middlemen—the commercial banking system—so that central banks can pour money directly into everyone's digital wallets (as Universal Basic Income, for instance) completely bypasses the existential dilemma that capital faces today: its inability to generate sufficient amounts of new value, and thus social wealth, through labor-intensive growth cycles. This is why it relies so heavily on mouse-clicked credit inflating financial bubbles. As I have argued, the trafficking of financial assets produces fictitious increases in value, which no longer have anything to do with the real profits derived from the entrepreneurial consumption of labor. Staggeringly, yet consistent with his position, Varoufakis prescribes more quantitative easing for investment in the green and digital transition, as if this worn-out Keynesian move could magically conjure a new accumulation regime from today's terminal stagnation and save capitalist societies from their grim destiny. It is a simple solution for a simplistic reading. In truth, neo-Keynesian and neoliberal recipes are both yesterday's news—they have repeatedly proven their inability to resurrect the capitalist mode of production, since they only confront it at the surface level. The deeper—and most urgent—issue we face is the structural crisis of value creation in a rapidly deflating economy, which is why centralized digital currencies can only work as cynical and *despotic* tools for the regimentation of mass decline. Any other hypothesis is, at best, jaw-droppingly naïve.

At present, CBDCs are being introduced as a "safe and effective" payment system, which, among other beautiful things, will guarantee safer banking and eliminate the risk of SVB-like failures. In all likelihood, however, the next serious crisis will show the true face of CBDC, coercing us to accept more misery and less freedom. As we saw with Covid, a state of exception leaves us with no real choice. For many people, maintaining a job meant taking the "vaccine." We are now moving toward a real economic slump that, regardless of whether it materializes as a deflationary market crash or a hyperinflationary cycle (or both in rapid succession), will likely be followed by a prodigious technological solution from the elites: deposits could be moved to "a central bank near you," meaning that whatever you owe would become the liability of that central bank, which would guarantee protection by managing your money flows digitally. As with Covid jabs, most citizens will take the "safe and effective" bait. Capitalism is really the gift that keeps on giving! The endgame is now writ large: a global economy undergoing slow-motion collapse can only attempt to perpetuate itself via some form of direct control over its debased currencies.

It is impossible to determine our proximity to a watershed moment that will prove to be shocking (i.e., convenient) enough for the introduction of the new monetary regime. Silicon Valley Bank, Signature, First Republic and the other banks that collapsed in 2023 provided just a small taste of things to come. The system is breaking at the seams, and a credit event is now long overdue—as heralded by the repo crisis of September 2019, the crash of March 2020, the UK guild implosion of October 2022, the regional banking crisis of March 2023, and the subsequent failure of Credit Suisse (a globally systemic bank). In this respect, we should not forget that Bear Stearns' trouble began in July 2007 (when two of its hedge funds imploded), a year before financial operators realized that the entire house of cards was about to collapse as the interbank sector began to freeze on counterparty risk (summer 2008)—whereas the average Joe had to wait until September 15, 2008, when he could see, on TV, Lehman Brothers' brokers and traders leaving their workplaces with cardboard boxes in their hands. Are we now living a historical parallel? Are the events of 2023 the anticipation of another Wall Street meltdown? There is little doubt that the Titanic is accelerating toward the iceberg, a major incident that will, in all probability, be used to draft in the miracle cure: a "digital monetary vaccine" that protects everyone—or so it will be claimed—against the economic virus.

We live in an age of extreme socioeconomic fragmentation, which is meant to be controlled from the top down. The decomposition of our world manifests as both the fracturing of the social bond (supported by the retail economy) and the extreme pressure on financial markets. Yet, as Ernest Hemingway reminded us in *The Sun Also Rises*, bankruptcy happens "in two ways. Gradually, and then suddenly." And as we brace for the hard landing, the distrust that rises from below begins to clash with the policies of crisis management imposed from above. This translates into an increase in economic, social, military, and cultural stressors. The first thing to do is accept that there are currently pockets of resistance and angry rebellion but no collective alternatives in sight. While capital still occupies most of us 24/7 (in the form of precarious and/or overbearing work, mass distraction, false polarization, cognitive dissonance, and emotional blackmail), it makes us superfluous at the same time. From the perspective of the reproduction of capital, which is our civilization's indisputable metaphysical dogma, most humans are becoming expendable, like cannon fodder. The problem here is the lack of collective awareness regarding the cause of this paradigm shift. Most people still behave as though they are central to the system's logic of reproduction—whether as voters, workers, or consumers. But the role of the masses in relation to capital's profitability is rapidly changing, as we are becoming dispensable. Whatever form a genuinely emancipatory postcapitalist society would take, it must replace the current mode of (re)production with a social bond through which we learn to make a radically different use of our time, creativity, and modes of enjoyment—that is to say, a different use of our freedom.

To this effect, economic science is of little help since it is undermined by a serious positivistic flaw—the same flaw that has always threatened traditional Marxism as well. As long as we link our crisis to empirical causes, economic science will keep missing the target. Hegemonic economic thought reduces all reality to quantifiable units that are observable on the surface. Whatever escapes empirical calculation is, at best, demoted to the rank of philosophical speculation. But in its epistemological arrogance, bourgeois economics proves inadequate to capture the social substance of economic relations. All it can do is offer us rebrandings of old formulas, from "Bidenomics" to "securonomics."[10] The latter neologism is the latest iteration of the "green neo-Keynesianism" recently mobilized by the UK's Labour Party. As usual, it promises to deliver an exciting mix of more state debt and investment in new technology (a £28 billion-per-year "green prosperity plan") that aims to create more jobs and a secure financial environment for all British citizens. In other words, it is yet another case of political denialism, only demonstrating that our political representatives are sleepwalking into the abyss.

To grasp our world's direction of travel, we had better leave behind the exhausted stimulus versus austerity diatribe and instead reflect on the deeper indicators: (1) the increasing contraction of the overall mass of surplus value; (2) the secular growth of credit; (3) the widening of the gap between this credit without substance (created out of thin air) and real surplus value (generated through the exploitation of productive labor); and (4) the global paradigm shift from liberal capitalism to the illiberal, ubercapitalist dystopia currently in the making. The last point is a direct consequence of the first three, and to ignore the causal relationship is to engage in a critique of the new normal that is tragically sterile and counterproductive.

The steady decline of economic growth that has been seen in recent decades requires an increase in money creation to chase the debt that is continuously put into circulation. Debt today is necessary and tautological. What should be emphasized is the delayed effect of this monetary phenomenon, since today's inflation is essentially the result of past credit expansion, which takes time to work its way through a system that struggles to generate sufficient amounts of new surplus value. Insisting that today's inflationary environment can be explained solely by empirically quantifiable factors means adhering to the positivistic myopia of dominant neoclassical economics, and thus to a hopelessly ahistorical view of capitalism. Today's secular devaluation is the inevitable result of the credit avalanche set in motion in previous decades and building since 2008 in particular. This avalanche is now rolling downhill ominously. Sadly, we have not seen anything yet in relation to its impact. In this sense, tinkering with the calculation of the effect that the current rate hike may have on inflation is pointless, not least because these rate hikes are limited by the destructive effect that, past a certain threshold, they unleash on the financial architecture. This was demonstrated emphatically by the banking collapse of March–April 2023.

Objections stating that interest-bearing capital and credit have always informed the history of capitalism are misleading, as well as intellectually lazy. What matters is the historical process that has led to today's grotesque dependence on credit creation. The transformation in the role of credit within the capitalist mode of production can be traced back to the early twentieth century, when supplemental liquidity began to be incorporated into the mass of value produced through investment in wage labor.[11] This recourse to exogenous credit soon morphed from an occasional phenomenon to the condition of possibility for real production itself. During the twentieth century, the credit lever that was used for the extraction of surplus value presented itself with characteristics slightly different from those described by Marx in the third book of *Capital*. According to Marx's reading, credit interest is derived from the surplus value produced in the real economy, which in the second half of the nineteenth century still formed the basis of capitalism. But that reasoning now needs an update.

Choking on credit

The historical growth of credit is an inevitable consequence of the development of the capitalist mode of production. As profits from individual capitals are no longer sufficient to cover increasing investment in what Marx called "constant capital" (e.g., machines and raw materials), credit injections become endemic. In other words, technological acceleration begins to tighten a credit noose around individual capitals, as the iron law of competition leaves no choice but to increase costly investment in new technologies. At this point, a mechanism is established that redefines the internal logic of the mode of production while leaving its purpose intact. In order to gain new market shares, capitals are forced to accept the external constraint of credit, which gradually subjugates workers not only in terms of labor exploitation but also via the mass of financial speculation on which such capacity for exploitation comes to depend. And while capitals struggle to reproduce themselves through profit investments, the dependence on credit becomes a chronic (and toxic) addiction.

Contemporary capitalism works as a feedback loop between the communicating vessels of compensatory credit and the decreasing mass of surplus value. Individual capitals must continue to appropriate a share of surplus value to service their debts; however, a segment of this surplus value has already been colonized by the expanding pool of credit. Hence, every increase in surplus-value creation is merely the form of appearance for exponentially larger monetary expansions. The widening of the gap between insubstantial credit and real valorization means that the retail economy itself ends up flooded with toxic liquidity. At this stage, the apparent valorization of individual capitals corresponds to a contraction in the total value produced with respect to the money supply put into circulation—a situation of systemic imbalance which, after a period of incubation, manifests itself today as irreversible currency debasement. An economy cannibalized by credit can only destroy the value substance of its fiat money.

As the gap between real capital and fictitious credit widens, so does the potential for systemic collapse. At the same time, transnational capital has no option but to try to control the narratives that guarantee a continuous supply of credit. Once again, here is the paradox of our time: for the credit chains to continue to extend into the future, the real economy must be radically downsized. In order to survive its own devastating contradiction, hyperfinancialized capitalism must destroy portions of real demand by turning the screw on workers and consumers. Today, the "curious copulation"[12] of science and capital brings about not only a fatal crisis of valorization but also the *dematerialization of the real* as such. Codes and algorithms now preside over the ideological reconfiguring of social reality into hyperreality, where virtual simulations are the only available referential frameworks. In regard to this depressing picture, the historical mistake of the left (including the "orthodox" Marxist left) lies in its continued fetishization of wage labor. The left believes that work (and workers' struggles) can either save capitalism from implosion or, more radically, lead us beyond it. Yet, the question should be posed differently. At issue is not the way to save or supplant capitalism through wage labor but the way to transcend both capitalism and wage labor, for the latter was always the lifeblood of capital—not only its dialectical opponent but also its vital ingredient and condition of possibility. Wage labor is what made capital possible by socializing it into capitalism.

The contradiction that defines labor power today is that there is too little of it for the valorization process but too much for the system's absorptive capacity. For this reason, labor power must be rationalized and regimented (while also being further oppressed and exploited). Capital's need to expand can no longer be satisfied by labor exploitation alone. Its profitability is engineered today by the financial simulation of growth, which is without value substance. Such profitability runs on oceanic masses of debt, which support both demand—otherwise tending to zero—and real production costs. We are already hostage to a future in which the mass of surplus value (and therefore real profitability) pales when compared to the mass of credit needed to keep it alive. This means that the very temporality of capital has shifted from the past (reproduction through profits that have already been accumulated) to the future (reproduction through profits that are not yet realized). While the two temporalities remain intertwined, the exponential growth of credit (in parallel with the growth of the share of constant capital) fosters a qualitative mutation in the composition of capital, which is the underlying cause of the ongoing collapse.

The irony of it all is that today's credit-addicted economy is choking on its own productivity. Whether it is military spending for armed conflicts or any other kind of technological investment, their origin is in the creation (ultimately via central banks) of more inflationary debt. There is simply no way to avoid this suffocating mechanism. As a neutral signifier, "globalization" itself hides the fact that global production is now chained to increasingly unmanageable deficit cycles and attendant financial bubbles. In this respect, the slow realization that globalization is now unravelling into socioeconomic ruin is the main driver of military conflicts whose criminal logic is utterly blind to actual systemic implosion. Since 2001, the United States has engaged in continuous warfare, which has, according to a conservative estimate from a research project at Brown University,[13] caused (directly and indirectly) roughly 4.5 million deaths in post-9/11 war zones, including Afghanistan, Pakistan, Iraq, Syria, and Yemen. If the scope of this carnage affecting "disposable populations" makes the news at all, it is only to appeal to a deeply hypocritical sense of guilt that is tragically unable to locate the root causes of the problem. What is rarely questioned, for instance, is the causal link binding US global economic dominance and its military-industrial complex, a multiheaded hydra that keeps wreaking havoc to delay the end of its hegemony.

At a time when dollar-based global domination is fading, the US continues to rely on the military-industrial complex as the backbone of both its currency and financial sector. The more indebted the economy, the more the military-industrial complex will find reasons to stretch its tentacles. To attempt to retain world supremacy, the debt-driven hyperfinancialized (unproductive) Western economic model must continue to channel billions into the military machine. The specific role of US-sponsored military conflicts is crucial here. Wars drive cash into Treasuries, because when war breaks out *and* the US military springs into action, US bonds still tend to be perceived as the safest assets, given the perceived dominance of the US. So, when the US military-industrial complex flexes its muscles in any war zone around the globe, either directly or by proxy, Treasuries get boosted as a rule, which in turn allows liquidity to move into the stock market. This is exactly what has happened with the Ukraine-Russia war and, more recently, the Israeli massacre of Palestinians. While global debt is increasingly unstable, the expansion of war can stabilize bond markets since it pushes cash into the perceived (for now) safety of debt.

This logic is perverse for two obvious reasons. First, it relies on chaos, devastation, and even genocide to prop up the financial sector and its desocializing model. Second, it is inversely proportional to what takes place in the real economy, where demand must be contained or destroyed to keep inflation from spiraling out of control. This is why we increasingly live in a state of perpetual war, which some commentators (including Pope Francis)[14] are now calling "World War III in instalments." Military conflicts are likely to escalate in rapid succession, presumably until our masters are ready to pull the plug and introduce a cross-border digital monetary prison of maximum control. The financing of a mammoth military at home and especially abroad through deficit spending works as an attempt to bolster the dollar (including the petrodollar) as hegemonic currency, hence the following paradox: even if, from an economic standpoint, every single leading indicator points downward, US GDP might even improve while government deficit spending vastly increases.[15] The world is now trapped in a vicious circle in which the funding of warfare fosters the *illusion* of a functioning economy—an illusion that will be propagandized remorselessly until no longer convenient.

It is important to emphasize that there are no victors in the current geopolitical contest, for the showdown occurs on the sinking Titanic, with social decline as the only shared outcome. It is objectively difficult, for instance, to see how the yuan could replace the dollar. The growth of the Chinese economy over the past five decades was characterized by its monopoly on manufacturing production, a phenomenon largely driven by investment from the deindustrializing United States. It therefore occurred within the framework of global deficit circuits, whereby debt dynamics in the West ended up generating demand for Chinese export, resulting in the inundation of Western markets with cheap products made in China (while, at the same time, productive countries like China also invested their net surpluses in dollar-denominated stocks and bonds, since the dollar remained the global reserve currency). However, this precarious equilibrium ended with the 2008 global financial crisis, when the bursting of real estate bubbles in the US and Europe caused the Chinese export-based surplus to decline. Since then, China's slowing economy has also been feeding on credit, following in the footsteps of its Western "business partner"—as confirmed by the magnitude of the Chinese real estate market bubble.

The Chinese economy has been operating on two primary pillars: unregulated shadow-bank lending (repos), and real estate, whose astronomical credit leverage perfectly reflects the logic of the entire financial system. However, events like the recent liquidation of Evergrande (China's real estate giant)[16] would seem to confirm that China is not in the position to emulate what the US did at the end of World War II. China's Belt and Road Initiative is no Marshall Plan. Furthermore, the Chinese central bank is now among the most active institutions purchasing physical gold, quite obviously because it is aware of how critical the global financial situation is. Consequently, should the self-destructive trend extend globally, the potential for a major war would become more real. At the same time, the latter can also be envisaged as a series of conflicts legitimized by a silent agreement between geopolitical enemies who know they share very similar economic destinies, as well as the need to impose a control infrastructure onto the masses.

As anticipated, modern wars are inextricably linked to the credit-addicted economy. Throughout the history of capitalism, wars have constantly been deployed to generate credit with which to finance armies, weapons, and new technologies. In this respect, the two world wars had already laid bare the interconnections between the state, capital, and credit creation. Technological competition imposed massive investments in constant capital, which turned credit into the new gold. Hence the gradual privatization of central banks, which now have the power to influence both geopolitical and sociocultural strategies. This explains why the recent "pandemic" was immediately labelled a "war against the virus," and why it was seamlessly replaced by real military wars (in Ukraine and then in Gaza and the Middle East), which are being prolonged into absurdity with typical capitalist contempt for human life. The war on Covid allowed the direct creation and issuance of colossal amounts of money into the system, condensing into a much narrower timeframe the perverse logic of the previous two decades of the "war on terror," which is now being reignited.

A new 9/11?

It is not surprising that the Western media unilaterally labelled the Hamas attacks of October 7 (operation Al-Aqsa Flood)[17] a "new 9/11." Of course, they referred to the official account of 9/11, indelibly impressed in its terrifying iconography (which typically excludes the response unleashed by the US in the Middle East over the two decades that followed, a protracted mass murder operation known as the "global war on terror"). What the "new 9/11" tag should evoke, in fact, is the opposite of what is implied by the mainstream media: since September 11, 2001, global emergencies have been rolled out with a diabolical sense of timeliness so that the proverbial can (the bankruptcy of the global economic system) is kicked further down the road.

If we seek a clue for what might have instigated the most recent iteration of the Israel-Palestine crisis, we could start with Joe Biden's speech of October 11, 2023: "When Congress returns, we're going to ask them to take urgent action to fund the security requirements of our critical partners."[18] Predictably, the US war chest expanded. On October 19, in a rare prime-time address from the Oval Office, Biden was explicit: "Hamas and Putin represent different threats, but they share this in common: they both want to completely annihilate a neighboring democracy… They keep going. And the cost and the threats to America and the world keep rising." Crucially, he stressed America's role as a "beacon to the world," "the essential nation"; "American leadership is what holds the world together. American alliances are what keep us, America, safe. American values are what make us a partner that other nations want to work with. To put all that at risk—if we walk away from Ukraine, if we turn our backs on Israel—it's just not worth it."

The truth content of Biden's speech needs to be extracted from his reassurances that the United States still protects the world. What Biden was desperate to hammer home was the message that, at the dawn of military escalation in the Middle East, US bonds were still the safest haven for investors. Biden wanted to send an assurance that the Federal Reserve would do "whatever it takes" to support the (increasingly shaky) Middle East petrodollar consensus, which was in turn expected to boost investment in US Treasuries. In other words, Biden was trying to convince his audience that skyrocketing US debt was still "good debt," safe to invest in. He was in essence selling a financial product that can still be regarded as nothing less than the pulsating heart of the global economy, despite being issued by a vastly unproductive economy. Hence, the US president's immediate request for billions of dollars in emergency security packages for Ukraine and Israel (as well as border security with Mexico and other "international crises").

Judging from the reactions of bond and financial markets, Biden was indeed successful in selling two wars for the price of one. In the weeks that followed Netanyahu's declaration of war on Hamas, markets throughout the Western world, and in the US especially, registered a "miraculous" recovery from the previous phase of major instability. More specifically, the 10-year Treasury yield—the benchmark indicator for the health of US debt—went from breaching the 5% threshold to the more sustainable 4.5% area after Biden's reassurance that the US would back Israel against "terror," and it ended up below 4% by the year's end. Because yields drop and cash flows into stocks when debt is purchased, the stock markets in turn benefited, rallying to unexpected heights across the Western world.[19] While the propaganda machine tried to sell the narrative that the financial rally was the effect of good economic news—e.g., data on a drop in core inflation for October 2023 and hints by the Fed regarding a pivot on rate hikes—the uncomfortable truth is that it took the murder of thousands of civilians to temporarily avert a catastrophic selloff in the bond market.

Covid, Ukraine, Israel; at a fundamental level, these cannot fail to appear as interchangeable emergencies released with clockwork precision. The common denominator in the crisis-to-crisis metanarrative is that global predicaments require funding, a continuous stream of liquidity meant to have much the same effect on heavily stressed bond markets as central bank QE does. This is why the saying that "war is the cure for Covid" hits the nail on the head (though it could always reverse into its opposite). Geopolitical crises are literally weaponized to pull easy money into the present and postpone the financial meltdown. Even the threat of expanding war and terrorist activity has the power to summon cash from nowhere (while also bombarding the masses with apocalyptic visions that gently nudge them to submit to the "only policing authority" that can provide safety). However, these are merely frantic, short-term strategies that follow one another in an absurd crescendo of violence and destruction that at present appears ineluctable.

In the West, it is likely that we are heading back to the old "war on terror" playbook, as demonstrated by "terrorist incidents" in France and Belgium immediately after the onset of Israel's carpet bombing of Gaza. On October 15, FBI Director Christopher Wray issued a warning about the rise of terrorism on American soil.[20] In fact, the resurgent threat of "jihadist terror" was announced months before the October 7 attacks. In May 2023, for instance, during a visit to the US, French interior minister Gérald Darmanin had asked for increased intelligence collaboration against "Islamic terrorism," which, with incredible foresight, he called "the primary threat in Europe."[21] This alert was repeated nearly verbatim in July by then UK Home Secretary Suella Braverman, who "identified Islamic terrorism as the primary UK domestic threat" and cautioned that "extremists could use artificial intelligence to plan more sophisticated terror attacks."[22] This is why the expansion of war from Ukraine to the Middle East, with the return of the threat of gory "Islamic terrorism," was always a predictable candidate for the "next crisis." The *déjà vu* of *déjà vu*.

If we adopt the moral standpoint, the truth of October 7 can be summed up with the words of Amira Hass, who wrote in *Haaretz* on October 10 that, "In a few days Israelis went through what Palestinians have experienced as a matter of routine for decades, and are still experiencing—military incursions, death, cruelty, slain children, bodies piled up in the road, siege, fear, anxiety over loved ones, captivity, being targets of vengeance, indiscriminate lethal fire at both those involved in the fighting (soldiers) and the uninvolved (civilians), a position of inferiority, destruction of buildings, ruined holidays or celebrations, weakness and helplessness in the face of all-powerful armed men, and searing humiliation."[23] In a more politically cautious manner, Slavoj Žižek argued that "Hamas and Israeli hardliners are two sides of the same coin. The choice is not one hardline faction or the other; it is between fundamentalists and all those who still believe in the possibility of peaceful coexistence."[24]

However politically motivated, moral criticism always tends to develop into insipid idealism, overlooking the elementary difference between oppressors and oppressed (or between domination and exclusion). Palestine has long been reduced to a concentration camp by a colonizing state that has, historically, acted as an outpost of US foreign policy. While some might argue that Netanyahu's extreme right-wing government was a huge headache for the Biden administration, the Israeli leader nevertheless received the unconditional support of the US (and all other Western governments), with sympathy, weapons, and dollars. Joe Biden provided Netanyahu with sophisticated military support, more than enough for what the Israeli leader himself ominously called "a long war." Furthermore, the US vetoed the UN security council resolution to pause hostilities while cynically and hypocritically cautioning Israel against inflicting too much damage upon Palestinian civilians. In other words, they should bomb the Palestinians "more carefully"—could it get more disgusting than this? The matter was summarized succinctly by Miranda Cleland when she said, "Rather than demand an immediate ceasefire, the Biden administration is actively working to further provide cover for Israeli atrocities in Gaza."[25]

Rather than parrot slogans like "all kinds of extremism are wrong," we should instead underscore the ways that genocide perpetrated in the Gaza Strip represents the "heart of darkness" for Western imperialist fundamentalism. In the last decade alone, numerous attacks against Palestinians have had thousands of victims, most of them civilians. And yet, it is somehow Hamas's terrorism that we should feel morally compelled to condemn *first*, before being allowed to even enter the discussion. And Palestinian resistance is only good for us when *we* decide what kind of resistance it should be—that is, passive resistance, not resistant at all.

Ultimately, any criticism of the mass slaughter in Gaza that posits two equally wrong sides is articulated from an opportunistic position of proximity to capital. This position assumes that capital's functional managers are capable of restoring some form of order, such as the "two-state solution"—the "thing" that everyone talks about and yet will never happen, because the very existence of the state of Israel is based on the *apartheid* of Palestine. What this standpoint conveniently fails to consider is that geopolitical events like ethnic cleansing in Gaza help those in power to preserve the criminal socioeconomic model they so loyally embody. Mass slaughter is baked into the rotten capitalist cake. Capital is utterly indifferent to the amount of pain it inflicts upon humanity, and so are its cynical agents. As an anonymous drive, capital is the obtuse repetition of its crushing law of movement. This increasingly defines not only its internal compulsion toward profit making but also the external determination of profit's conditions of possibility, including the fabrication and manipulation of global threats and the authoritarian repression of dissent, from the criminalization of "antivaxxers" to the crackdown and censorship of pro-Palestine voices. Consciously or not, the elites are the anthropomorphic expression of ironclad systemic imperatives. Increasingly pressurized by economic decline, it is the West especially that once again reveals its true colors—with the assistance of a motley crew of intellectual cheerleaders that, sadly, includes "leftists" of all stripes.

The main shortcoming of moralistic approaches to Ukraine and Gaza is that they lose sight of the key contradiction: we live in an age of compulsive global shocks, which cannot be allowed to stop. When the Ukraine crisis is over, the void will be filled by another global emergency. From the perspective of the reproduction of the financialized economy, war and destruction can be neither avoided nor paused. The implosive inertia of capital calls for increasing amounts of violence and mass deception. While this view does not intend to overlook the uneven, self-contradictory, and haphazard characteristics of human history, it nevertheless emphasizes the inevitability of our decaying civilization's growing appetite for barbarism. Any moralistic critique of capital is therefore pointless, because "capital doesn't give a damn about the idea of the contract which is imputed to it—it is a monstrous unprincipled undertaking, nothing more."[26] Capital was never supposed to follow any moral rule, so it is nonsensical to reproach it on that level. The true and very urgent problem we face—both philosophically and politically—is *how to intervene in the ineluctable*; how to conceive of interventions that are not caught in the deadly spiral of socioeconomic implosion.

The parallels between 10/7 and 9/11 that have been presented via alternative media have drawn on their common "Frankenstein syndrome." Just as the US was hit by its own CIA-nurtured "lab creature," Israel now faces the blowback of a "monster" that Tel Aviv's intelligence services have fostered for decades, initially with the aim of weakening Yasser Arafat's secular PLO (Palestinian Liberation Organization). While this reasoning is plausible, it remains inconsequential if we fail to develop a critical analysis with a deeper level of context. The media-fueled fog of war conceals the opportunistic motif behind the conflict: wars are meant to (threaten to) escalate so that liquidity creation can be expanded. The illusion of a debt-soaked economy will be kept alive along with its eschatological demon, the fear of impending apocalypse. This will require more and more sacrifice of "human animals"[27]—to quote Israel's Defense Minister, Yoav Gallant (the irony being that, strictly speaking, all humans are in fact "human animals," some are just more equal than others).

A warlike enterprise

Capitalism has always been a warlike enterprise. Its self-congratulatory functional managers have never hesitated to send millions to the slaughterhouse. Have we forgotten the passionate liaison between Anglo-American corporate elites and Nazi Germany? JP Morgan & Co., Standard Oil, General Motors, Ford, Harrison Brown, Vickers-Armstrong and many other giants of the Western "free world" financed Hitler's resistible rise to power and continued to invest in Nazi Germany throughout World War II (mostly via the Bank of International Settlements, based in Basel).[28] Autobahns, dive-bombing Stukas, U-boats, Zyklon B, death camps, etc.—they all exhibit "big money" fingerprints. These bankers, investors, and CEOs were not just rotten apples looking for easy profits—there was more purpose in their actions. This was the same devastating purpose that lay hidden in the Treaty of Versailles, which, as prophesized by Thorstein Veblen as early as 1920, was "a diplomatic bluff" meant to foment radicalism in Germany while purposely sparing the country's "absentee owners" (its "imperial establishment"), thus reinstating a "reactionary regime" and preparing "a continuation of warlike enterprise."[29] We cannot grasp the destructive character of modernity if we disconnect it from the will of capital as a *compulsive social disorder* that today—let us reiterate the central point—is weaponized without shame to conceal systemic bankruptcy. Behind the horror of modern wars and their actors, there is always the impersonal, merciless drive of capital. In Marx's words, "As a capitalist, he is only capital personified. His soul is the soul of capital" which "has one sole driving force, the drive to valorize itself."[30]

Can we even begin to fathom the destructive potential of today's emergency capitalism? The social architecture of the commodity-producing system—which is truly a religious cult, as such requiring human sacrifices—is experiencing such terminal malaise that only the brutal butchery of "just wars" (as well as "whatever wars") can conceal the breakdown of its modus operandi. The "just wars" of the democratic West act as moralistic shields against "enemies" that the West has either nurtured consciously or generated through unrelenting oppression. There is never a shortage of such "enemies," precisely because oppression has never stopped. But even more crucially, these wars are liquidity *magnets*. They are deliberately initiated to increase the amounts of credit that can be pulled from computer screens into the banking system. No human activity creates a greater need for borrowed dollars than war. In this respect, we should not lose sight of the fact that, today more than ever, the political leaders, military organizations, and intelligence and counterintelligence forces that coordinate the war games are all more or less "priced in" as commodities in capital's marketplace. And the mainstream media are nothing but public relations agencies for corrupt governments.

As of November 8, 2023, the total amount of US dollars in circulation globally is $2.326 trillion,[31] while the US national debt is $33 trillion and counting. Even intuitively, this alone should explain why a full-blown liquidity crisis is upon us, which means that more electronic (digital) debt must be exponentially borrowed into existence. Moreover, when you raise the cost of debt without having the funds to pay for it, you will inevitably need to fabricate reasons to create synthetic liquidity through the central bank as "lender of last resort," if only to cover the servicing of that debt. In short, we exist in *a debt-fueled economy that requires more debt (and more reasons to generate it) in order to maintain the illusion of stability*. Real growth today will never catch up with debt since it is increasingly squeezed by technological productivity while tax revenues have nothing to do with growth. The Truman Show choreography that surrounds us was set up so that we do not realize that the financially swollen world is now *permanently insolvent*—perennially on the verge of a tsunami of margin calls that would annihilate it in one fell swoop. This is why the only true demand that matters today is the demand for disaster-related monetary measures, namely the (massively inflationary) magicking up of heaps of electronic cash to be pumped into the monetary architecture to postpone a liquidity freeze whose devastating potential these injections only increase. But this subject does not end up in the news. Like in 2008, we prefer to wait for the crash and then say we are surprised that it happened.

In the meantime, we are (literally) entering uncharted waters. Shipping lanes have been affected by the expanding conflict in the Middle East, which means that trade and commodities (including energy) are at risk of bottlenecks—an accelerator for a global recession. As with Covid, this could eventually force central banks to "print and support" in order to paper over the massive cracks in the system. World Bank President Ajay Banga immediately called the Gaza war a "global economic shock."[32] Furthermore, growing budgetary deficits and debt servicing costs have long since begun to hurt. Without bad news, rates were likely to stay higher for longer, and yet the longer they stay higher, the more likely a credit event would be. On the Friday before the new 9/11, losses on the held-to-maturity assets of US banks had broken the all-time record of $400 billion.[33] These are "unrealized losses," i.e., bank assets whose prices have decreased due to prevailing interest rates but whose losses won't appear in financial statements until the assets are sold. Perhaps this had something to do with "big banks quietly cutting thousands of employees";[34] perhaps there was a connection between Bank of America's massive layoffs[35] and its monumental $131.6 billion in unrealized losses.[36] But what really matters is that an entire financial ecosystem collateralized with Treasuries is exposed to a trillion-dollar mega margin call. And perhaps this has something to do with the timing of the new 9/11.

It is equally significant that the United States has record numbers for both the homeless[37] and the inactive workforce (people no longer seeking work).[38] As of 2020, inactive workers totaled approximately 100 million adults (compared to the 161 million employed or looking for work), up 58% from 1990.[39] Furthermore, 36% of Americans have no savings, and another 19% have less than $1,000 saved.[40] If we place this bleak picture against the backdrop of the ruthless US debt clock,[41] it should become clear to us why our "growth system" sponsors not only "low energy consumption" (green capitalism) but also continuous warfare.

Gaza, like Donbas, was a time bomb waiting to go off. Is it not legitimate to ask why Israel, a colonizing state literally based on intelligence and security (Mossad and Shin Bet), missed the entry of Hamas soldiers into its territory by land, sea, and air (with paragliders)? The story of Hamas's easy breach of Israel's "unparalleled security system" (unseen, unobstructed, without response or alarm) will sound as preposterous to many as the other official stories we have been told in recent times and since November 22, 1963. Of course, such an attack need not be a complete false flag. More realistically, it could have been allowed to take place, or even have been facilitated. But regardless of how it occurred, the point is that we are left with chaos and destabilization.

What is of course paramount for the correct ideological functioning of the emergency scenario is the shocking representation of horror, which functions as a quilting point that holds together the intricate layers of the entire narrative. The official story must be condensed into images of unspeakable revulsion, whose immediate purpose is, in this case, to remove any opposition to the legitimacy of "proportionate" retaliation. To understand the ideological use of horror, we could refer back to Immanuel Kant's late eighteenth-century definition of the sublime in the *Critique of Judgement*: an overwhelming aesthetic experience that transcends our sensible forms and intellectual capacities. Whether it is planes hitting the twin towers, Isis decapitations, Italian army trucks transporting Covid-19 victims "as crematoriums were full," the Bucha carnage of Ukrainians, or the Israeli kibbutz massacre "with 40 beheaded children," we face what we could call UMOs, Unidentified Media Objects. Whether true, partially true, or false, their mission is to capture the mind-blowing horror of the real, thereby "surpassing every standard of Sense."[42] The traumatic power of formless, unimaginable horror—like the fake news about 40 beheaded Israeli babies, which was floated into the infosphere and immediately withdrawn—lies not so much in moving us but in forcing us, as the Kantian sublime does, to suspend critical judgement and accept the "official narrative" (since there are now only narratives, not interpretations). A quote attributed to Malcolm X comes to mind: "If you're not careful, the newspapers will have you hating the people who are being oppressed, and loving the people who are doing the oppressing."

6.

The Great Denial

> Are we really pissed off or not that our lives are based on a model of neocolonialism which, through capitalism pushed into our societies, mashes children's bodies as if it were a video game?
>
> —Gabriele Rubini[1]

THE ABOVE QUOTATION from Italian chef, pro-Palestine activist, and former rugby player Gabriele Rubini is worth more than any "balanced" statements from prominent philosophers like Jürgen Habermas, who claimed in November 2023 that the Israelis' genocidal retaliation in Gaza was "justified in principle."[2] In today's metaverse, philosophy is lost, seeming either unwilling or unable to reflect upon the fact that we are undergoing a totalitarian reset whose cause lies within a rapidly decaying economic "rationality." In every totalitarian order, those in power claim to pursue "the good" on behalf of the totality of the people. However, achieving total control is impossible *per se*, since every order of sense is predicated upon exclusion—on a "part of the whole" that is left out and that cannot be totalized. Any dystopian vision based on the implementation of a closed control system is therefore destined to fail or backfire. While being the only source of hope, such an understanding acquires sinister connotations when applied to those who must, in the meantime, exclude themselves to protect their hegemonic position. If people still cultivated the power of intuition, perhaps they would have realized by now that we are moving toward a dystopian constellation in which we are all presumed guilty until proven innocent. As in a novel by Franz Kafka, *anyone* could soon be investigated without knowing why. Surveillance technology is everywhere. In the United States, more than a hundred "fusion centers"[3] allow police agencies to scrutinize and share enormous amounts of personal data culled from CCTV cameras, facial recognition technology, social media monitoring, drone cameras, gunshot sensors, and predictive crime algorithms run by artificial intelligence. In short, the infrastructure for a digital police state is already here, it just needs to be fully activated. When the next "apocalyptic emergency" is rolled out, let us not pretend we did not know about it.

The icesheet is cracking

It is increasingly the case that things are the opposite of what they seem. Inaugurating Davos 2022, IMF director Kristalina Georgieva blamed Covid and Putin for the "confluence of calamities" that the world economy faces.[4] No surprise there. More than merely a conspiracy hub, Davos is the platform for the increasingly panicky reactions of the elites to unmanageable systemic contradictions. While the Davosians told us in 2022 that the economic downturn was the *effect* of global adversity that took the world by surprise, the exact opposite is true: the tanking economy is the *cause* of those "misfortunes." What are sold to us as external threats are in fact the ideological projections of the internal limit of capitalist modernity. In systemic terms, emergency addiction keeps the comatose body of capitalism alive artificially. Thus, the figure of the enemy is no longer fabricated to legitimize the expansion of empire. Instead, it serves to conceal the impotence of the capitalist discourse.[5]

Since the fall of the Berlin Wall, the deployment of capital's full potential, also known as globalization, has gradually undermined capital's own conditions of possibility. The systemic response to this implosive trajectory was the unleashing of global emergencies, which must be supplemented by ever-larger injections of fear, chaos, and propaganda. Regardless of the degree of awareness exhibited by the (dis)functional elites, this response represents capital's knee-jerk reaction to its inevitable historical demise. We all remember how it began at the turn of the millennium, with Al Qaeda, Colin Powell's tiny vial of white powder, and the "global war on terror." This military offensive, which was sought actively, released the Taliban and the Islamic State, and it was followed by the Syrian civil war, the North Korean missile crisis, the trade war with China, "Russiagate," and finally Covid-19—in an irresistible crescendo of emotions. It now appears that something between a new Cold War and World War III has arrived, which could act as the mother of all emergencies for many years to come. The basic reason for this course of events is that the closer the system is to collapse, the more it requires exogenous crises to conjure up liquidity while further manipulating populations, thus laying the ground for its totalitarian changeover.

History tells us that when empires are about to fold, they ossify into oppressive regimes of crisis management. It is no coincidence that our age of serial emergencies began with the bursting of the "dot-com bubble"—the first global market crash. By the end of 2001, most tech-heavy companies had gone bust; by October 2002, the Nasdaq index had fallen by 77%, exposing the structural frailty of a "new economy" powered by debt, creative finance, and the slow bleeding to death of the real economy. Since then, the *simulation* of growth via financial asset inflation has been enabled by the manufacturing of global threats, duly packaged and sold to the public by corporate media. In truth, the rise of the "new economy" in the late 1990s was less about the internet than it was about the creation of an immense apparatus of *prosperity simulation*, which was somehow supposed to function without the mediation of mass labor. As such, it cleared the way for the wacky neoliberal ideology of "jobless growth"—the illusion, embraced enthusiastically by the Third Way social-democratic left (from Gerhard Schröder to Tony Blair), that a financial-bubble economy could ignite a new capitalist El Dorado. While this illusion has blown up in our faces, nobody seems to have any desire to acknowledge it.

In fact, since Virus stepped in to raise the bar even higher, we have returned to the same financial shenanigans. While Russia became the West's brand-new infectious disease—not least because of its proven historical record as the former USSR—it is crucial to appreciate that the haste of enemy-making and fear-mongering is a sign of desperation, based as it is on the aggressive denial of structural failure. Like Virus, the Ukraine war, followed by the devastation of Gaza and the escalation of war in the Middle East, screens us from the real horror of total societal breakdown via debt and stock market crash. This perverse situation must be developed into its proper dialectical conclusion: *the only way to stop the destructive succession of emergencies is to put an end to the self-destructive capitalist logic that feeds them.*

After the last period of mass labor mobilization—the postwar Fordist boom—collapsed, capitalism entered its terminal crisis, where fictitious *money* is increasingly dissociated from labor mediated *value*. By the 1980s, the irreversible erosion of capital's labor-substance, triggered by the third industrial revolution, had already given rise to a transnational system of credit and speculation that quickly penetrated all forms of money capital. This spectral monetary mass has continued to grow by self-fertilization, to the extent that only its artificial expansion—as has been pointed out by Robert Kurz,[6] among others—will enable the mobilization of liquidity in the real world. Economic growth in the 1990s was fueled by a "recycling mechanism" whereby demand, purchasing power, and the production of goods and services were sustained by "fake" (insubstantial) credit. The real economy was no longer grounded in the incomes and revenues of productive labor; rather, it was being colonized by the profitability of price speculation on financial assets—heaps of fictitious money without value substance. This type of pseudoaccumulation, based on the flow of financial liquidity into production and consumption, is the defining—but vehemently disavowed—metaevent of our dark age. By necessity, ever-larger amounts of fictitious capital end up supporting production, which means that a growing share of real accumulation is stealthily appropriated by the speculative process. This is an epoch-defining mechanism, which as such keeps the world hostage to its logic.

The current grotesque overvaluation of all risk assets (stocks, bonds, and real estate) suggests that the elites will continue to use their geopolitical playbook to buy more time and postpone the bursting of a debt bubble they began to inflate years before Covid and Putin became the favored scapegoats. The guardians of the capitalist grail have planned a perpetual state of exception in a desperate bid to delay the currency devaluation shock that has been brewing for decades. While they do so by increasingly violent and cynical methods, they seem to be the only ones to realize that such a shock would bring the world system to its knees. They therefore demonstrate a greater understanding (intuitively, at least) of our condition than those who should, in theory, be better positioned to assess it: the so-called post-Marxist intelligentsia and the postmodern left in all its inconsequential iterations. Regrettably, the "useful idiots" on the left have long betrayed their fundamental mandate to *critique political economy* and are therefore directly implicated in the unfolding breakdown. The left's traditional sense of moral superiority, legitimized by its willingness to fight for the exploited, has now been successfully co-opted by the capitalist discourse. More often than not, emergency capitalism speaks the language of the left, advancing its destructive interests on behalf of what we are told is the "common good."

The technocrats at the helm have more than a hunch that the iceberg is approaching. Having run out of policy bullets, they understand what appears absurd or counterintuitive to most of us: the failure of our obsolete mode of production can only be concealed through the release of global chaos, the gradual demolition of the increasingly unproductive real economy, and the authoritarian makeover of liberal democracy. Today's managers of "crisis capitalism" realize that control of the current model's hard landing is necessary for a tighter system of monetary enslavement to emerge. A quasi-deterministic logic is unfolding: food and energy rationing, mass immiseration, social credit, and monetary control via centralized digital currency have long been baked into the capitalist pie of the near future.

The Ukraine war has provided us with a literal image of this mechanism. Behind their morality tales, Western politicians, under pressure from their financial bosses, have sabotaged diplomacy by sanctioning Russia and pumping an abundance of weapons and military intelligence into Ukraine, as well as billions in financial aid. Aside from the parallel convenience of shady arms and cash deals, the aim is clear: to extend military operations that turn thousands into cannon fodder, slaughter civilians, and fan the flames of eschatological nuclear escalation. As with Covid, the fear paradigm is essential to beat the public into obedience. The perversely voyeuristic spectacle of daily massacres is intentionally deprived of any meaningful sociohistorical and economic context, which confirms that the underlying purpose is to blame Putin, Hamas, and the next incarnations of evil for the ineluctable economic downturn.

The sad truth is that continuous warfare delays the popping of the "everything bubble." The real aim of these conflicts is to exorcise the nightmare of another much more violent "Lehman shock," which—given the current conditions of obstinate, childish denial vis-à-vis the terminal crisis of capital—would plunge the world into chaos. The bottom line is that mouse-clicked instant liquidity is the only object that matters to the financial industry. And by deflating debt bubble quotas through the erosion of purchasing power and the compression of demand, the elites have stealthily set themselves up for more quantitative easing programs. But new QEs, perhaps with different names, require the nudge of controlled accidents that must be serious enough to guarantee immediate printing action. In this respect, the 2018 precedent should not be ignored. Back then, the pretense of quantitative tightening (reduction of the central bank's balance sheet) only lasted a couple of months before forcing the Fed into a U-turn. And when the gamble was attempted again in the summer of 2019, the repo market crisis of mid-September had the central bank liquidity bazooka swing into action. This is what the surface of extreme crisis management looks like. Yet, if we merely scratch the thin monetary icesheet, a deeper cause emerges: the irredeemable melting away of capital's value substance.

The empty ground

As we have seen, the inflation genie that escaped the Covid bottle was immediately blamed on Putin, including its "apocalyptic" effect on the poor.[7] However, inflation originates in the prior creation of immense amounts of "money without value" (i.e., money that is not "covered" by real accumulation), which, by flowing or trickling into the real economy, devalues the money medium itself. Commodity prices no longer grow in accordance with the market law of supply and demand. Instead, any increase in demand is paid for by money generated from economic nothingness. While currency devaluation by loose monetary policy was exacerbated by the negative supply shocks caused by Covid and geopolitical conflicts, it is in truth a secular phenomenon rooted in the unstoppable dissolution of capitalist value.

It is common for empires to suffer a slow and painful death as they deny the main cause of their implosion. The decay of the US-led capitalist world began over half a century ago, and it has only been delayed by waves of fake prosperity fueled by money creation, which have benefitted a small elite while burdening the masses with debt and slow immiseration. Over the past 50 years, US federal debt has seen an 85-fold increase (from $400 billion to more than $34 trillion and growing).[8] For over half a century, the US has imposed the hegemony of its currency by initiating unprovoked (or self-provoked) "military operations" abroad. Any temporary illusion of prosperity was bought by war and inflationary credit. As most currencies have been linked to the dollar since World War II, their devaluation is also inevitable.

Today's variety of inflationary devaluation first emerged as a qualitatively new phenomenon in the twentieth century. At the beginning of the industrial age, the substantial character of currencies was safeguarded by the fact that they were pegged to precious metals, which eventually took the form of the gold standard and the central banking systems based upon it. The final closure of the gold window (August 15, 1971) marked the inception of the ultra-financialized economic model that, half a century later, is taking us closer and closer to a catastrophic *redde rationem* via colossal debt expansion. Capital's global and structural crisis now appears in the guise of a new bout of stagflation (a stagnant economy with rising inflation), which evokes memories of the 1970s. Current supply bottlenecks and a price explosion for raw materials and energy is reminiscent of the oil price shock of 1973, when OPEC reduced its output in response to the Yom Kippur War. These comparative external factors, however, must be linked to a common internal cause, which has to do with capitalism reaching the conclusion of its internal expansionary journey. The stagflation of the 1970s ended the postwar boom, which coincided with a substantial fall in the rate of profit, caused by exponential advances in the technological automation of production. The Keynesianism of the time failed because it reacted to economic contraction with stimulus programs that only managed to boost inflation further. Accordingly, capitalism entered a new inflationary cycle. Neoliberalism provided a temporary way out of this impasse. It smashed the unions in the 1980s, together with the price-wage correlation and the social-democratic illusion that capitalist societies could operate through a politics of wealth redistribution—as if capitalist wealth was a *metaphysical* rather than a *historical* category, limited by the dialectic of money capital invested in value-productive labor.

In the early 1980s, inflation was fought through the "Volker shock," i.e., by hiking interest rates (the cost of money) beyond or very near the rate of inflation. This triggered a recession in the capitalist center and led the periphery of empire (especially Latin America) into a severe debt crisis. But it saved capitalism from systemic collapse, which further benefitted the billionaire class. US financial markets rapidly expanded to become dominant, while goods production in the American rust belt declined. The United States evolved from the "workshop of the world" to the "financial center of the world," a transformation facilitated by the US dollar being the global reserve currency. It was already in the 1970s, then, that capitalism had begun to falter under the weight of its internal contradiction, where productive labor serves as both the foundation of capital and a cost that needs to be curtailed in the competitive war between individual enterprises. This contradiction, which is at the very heart of the anonymous capitalist drive for profit making, turned openly self-destructive in the 1980s, when debt creation and growth simulation became endemic to make up for fading value production.

Since the 1980s, global debt has risen much faster than world economic output. Global debt needs to be contextualized: it feeds the fundamental delusion that financial speculation anticipates future capital valorization, which must however be moved further and further into the future since it is unmatched by corresponding valorization in the real economy. Today's financial capitalism is the ultimate self-fulfilling prophecy, a mechanism based on the creation of ever-increasing amounts of insubstantial money to compensate for rapidly vanishing surplus value. If the US and the Western world enjoyed a period of relative growth in the 1990s despite low wages and rising productivity, it was because consumption was increasingly sustained by credit.

While neoliberal globalization provided an escape route for the exhausted Fordist mass production model, it simultaneously tied itself to ever-larger pyramids of debt (or credit creation programs) and speculative excess, making the system increasingly unstable. It is no surprise that the 1990s ended with the formation of the first global bubble (the dot-com or internet bubble). This was followed by the financial crash of 2008, the response to which was the implementation of QE programs, i.e., *more of the same*: monetary expansion through central bank purchase of debt securities and other assets. The same capitalist contradiction reappeared in the form of the European sovereign debt crisis (2009–12) and as a potentially devastating liquidity trap in autumn 2019, which officially inaugurated the era of pan-emergency capitalism. The pandemic was used as a global shield for money printing and borrowing at unprecedented levels; under Covid, the Fed printed more fiat money in one year than through all combined QE programs since 2008.

In recent times (until March 2022) we have also been treated to a neoliberal adaptation of Keynesian crisis management through the implementation of extremely low interest rates—the opposite of what was done in the 1970s. In the past 40 years, interest rates were lowered further and further to allow fresh liquidity to flood financial markets. Since 2008, however, even 0% interest rates were no longer sufficient, which is why central banks (beginning with the Fed) have pulled quantitative easing out of their magician's hat, literally becoming open waste dumps for the financial markets. Throwing caution to the wind, they have inundated the economy with free money using junk paper as collateral, without even bothering to go through the banking system. The downhill slide of the devaluation avalanche that began in autumn 2008 is now unstoppable. Yet, somehow, the world still believes that central banks will solve a debt crisis by printing more money. The final attempt by Western economies to save their broken system is now failing miserably, as these economies continue to decay in a mixture of currency debasement, deficits, and history's largest asset bubbles—while most people persist in their faith in capital as an eternal and basically indestructible entity. The choice we are presented with is the same we have been given throughout the history of advanced industrial societies: inflation or deflation. Either money is devalued as a general equivalent (inflation) or the devaluation process affects capital directly, with production (factories and workers) suddenly becoming superfluous. Unlike in the past, however, both inflation and deflation now mean fiat money debasement *with the added bonus of systemic breakdown*.

Despite their claims to the contrary, the current preference of technocrats is not to fight inflation but to instead use it to inflate away portions of the public debt. This is equivalent to a transfer of wealth (an invisible tax) from the lower and middle classes to the custodians of the "everything bubble," for the purchasing power of Main Street gets battered while part of the debt on Wall Street is deflated. Despite this cynical ploy, however, central banks continue to drink-drive toward the precipice. Whichever move they make, they lose. If they hike rates significantly and for longer while managing to reduce their balance sheets (quantitative tightening), the debt bubble will pop, with catastrophic consequences. If, however, they once again turn to quantitative easing, inflation will soar at a fast pace, eventually into hyperinflation. The choice is between a deflationary debt crisis and stagflation. Both are worse. Stabilizing this scenario is virtually impossible.

In all likelihood, the debt and stock market crisis will continue to be delayed. The grand finale—a biblical crash beyond our wildest imaginations, ignited by the explosion of the debt market hyperbubble—is being postponed through the gradual depression of the real economy. This means that the "misery index" (the combination of inflation and the unemployment rate) will grow even further. Central banks can tame inflation only in words, knowing that any tightening of monetary policy is constrained by the opposite necessity of continuing to monetize public and private debt by creating liquidity out of nowhere. In a certain sense, we are returning to the prehistory of capitalism, once again dealing with the problem of "money without value." We have almost come full circle. However, the current debasement of the money medium presents itself as the catastrophe of the "work society," the system of abstract labor mediated by the market. The current bio- and geopolitical violence is an integral component in this self-destructive trajectory. We only have one *real* choice: we either begin to emancipate from the commodity, value, and money forms, and thus from the *capital form* as such, or we will be dragged into a new dark age of violence and regression.

To summarize, here are the main drivers of senile capitalism:

1. *Debt*. The only road into the capitalist future continues to be signposted by liquidity creation programs. Creating cash on computer screens and setting it in motion as credit is the intrinsically puerile monetary strategy that keeps our societies from staring into the abyss—like the cartoon character who, having run off the edge of a cliff, floats in midair before acknowledging gravity. However, the pull of gravity is now irresistible, and the descent has begun with a violent bout of currency devaluation.

2. *Bubbles.* Financial bubbles, inflated by cheap credit that feeds a delusional mechanism of perpetual motion, are the only meaningful measure of wealth-production left. Preventing the bubbles from popping is the only thing that matters to the minions of the "beautiful machine." While the financialized economy balloons away from its social bond, human existence turns into collateral for the speculative algorithm.

3. *Controlled demolition.* Wage dumping and downward competition for fewer and fewer jobs is the *necessary* other side of the bubble paradigm. For the speculative markets to persist, the "work society" must be gradually downsized, since today's artificially inflated financial assets and real demand are mutually exclusive. Simply put, Main Street is a liability for Wall Street, which is why consumer capitalism is now morphing into the manipulative, ideological management of collective immiseration.

4. *States of emergency.* Our existential condition during the terminal phase of bubble-to-bubble capitalism is an intrinsically terroristic metaemergency ideology, a permacrisis that must accompany us from cradle to grave. In this respect, the self-fulfilling pandemic of 2020 was only the icebreaker.

5. *Manipulation.* Media propaganda in the age of digital hyperconnectivity comes naturally, so it is only natural that senile capitalism, sensing its collapse, makes the most of it. A stubborn confluence of blind stupidity and cynical calculation is at work here. As George Orwell predicted well before the internet, it comes down to *telling lies while believing them*: "The process [of mass-media deception] has to be conscious, or it would not be carried out with sufficient precision, but it also has to be unconscious, or it would bring with it a feeling of falsity and hence of guilt."[9] Jean Baudrillard called the result of this process "hyperreality."

Capital's perpetual motion machine

Having run out of monetary tricks, the financial elites have painted themselves into a corner. The speculative system they have pumped for decades through money printing and the artificial suppression of interest rates can no longer be sustained without significant "collateral damage." The illusion of bourgeois economic theory that money can move autonomously, as if through a perpetual motion machine, is finally being exposed. The current inflationary environment is the first obvious symptom of a cancerous disease rapidly spreading throughout the social body, forcing a large share of the population—including the increasingly insolvent middle classes—to choose between putting food on the table and paying the bills. It should be clear by now that any money-creation program will cause further erosion of purchasing power, therefore requiring new creative methods to control the impoverished masses. The alternative to this scenario is for central banks to keep raising rates until the market bubbles pop—which would get us straight to the hard-landing scenario.

The illusion of perpetual financial motion works as follows: the expansion of credit pulls money into risk assets whose valuation grows as demand increases; soaring financial assets then serve as collateral for more borrowing, setting in motion a feedback loop in which credit feeds asset valuation feeding collateral feeding credit. Under the illusion of eternal liquidity expansion, the leveraging of capital to buy assets for use as collateral for more credit is all that matters. And as long as the self-fulfilling loop holds, debt-service obligations can be rolled over. But if interest rates rise and collateral drops in value, the borrower suddenly begins to sweat and starts selling assets, which soon becomes herd behavior. With the deterioration of collateral, assets are at risk of dropping below the outstanding debt, which causes liquidity to dry up and, eventually, bubbles to pop. This is the stage we are approaching, where the fake wealth-creation loop reverts to a death spiral: asset valuations fall, collateral shrinks, credit collapses.

It is worth reminding ourselves that in the globalized West, we have already pawned everything we own. That is to say, most of us (states, businesses, families) *own nothing but our debt,* which is falling underwater. And, as the global casino threatens to go bankrupt, our puppet masters understand all too well that they must act swiftly if they are to retain power and privileges. Crucially, they know that their only chance to continue flooding markets with the necessary amounts of artificial liquidity requires controlling the freefall of the real economy as it shrinks into stagflation. Inaugurated in style by the pseudopandemic, this process continues to take place under the coordinated watch of central banks, whose rate hikes only tickle inflation but further depress real demand.

In this respect, the contextual rise in the cost of energy must also be viewed as part of the wider attempt to decompress a highly flammable system—the equivalent of carefully defusing a bomb. We have seen that the sanctioning of Russia was close to a farce—and, for Europe, a masochistic exercise. Similarly, one of the key secret aims of the corporate-led "fight against climate change" is to impose lower living standards upon the working and middle classes which, until only a few years ago, were still being lured into embracing the utopia of endless growth and mindless consumption. Ukraine can be seen as today's tragic symbol of such economic downsizing. Thanks to a cynically prolonged proxy war, the country faces the obliteration of its industrial infrastructure. Significantly, on December 28, 2022, BlackRock CEO Larry Fink and Volodymyr Zelensky agreed to coordinate investment to rebuild Ukraine,[10] confirming the familiar pattern whereby the devastation (and depopulation)[11] of an entire society is an opportunity for financial expansion.

Unfortunately, this dark phase of "crisis capitalism" has been vastly underestimated—to use a euphemism—by our "radical" left-wing intellectuals, who, like Pavlov's dogs, have greeted the "return of the state" as a sign of emancipation. Their inability to grasp the elementary nexus between a global economy hooked on growing mountains of credit without substance and state authoritarianism suggests they now support a sinister type of conservatism.

The depressing short-sightedness of the left was particularly painful to observe as the global health emergency unfolded. Ironically, or maybe predictably, what the left seems unable to accept is that capitalism itself, with all its familiar categories, is fading into obsolescence and can only fake a life it does not have by mobilizing terror. Covid-19 was above all a *pandemic of fear*, whose damaging consequences on the human mind and body remain unknown. With "vaccines" mandated as a magic bullet (95% efficacy, we were told!)[12] against a disease with a 99.8% survival rate,[13] how could our "radical" philosophers fail so spectacularly to smell the ideological rat? By the same token, none of our anticapitalist gurus batted an eyelash when Pfizer admitted it did not have a clue whether its serums actually stopped transmission,[14] despite the fact that it was precisely "stopping transmission" that was sold to the public as the indisputable scientific truth behind the discriminatory mandates. Similarly, no outrage occurred when the Twitter Files were released on December 26, 2022, which revealed the extent of the pressure exerted by US government agencies to manipulate the scientific debate on Covid-19 and silence critical voices. How far right has the "radical left" moved if it fails to recognize emergency capitalism's criminal sleight of hand? By supporting global discrimination and destruction under false ethical pretenses, most of today's left does the work of the right more efficiently than the right itself.

While awareness of mass deception is now slowly emerging, most people still prefer to keep their head in the sand. And yet, there is little point recriminating. What instead remains crucial is to remind ourselves that Virus was the invisible shield utilized to avoid a banking and financial crisis that would have made 2008 seem like a walk in the park while simultaneously ushering in a pan-emergency strategy for the coordinated management of mass impoverishment—not only in the peripheries of the capitalist world but also in its center. It is especially revealing that we are now being persuaded to accept the economic freefall *as fate*: a somewhat mythical stagflation originating in external and largely uncontrollable triggers rather than in the rotting away of our economic model. In retrospect, one could even appreciate the evil genius of a system that conceals its massive social, economic, and cultural implosion behind what seems an endless series of scapegoats.

During 2022, many critical issues have threatened the global financial casino. In total, equities and bonds lost more than $30 trillion.[15] The Nasdaq index closed the year at 33%—its worst performance since 2008.[16] The global volume of negative-yielding debt shrunk from $18.4 trillion in December 2020 to $686 billion in December 2022 (which, despite misleading media reaction, was bad news for the global debt bubble since it meant that bonds tanked).[17] Naturally, rate hikes were held responsible for the loss of market value. The latter, however, took place against the backdrop of record-breaking corporate buybacks (which artificially increase share prices and boost corporate profits).[18] Ergo, while taking a hit, the markets continued to behave like casinos on the Vegas strip, with central banks happily playing the house (which always wins).

Moreover, if in 2022 the global liquidity index was deteriorating fast (after more than a decade of artificial growth), the last day of that year registered an all-time high in reverse repo deposits at the New York Fed: $2.5 trillion by 113 counterparties.[19] This means that while ordinary people tried to figure out how to pay mortgages and bills, large investors parked inordinate amounts of cash at the Fed since the reverse repo facility guarantees higher returns than the markets. While it would only take a small increase in counterparty risk for this repo business to backfire, it still means that large volumes of *insubstantial liquidity*, carrying a massive inflationary potential, are trapped in the financial markets, thereby not appearing *directly* as real demand—precisely the mechanism that has, since the 1990s, kept inflation suppressed. However, this expedient has now passed its use-by date, for the heap of fictitious capital has swollen to such a magnitude that it can hardly be contained.

Since the beginning of the millennium, our world has been held captive by the cloning of financial bubbles, from tech to housing to sovereign bonds, each of which depends on both frantic liquidity creation and bond rate suppression by central banks. More importantly, this is what sustains real capitalist production (i.e., our societies). As we have seen, an enormous share of real production is already part of the speculative process. At the same time, the financial conveyor belt has reached near-total disconnection from the work society. We have been kidnapped by an invisible self-perpetuating apparatus whose abstraction is so great that its comprehension eludes most of us.

Let us recap the key point: bubble inflation requires "hot air" in the form of borrowed liquidity. The lung capacity of the system is its bond market, the place where debt securities are traded. If capital needs to be raised for asset investment or to finance state expenditure (including wars), bonds are issued, which oblige the issuer to repay their cost at a negotiable maturity date and interest rate. Corporations issue bonds, and so do governments. Our system is now existentially dependent on skyrocketing piles of bonds, through which investors secure the credit they need to speculate in financial markets. Borrowing aggressively in order to invest is the risky strategy known as leveraged finance, which makes up the DNA of contemporary capitalism.

We are now approaching what for bubble capitalism is an existential moment of truth. The fuse for the next bomb is the debt market, and it has already been lit. Bonds are no longer "fairly priced" in line with the mythological law of supply and demand. According to this law, a bond's price rises when it is in high demand, while its yield (and therefore its repayment rate) falls; conversely, when bond demand drops, so does its price, with its yield (and repayment rate) rising. Higher bond rates should provide a release of "hot air" in any asset bubble, since less affordable bonds drain liquidity from the system. This is to say that the bond market is supposed to blow off steam when bonds carry high rates. However, the entire financial metaverse is now systematically distorted by central banks, which, through the massive liquidity injections of the past have created a Frankenstein "bond monster" they need to feed constantly but struggle to control. If, in principle, there is no end to credit creation, the consequences of uninterrupted artificial asset inflation are no longer manageable through economic policy alone.

The destructive potential of the debt avalanche is immense, to the point that it can no longer be hidden. Or rather, it is so threatening that *it must be hidden*. In December 2022, the BIS issued a warning about the staggering $80 trillion-plus off-balance sheet debt held by financial institutions and funds—an amount greater than the combined total stocks of dollar-denominated Treasury bills, repo and commercial paper in circulation.[20] This is *derivative debt* that is not being captured through regular statistics, mostly complex speculative instruments like foreign exchange swaps and forwards. The BIS claims that this invisible debt has grown from $55 trillion to $80 trillion in a decade, with daily foreign exchange (FX) swap deals totaling a whopping $5 trillion per day. US financial institutions and pension funds have twice as much FX swap dollar obligations as the amount of dollar debt listed on their balance sheets. Foreign banks have $39 trillion in derivative debts that are also not showing, which amounts to "more than 10 times their capital." This debt burden is a ticking time bomb at the heart of the global economy.

If, in the wake of the 2008 global financial crisis, the Fed claimed that it began running stringent stress tests for the Global Systemically Important Banks,[21] the BIS disclosure of undeclared derivative debt brings us back to Alan Greenspan and his 1987–2006 Fed chairmanship, when Wall Street was allowed to build the pile of toxic derivatives that blew up in 2008. That nothing has changed is an open secret, for credit bingeing has been the system's modus operandi of the last four decades. In an interlocked environment, however, contagion is always lurking. When dollar-denominated debt is more expensive due to rising interest rates, the default of a globally interconnected bank, or the fire sale of financial assets, are concrete possibilities, as is an ensuing meltdown. For this reason, *the system must find reasons to keep itself liquid at all costs*, while also managing the dire consequences.

In fact, the only option left for a debt-soaked bubble regime would seem to be currency debasement. As some financial analysts have forecasted for a while, the prospect we face is that the greatest bond heap in history will be washed away by a tsunami of mouse-clicked liquidity. Despite the central bankers' hawkish posture that began in March 2022, they will soon be forced to make drastic decisions that will further damage fiat currencies in order to protect bond markets. Then, a debt bubble morphing into a monetary bubble could pave the way for the widely announced CBDC-based system. In fact, more inflationary money printing was already at work throughout 2022 and into 2023, as evidenced by the Fed's injections of repo liquidity, which dwarfed Powell's quantitative tightening. The bottom line is that our social existence remains hostage to the expansion of artificial liquidity, for the capital-labor dialectic is defunct. In this respect, the problem faced by transnational entities like the BIS, the WEF, the IMF, the World Bank, and so on, is how to save the wobbling bubbles while selling us the story that economic contraction is the consequence of an unfortunate series of events.

A sense of perspective

The real paradigm shift within capitalism occurred a few decades ago when a new form of financial capital emerged, one that is *qualitatively* different from its precursor. Since the 1980s, financial speculation on asset prices is no longer an appendage to a thriving and expanding "real economic abstraction"—the sociohistorical discourse based on the correspondence between a given amount of labor time and a given amount of monetary compensation (wages). Rather, the financial "industry" is now both the driver and the escape route for the social narrative that founded capitalism around five centuries ago—when labor power first appeared as a commodity exchanged on the market. As previously discussed, there is now a growing cleavage between the massively stretched credit chain and the total mass of value originating from labor, which means that keeping up appearances is increasingly problematic. We live in a "lipstick on a pig" form of capitalism. Since 2001, there has been a huge transfer of liquidity into the bond and real estate markets, generating unprecedented bubbles, not only in the US and the UK but also in China and Europe. This has created a *qualitatively new* mixture of speculative growth and an economy based on the real production and consumption of goods.

During an incubation period, the escape of insubstantial credit into the future did not generate inflation. Today, however, it is pointless to continue believing that the mass of fictitious and speculative capital remains trapped in the financial sector. Rather, it has colonized the real world, eroding both our purchasing power and the economic model we still believe we live in. The internal limit to real accumulation acts as an external propeller, pushing capitals toward the virtual space of transnational circulation of financial assets, which is powered by growing stacks of self-cannibalizing debt. This is not a pathological corruption of the original capitalist model but the logical consequence of its structural crisis: the overall fall in the mass of surplus value is larger than the increase in the relative surplus value of individual capitals competing through reductions in the cost of labor power.

This means that the capitalist discourse is broken, having irreversibly damaged the pillars of its sociohistorical narrative. The use of cost-cutting technology has made productive wage labor increasingly redundant, thus inhibiting the creation of new surplus value and triggering an implosive spiral. Since then, the financial supplement to the work society has turned into its *basis* and *raison d'être*. Financializing the economy was the historical answer to the demise of Fordism. Today, our lives are held captive by the grand illusion that financial capital can become a perpetual motion machine while making its original formula obsolete. Yet, because the global mass of unproductive labor has crossed a critical threshold, currency devaluation is inevitable, an economic shock that is bound to become a violent shock for social consciousness in general.

A bubble system of the current magnitude cannot coexist with real growth, i.e., flourishing mass consumption and mass production. If today's volume of fictitious capital were to circulate freely in our societies, it would instantly trigger hyperinflation—a scenario that has thus far been exported to the neglected peripheries of the globalized world.[22] The endgame phase we have entered results from the extraordinary growth of credit dependence during the twentieth century, which means that money could not preserve its previous form, i.e., its convertibility into a hard asset. World War I demonstrated that it was no longer possible to finance a war with gold-backed currency. The increase of debt that came with World War II and the subsequent Fordist boom eventually lead to the decision, in 1971, to abandon the gold standard. With this, money lost its historically specific substance, and bourgeois economic theory (or neoclassical economics) could never quite comprehend the radical implications of this event. Even Keynesianism was merely an attempt to save capitalism from itself by reigniting the labor economy via increased state debt (deficit spending). At the same time, Marxist labor movements never fully assimilated Marx's radical critique of value. Instead, they focused on struggles for redistribution, but always within the ontological horizon of capital. After 1971, money as a "store of value" became a mere convention without objective foundations in the social bond. The logical and inevitable consequence of this loss of value substance is structural devaluation, with either inflation or a violent deflationary wave being triggered by a market crash.

This trend is irreversible. No sector of the economy can return to real growth and bring us back to something even vaguely resembling the Fordist period, which was already being powered by extraordinary injections of state credit. When the Fordist accumulation cycle hit the buffers, no new mass reabsorption of labor could be mobilized, which is why fictitious capital has achieved ontological status, compensating for the permanent loss of surplus-value creation. The dream of constant growth sustained by mass consumption is turning into a nightmare, with most of today's consumers already tapped out. The inherently dystopian capitalist phase we have entered is characterized by *productivity without productive labor*, which means that the work society as a whole is digging its own grave. Many businesses, of course, will keep competing for market shares by making use of increasingly sophisticated technologies while exploiting the immiserated workforce; but in the current conditions of technological productivity, competition can only result in the shrinking of total capital.

Gaining a critical perspective on the implosion of today's senile capitalism is essential. It requires, as a fundamental precondition, resisting the onslaught of deception and distraction churned out by the controllers of the infosphere. Mainstream media will never inform us about the causes of a *structurally insolvent* economy, for the simple reason that it is a branch of the same bankrupt system. On the contrary, it will attempt to persuade us to look elsewhere: diseases, wars, cultural prejudices, political scandals, natural catastrophes, mass protests, etc.—each of these can be exploited against the people. In truth, our economic predicament is the second instalment of the 2008 crisis, part of a systemic collapse so acute that its cause is now systematically and preemptively denied.

Arguably, understanding our condition requires the effort to think *against* ourselves, since, as a rule, a subject who "organically belongs to a civilization cannot identify the nature of the disease which undermines it."[23] Conformity and willful ignorance are infinitely more contagious than the strength needed to overcome the biases of our time. Most of us are determined to remain asleep, preferring to believe that what we are experiencing is only a temporary glitch. Yet, we must gather the courage to see through the smokescreen that hides the decaying substance of our world. Defensive reasoning crushes the vitality of thought. It colonizes not only consciousness but especially our unconscious attachments to the obsolete categories of a collapsing civilization.

Every civilization immunizes itself by drawing a line between its own constituent order and a malevolent other. Evildoing must be projected outside the dominant social body if the latter is to retain its illusion of consistency. Yet, a global civilization on the verge of defaulting on its value (the *self-valorizing value* called capital) can no longer rely solely on fighting localized enemies—it must unleash ubiquitous global villains. This is why we are constantly reminded that a "Dr. Strangelove moment" is just around the corner. Since 2022, the fear of Virus has been replaced by the Doomsday Clock,[24] whereby war becomes an ideological screen that dissimulates the pain of ordinary reality, from recession to structural inflation and mass layoffs. Furthermore, wars allow not only monetary expansion but also systemic self-immunization by redrawing the line between us (the morally and culturally superior) and them (the barbarians). In this respect, the geopolitical tension between the US-led globalized Western model and the multipolar world in the making (BRICS+) is, strictly speaking, an *effect* of the ongoing economic collapse.

Regardless of where you are on the geopolitical chessboard, the common problem faced by every capitalist state and its overseeing transnational aristocracy is, and will remain, how to control the waves of mass discontent that will stem from increased immiseration. We only need to browse the G20 Bali declaration of November 2022[25] or the latest WEF program at Davos to see that the elites' main concern is to make sure that growing levels of global poverty are met with "global solutions" that range from vaccination-linked digital IDs to the release of Central Bank Digital Currencies. *Global cooperation* is the ideological catchphrase of the jet-setting ultrarich who seek to regiment the increasingly stagnant world population. In this regard, the neofeudal spirit of our time is best captured by the "lockdown model." On one hand, we tend to forget that millions of socially excluded humans were already living under "lockdown conditions" before the pandemic, confined to suburban slums and rural peripheries without access to work and basic goods; on the other hand, iterations of the lockdown model will be extended to most of us in the near future, ostensibly to protect us.

It is crucial, then, for us to realize that we face the prospect of total socioeconomic breakdown. Those who drive the financial gravy train will keep promoting all kinds of conflicts and divisions in order to hide systemic collapse. Each conflict today begins and ends within "crisis capitalism." The demise of socialism in the 1980s lifted the veil of Maya. Since then, "duality is a delusion," as a Buddhist would say; there is only one socioeconomic dogma, *and it no longer works*. Keeping consumer capitalism alive while also expanding debt toward infinity is now impossible. The pile of IOUs reaches beyond what we own as collateral (essentially, our assets, labor power and lives) while fiat currencies have long since begun their journey to the land of rubbish. The entire banking system is approaching collapse. The great reset is our owners' authoritarian attempt to respond to this systemic threat by taking control of the collateral (our lives) and remain in the driver's seat. All the rest is perception management.

7.
Welcome to
"Lower Energy" Capitalism

> As we transition to a lower energy system (renewables replacing fossil fuels), growth-based economics will be phased out and replaced with something else.
> —Simon Michaux[1]

WE HAVE ENTERED A GLOBAL CYCLE of secular inflation that is pushing communities to embrace an ideology of "low-energy" mass impoverishment. The cynical attempt to preserve a system based on permanent monetary inoculation translates into the devastation of entire societies. The immediate consequence of this dynamic is not liberation from capitalism but a new capitalist phase of brutal crisis management, which is now upon us. Jean Baudrillard foresaw this trend in the early 1980s when he claimed that nuclear power constituted both the maximization of energy and its control, adding: "Lockdown and control grow as fast as (and undoubtedly even faster than) liberating potentialities."[2] It would therefore seem pointless to speculate on when capitalism will end, since each eschatological fantasy is dissolved by the capacity of the financial machine to, literally, "buy more time."[3] Finance is, among other things, a temporal apparatus, redefining the meaning of our historical time *before* we have a chance to grasp it. The bottom line is that each step in the global downfall will continue to be matched by shock-and-awe narratives of corresponding gravity; endless terror as endless deterrence. Power can stage *any* crime to safeguard its legitimacy. This is why any meaningful resistance to the status quo in the making entails a struggle to define the cause of our predicament as immanent to capital.

The inflation genie

What sort of world do we live in? I have argued throughout this book that there is one answer that takes precedence over all others: our globalized world is a debt-making machine that feeds on central bank ATMs. Our civilization is addicted to money printing and asset bubbles, a form of dependence that can hardly be broken. Today, nothing is more dangerous than interfering with the expansion of fake liquidity; nothing more threatening than a sudden "credit crunch." In seemingly postpandemic times, we remain hostage to a Ponzi scheme in which toxic liabilities act as collateral for other toxic liabilities in an endless trail of insubstantial assets. Central banks expand their balance sheets to purchase these liabilities merely to prevent their loss of paper value, and putting an end to such monetary expansion is like provoking a cardiac arrest. The choice faced by most countries, including the affluent ones, will soon be to either default on their debt or embrace hyperinflation of the currency needed to repay the IOUs. This means that capital accumulation itself is now *on life support*. What takes place today as a matter of monetary normality is typical of wartime economies, namely *direct* financing via the money presses. While this can only result in the depressing of society, simultaneously generating the highest wealth inequality in history, what should give us pause is the thought that a world held captive by bubble inflation inevitably "melts into thin air," losing its social grounding as well as the language to articulate any form of resistance. Collapse is at once economic, sociopolitical, and cultural. This is why we live in times of generalized perversion, by which I mean that nobody dares to acknowledge the impotence of capitalism.

The key to understanding our predicament is to realize that the calamitous devaluation of the money medium is now a secular phenomenon, since the simulation of monetary growth has penetrated all forms of money capital. Insubstantial financial "wealth" colonizes commodity production and consumption, making both hostage to the credit spigot. The financial sector responds to what happens in bond markets, which are increasingly propped up artificially by liquidity boosters from central banks. Bonds are issued to raise money and pay regular fixed interest to the bondholder. However, bonds are also tradeable, which means they give returns called "yields." When bond yields rise sharply and in seemingly uncontrolled fashion, as occurs in a critically stressed economic environment like ours, it is a sign that bond prices are falling at a similarly dramatic pace. This indicates that investors are pulling out and, consequently, the bond market is tanking—which, as we have seen, is bad news for stocks. In short, the cost of financing one's debt surges rapidly, and the insolvency ghost rears its ugly head. Because debt-bingeing went through the roof after 2008, any turbulence in bond markets is simultaneously a shock for stock markets. It functions very much like clockwork: when bond yields rise quickly, stocks get hit, which normally prompts the central bank cavalry to act. The most common way to keep bonds from deteriorating is for central banks to use their unlimited firepower to print more cash with which to buy the unloved debt securities, which is intrinsically inflationary.

Consider the benchmark yield on the 10-year Treasury note. When the yield spikes rapidly, it suggests that investors in US debt are running to the door, which spells doom for Wall Street's "creative finance." So, what happens when investing in debt—the lifeblood of our world—loses its appeal? Here is an example. On June 13, 2022, the Italian bond yields breached 4% for the first time since 2014,[4] causing what was then called a "fragmentation" in the cost of borrowing across the EU. With lightning speed, the

European Central Bank ran to the rescue by selling German and other Northern European bonds close to maturity to buy Italian and other Southern European bonds (a subterfuge that hardly thrilled the "frugal" northerners).[5] Moreover, the ECB instituted the TPI (Transmission Protection Instrument),[6] also known as the "antispread shield," which allows for targeted and *unlimited* debt purchases—in effect, putting the countries who need TPI under external (ECB) administration. The upshot is that while the rule of today's central bank resembles that of an absolute monarchy in premodern times, its interventions are inflationary—which brings us back to the original quandary of *irreversible money debasement.*

Despite first denying inflation, then calling it "transitory," and eventually blaming it on Putin and other "baddies," our political leaders (the executors) and their central bankers (the enforcers) eventually had to admit that "Houston, we have an inflation problem." So, when President Biden read from his White House podium on August 10, 2022, that the US had been blessed with 0% inflation the previous month,[7] adding that the economy was in fact booming, we should have smelled a rat. This blatant distortion of reality served both as an electoral stunt and as a means to prepare the ground for a "Fed pause" (a rate hike stop). This is because if the cost of money were to continue ticking higher, the debt-saturated markets would crash along with currencies and everything else. In fact, by autumn 2023, a return to lower rates legitimized by a *narrative* of peak inflation (including oil prices) appeared the most credible scenario. However, while a strategy of lower interest rates would assist in maintaining market liquidity, it would simultaneously lead to the resurgence of inflation together with the adoption of "unconventional" measures to address it.

In 2010, the Rockefeller Foundation published a pamphlet on world crisis containing a "lock step" scenario,[8] which accurately predicted both a deadly zoonotic pandemic ("the pandemic that the world had been anticipating for years finally hit") and the ensuing imposition of "airtight rules and restrictions, from the mandatory wearing of face masks to body-temperature checks at the entries to communal spaces like train stations and supermarkets." It also foresaw that "the Chinese government's quick imposition and enforcement of mandatory quarantine for all citizens, as well as its instant and near-hermetic sealing off of all borders, saved millions of lives, stopping the spread of the virus far earlier than in other countries and enabling a swifter postpandemic recovery." And it prophesized that, "after the pandemic faded, this more authoritarian control and oversight of citizens and their activities stuck and even intensified. In order to protect themselves from the spread of increasingly global problems—from pandemics and transnational terrorism to environmental crises and rising poverty—leaders around the world took a firmer grip on power."

What is spelled out in this remarkable piece of prophetic writing from the Rockefeller think tank is, ultimately, the connection between *lockdowns* and *poverty*: "authoritarian control" helps against "global problems" like "rising poverty." Is this authoritarian world not the world we *already* live in? Is the fiction not more real than reality itself? The normalization of surveillance and control ushered in by 9/11 and accelerated by Covid-19 can only become more oppressive, because it is the only "political" response available to confront a collapsing socioeconomic dynamic. In the meantime, the globalized West is engaging in a wacky race to the bottom. As of today, Europe is still firmly in the lead, thanks to the all-too-predictable backfiring of the sanctions against Russia, which have already caused upheaval in Germany (the former locomotive of Europe's economy)[9] and elsewhere. Being dependent on cheap Russian gas, Europe scored the clumsiest of own goals— *intentionally?* one could legitimately ask. For how could European leaders who invoke and even engineer package after package of sanctions not see that said sanctions would boomerang to hit Europe (Germany first) on the head? It is either a case of extreme incompetence or blind submission to external (US) dictates—or a combination of both. The outcome seems inevitable. With recession, central banks have no choice but to move from hawkish (rate-hiking) to dovish (rate-lowering), returning to a policy of cheap money and inflationary large-scale asset purchases. If the global banking system locks up, the world will hit the deflationary spiral, like drink-driving at full speed against a wall. Whatever can no longer be financed through credit will be brought to a standstill. Banks will refuse to lend and bank accounts could be frozen. Deflationary capital destruction through the meltdown of debt and stock markets would annihilate currencies and devastate livelihoods. The least one can say is that for this to happen as a controlled accident, the dystopian infrastructure for managing poverty and social unrest must already be installed.

For most of us, the future seems to offer a choice between structural stagflation (stagnant economy with high inflation) and an abrupt deflationary depression—like a choice between death by a thousand cuts and a heart attack. Either way, the divide between the superrich and the rest can only increase further. It is no longer the classic swing between boom and bust, or a financial cycle that ends in a "Minsky moment" (where levered-up finance tips over into insolvency), for we have reached the absolute limit to capitalist expansion. It is important to reiterate that we face systemic implosion, not merely a crisis engineered by evil banksters motivated by greed. While greed is inscribed in the capitalist drive as such—since capital is nothing but a compulsive end in itself—the current implosion reflects *the historical exhaustion of the value-creating substance of capital*; the fact that the fundamental ingredient of value itself—labor—is vanishing irreversibly while technological productivity takes off. It should be enough to observe that in a healthy capitalist economy the price of labor would rise. Instead, labor has been devalued for decades, which dramatically confirms that any monetary boost to the economy is *without value substance* and destined to produce further misery. It is therefore inevitable that, sometime soon, capitalist reproduction will be brought back to the ground through the severe contraction of insubstantial bubbles of paper value. Fictitious liquidity, created without any basis in real production, will be violently debased.

From denial to sacrifice

What continues to be stubbornly denied is that the devaluation of the money medium is today's key symptom of the implosion of capitalism as a global commodity-producing work society mediated by the market and driven by the pursuit of profit as an end in itself. What is most painful about this denial is that it has long since conquered the heart and soul of (what still dares to call itself) the left. The political left is either opportunistically ignorant or still caught up in the neoliberal chimera that a virtualized type of financial capitalism is not only possible but even desirable ("with a human face," of course). As a result, hardly anyone on the left is able to connect the rapid deterioration of socioeconomic conditions with the totalitarian turn of today's world—already explicit in the rising tide of mainstream media propaganda and the brutally discriminatory treatment of "the unvaccinated." Is it not yet clear to the left that the political face of "breakdown capitalism" is fascism, albeit articulated in new and more sophisticated (progressive!) forms of repression? The only way our comatose system can prolong its lifespan is by ditching its liberal façade and dramatically increasing its inherent capacity for barbarism. Capital is now desperately fighting for its life—against us.

In capitalist terms, we are facing an ironic twist on Margaret Thatcher's infamous TINA, "there is no alternative." Whatever happens next, we will continue to see the drastic devaluation of fiat currencies and the corresponding dissolution of the capitalist social relation. Most people will comply with the status quo out of fear and the internalization of a novel system of values based on collective guilt, responsibility, sacrifice, and obtuse, machine-like obedience. In other words, we will not only have nothing but, most crucially, we will be persuaded "to enjoy it." The consumerist ideology that drives modern capitalism is already being replaced with the injunction to "enjoy (having) nothing." Any battle for greater equality (with regard to gender, race, health, etc.) already occurs against the invisible background of "equal opportunity immiseration," where (nearly) nobody will be left behind.

Whether such a conversion to a punishing form of capitalism will succeed remains to be seen. Undoubtedly, a paradigm shift of this caliber needs the support of a belief system capable of transforming consumerist hubris into slave-like submissiveness masquerading as "empowerment." Humanity (particularly the increasingly depleted middle classes) will need to be convinced to commit to common causes that might justify being deprived of the "gift" (even as a fantasy object) of boundless consumption—fear alone will not suffice. For the neofeudal paradigm to succeed, the "work hard and play harder" ideology that keeps the modern consumer ticking must be replaced by a new ethics of sacrifice disguised as "self-affirmation." As spelled out by Emmanuel Macron in his "end of abundance" speech of August 2022,[10] we are at a point where "our system based on freedom [...] can demand sacrifices from its citizens." The ideological ruse of senile capitalism requires an endless wave of global crises to induce us to forfeit fundamental freedoms *in the name of preserving the freedom of capital.*

What changes here is the subject's relation to nothingness. If in consumer capitalism "nothing" is disguised as "more" (since the capitalist logic of desire relies on never having enough of "it"), in neofeudal capitalism "more" will be sold as "nothing," that is to say, a quasireligious, stubbornly egotistical attachment to renunciation. Harnessing human desire to a new social contract predicated upon protecting us from global calamities or the malevolence of "others" will be crucial for the system's capacity to reproduce itself. The potential of the modern-day leviathan could be unlocked by a new spirit of collective sacrifice, which is why contemporary capitalism is so eager to hijack the rhetoric of the left, knowing that only in the name of "progressive ideals" can the exploited masses accept new forms of domination disguised as necessary sacrifices. If that is the case, supposedly progressive and humanitarian narratives will translate into higher forms of conservatism and tyranny.

This logic emerges clearly with the emotional blackmail concerning climate change. Progressive citizens are expected to take on drastic lifestyle changes (for the worse) through sharing the guilt for the harm caused to Mother Earth, all while the planet continues to be exposed to the (re)productive, market-mediated dynamics of capital. This attitude can be recognized in the well-known phenomenon of "celebrity ecowarriors," a spin-off of "philanthropic capitalism." Leonardo DiCaprio, for instance, routinely tweets about the collective fight against climate change (e.g., "If we don't act together, we will surely perish!"), but he does so from his 315-foot, 110-million-dollar, helicopter-decked superyacht, which pollutes as much over a couple of miles as the average car does in a year—hardly "acting together." It is precisely as an actor, however, that he should know better, since he achieved international stardom with *Titanic* (1997), and we all know how that story ended. In other words, the devious elitist attempt to co-opt the leftist spirit of engagement for a collective cause might, at some point during the system's downfall, backfire—which is probably the only hope we have.

Rolling out fear to rollover debt

The first week of September 2023 began with the official return of the deadly virus. On Tuesday, September 5, pictures of Joe Biden wearing a black face mask were released into the global infosphere.

Simultaneously, mask mandates were issued at an elementary school in a small Maryland town in response to a new Covid outbreak in which three pupils tested positive.[11] In late August, face masks were mandated at Lionsgate Studios in Hollywood, Morris Brown College in Atlanta (with social distancing),[12] and Dillard University in New Orleans,[13] followed by other public places across the Western world. As of September 25, each US family could request four free Covid home tests, as the Biden administration resumed the program that was ended in June the previous year.[14] Testing was also scaled up in the UK,[15] where Covid-related flight disruptions brought back vivid memories of the recent past.[16] By the end of 2023, the specter of a new Covid variant (JN.1) still haunted the world. While most people opted out of mass hypnosis this time, governments around the world were still busy pushing "vaccines" (while hiding their adverse effects), testing, face masking, and surveillance.[17] By that time, the WHO had already warned of a mysterious Disease X, claiming, "Disease X represents the knowledge that a serious international epidemic could be caused by a pathogen currently unknown to cause human disease."[18] The same organization cautioned (without providing any data) that the imaginary Disease X could result in 20 times more fatalities than Covid-19 did.[19] Later in 2024, the pandemic ghost was still circulating, whether under the guise of Monkeypox[20] or Eastern Equine Encephalitis (with curfews implemented in Massachusetts).[21]

The first thing to do when faced by the formidable ideological firepower of the ruling class is to keep calm and not lose sight of the deeper causality. Signifiers like "Covid" do not belong—primarily at least—in the semantic field of epidemiology but in those of socioeconomics and behavioral psychology. Their intrinsic and overarching purpose is to shepherd us into a world of "lower energy density" where implosive capitalism seeks to extend its lifespan by turning the screw on entire populations. The flow of interchangeable shocks, even when purely hypothetical, feeds a fear paradigm that attempts to keep us subjugated. The management of perception in the digital era dissolves the boundary between true and false. This is perhaps nowhere more palpable than in the increasingly frequent emergency test alerts sent to mobile phones,[22] punishing reminders that we must live in a constant state of apprehension.[23]

By now, this much should be clear: crisis capitalism operates as a diabolical poverty management exercise based on the controlled release of panic, anxiety, and guilt, supplemented by endless distractions and fake or scarcely relevant polemics for herd consumption. Since 9/11, emergency is a state of mind that must be systematically nourished to maintain control over the people. Nothing must be left to chance. In this respect, Virus is only one of today's symptoms of a collapsing form of life. While humanity possesses the material and intellectual competence to provide for food, shelter, and a meaningful shared existence, it spectacularly fails to do so by subordinating those rights to the blind drive for profit making, whose viciousness grows as we edge closer to full-blown economic meltdown.

What the media and the political class will never tell us is that the next major lockup of the financial system would be followed by the collapse of the economy and the inevitable breakdown of society. In the dramatic meeting that took place on Thursday September 18, 2008, Ben Bernanke (then chairman of the Federal Reserve) famously stated: "If we don't do this [pump hundreds of billions of dollars into the system] tomorrow, we won't have an economy on Monday." Today, the consequences of a financial crash would be infinitely worse, and there is no guarantee that another rescue operation to unblock the system via massive cash injections—as already experimented with during Covid—would work. Essentially, this is why we are being conditioned to accept, if not actively desire, "low-energy" capitalism.

Let us once again recall that in September 2019, repo rates exploded overnight, shaking the core of a shadow banking system addicted to cheap credit. To avoid a contagious liquidity freeze, the

Fed immediately began mouth-to-mouth resuscitation via "quantitative easing on steroids": cash injections, first weekly and then daily, to the tune of billions of dollars. They reassured us that the technical fault would be resolved in a couple of weeks, and yet they went on flooding the banking sector with inordinate amounts of magic money until April 2020, when the baton was passed to the various pandemic support packages. At that time, the nature of crisis capitalism emerged clearly in all its absurdity, and a virus was weaponized to gag the global economy while the financial sector was once again bailed out. This is how the most efficient economic system we can think of makes its own greed "sustainable."

Four years later, pandemic angst is still exploited as a biopolitical tool against excess demand. Concealed by the usual barrage of meaningless "news," the debt-soaked system is again reaching a point of extreme saturation, in a context that sees us moving "from a capitalist-productivist society to a neocapitalist cybernetic order that aims now at total control,"[24] as Jean Baudrillard foresaw back in 1976—a time when the left was not yet *paranoid about being paranoid*, having not succumbed to the ubiquitous "conspiracy theory" blackmail. As more monetary injections are needed to support the debt bubble that keeps financial markets from cratering, real demand must be compressed to prevent an inflationary spike that could easily get out of hand. The scenario the elites want to avoid (at least for now) is depicted at the end of Alan Pakula's 1981 film aptly titled *Rollover*, when, after a financial crash, the world's currencies become worthless, and riots develop across the globe irrespective of political boundaries (East and West blocs) or economic differences (developing and industrialized countries). The implicit lesson of the film is that for today's financial travesty to continue, the skyrocketing debt stocks must be rolled over, which requires the assistance of an endless sequence of exogenous "accidents."

On the surface, things are bad enough. The financial system is a speculative black hole that must be fed greater and greater amounts of cash, and yet it can never be made whole. As the debt multiplier ticks higher, bond selloffs are increasingly common, which means that bonds (debt securities) lose value while their yields rise. At the end of September 2023, the US 10-year Treasury yield topped 4.5%, the highest point since October 2007, which pressurized stock markets as risk increased. Consistently rising bond yields are a major concern for both Wall Street and Main Street economies no longer able to refinance their way out of the debt trap.[25] By the end of 2023, it was clear that an inflationary monetary response would again be required. But the pathetic attempt to save an indebted system by adding more debt to it can only exacerbate the problem.

If we look beneath the surface, it gets even worse, as the entire structure is crumbling. I have stressed that sovereign debt is the backbone of modern financial systems, which means that demand for government bonds must be constantly stimulated—especially in the unregulated repo markets, where lending is mostly collateralized by government bonds. The key role that repo lenders play in keeping the system liquid hinges on their confidence that the value they receive as collateral will not drop sharply. When that happens, it triggers margin calls (requests from the lender to cough up additional funds) and then fire sales (asset sales at very low prices due to impending bankruptcy)—a vicious circle that usually leads to a crash. This is to say that, since debt is the epicenter of our world, its volatility shakes the foundations of the entire socioeconomic structure. The problem we face is that the borrowing binge of capitalist states has no end in sight, because revenues are chronically insufficient. However, servicing public debt presupposes *real growth*, which the state cannot provide. The state does not produce value, it can only manage it for social consumption. It is therefore delusional to think that the central bank allows the state to have real command over money. In economic terms, the authority of the central bank is purely formal, for its money creation programs can only *represent* real value, not generate it. This is why Marx defined government bonds as titles of *fictitious* capital; they are "illusory" from the outset since they are "nominal representatives of non-existent capital."[26]

Poverty is the new green

The premise I have outlined goes a long way toward explaining why we have been inundated with moralizing narratives concerning a "green transition" to "lower intensity" capitalism. Simply put, the latter translates into more poverty and less freedom for anyone not fortunate enough to belong to the 0.1%. Let us consider the recent Saudi move, in September 2023, to extend oil production cuts to the end of the year,[27] which immediately sent crude oil (Brent) beyond $90 per barrel. US strategic reserves were at their lowest level since the early 1980s[28] while the global oil market faced a deficit of 3 million barrels per day.[29] The fact of the matter is that, despite the anti–fossil fuel hysteria, oil is still by far the most efficient energy source for the capitalist engine, which also means that when its price goes up, it bleeds into a myriad of petroleum-based commodity prices.[30] This provides a further tailwind for inflation, which in turn suggests that, one way or another, (energy) consumption demand must be kept in check.

In the context of "capitalist realism," then, what is the battle against climate change really about? First, we are rapidly moving to a multipolar world in which the BRICS+ nations consume more fossil fuels than the West, since they have replaced the West as the "factory of the world." This new multipolar order has been in the making for a long time and is in many ways already in place. The most obvious practical problem with net zero is therefore that the "growth fetish" of the global productive machine is existentially dependent on so-called fossil fuels (oil, gas, and coal) insofar as their unique applications cannot easily be phased out and replaced by renewable transition technologies (wind, solar, etc.). Simply put, renewable energy systems have lower Energy Returned on Energy Invested (ERoEI) ratios than fossil fuel-based systems do, as even the "progressive" liberal press now acknowledges.[31] Thus, Big Oil will continue to profit for the foreseeable future, since fossil fuels represent around 80% of world energy use,[32] with petroleum being the largest single energy source in the global economy (a third of world energy consumption).

To understand one of the key issues at stake in the climate change conundrum, we should perhaps begin with some recent illustrative U-turns on radical net zero commitments, including those by Bill Gates,[33] Rishi Sunak and Larry Fink.[34] The story of BlackRock's change of heart is perhaps the most revealing. On June 26, 2023, the United Nations Human Rights Council filed a complaint against Amin Nasser, CEO of Saudi Aramco, the world's largest oil-producing company (98% of which is owned by the Saudi state). The missive,[35] which was also sent to Aramco's global financial partners (including JP Morgan Chase, Citigroup, Morgan Stanley, BNP Paribas, Goldman Sachs, Crédit Agricole, and other megabanks) challenged Aramco on human rights violations tied to fossil-fuel induced climate change. Two months later, the correspondence was released to the public, accompanied by jubilant headlines in Western mainstream media. What those media were less keen to report, however, was that in July 2023—only a month before the UN letter was made public—the same Amin Nasser, CEO of Aramco, was named independent director of BlackRock.[36] Now, if we consider that BlackRock is not only the world's top asset manager and the most powerful economic entity on the planet but also a staunch supporter of decarbonization, should we conclude that BlackRock CEO Larry Fink has decided to scrap his cuddly environmentalist agenda? Not exactly, for both he and his new Saudi board member have stated that they will continue nudging fossil fuel companies to adopt decarbonization plans, despite abandoning the ESG (Environmental, Social, and Governance) lingo.[37] Put differently, the Green New Deal agenda continues to be useful as an ideological tool, but not necessarily for business, since Big Money invests in all of the profitable industries it tells climate change aficionados to boycott.

Of course, "capitalist realism" is inherently hypocritical, combining "rapacious pursuit of profit with the rhetoric of ecological concern and social responsibility."[38] In light of the unstoppable economic decline we are facing, the official ecological narrative, based on the virtuous phasing out of fossil fuel emissions, is a pseudohumanitarian façade whose aim is not only to promote a delusional Green New Deal as a sustainable blueprint for postcrisis capitalism (for the superrich)[39] but also to escort impoverished populations into a digital panopticon designed to optimize mass control. Noble climate change hyper-activism is perhaps closer than it cares to know to the promotion of a centralized capitalist ecosystem regulated by avatars, tokenized digital assets, blockchain infrastructures, bio-nanotechnologies, the Internet of Bodies, and so on. The ubiquitous "veil of technology," with its smart rhetoric, is a wonderful opportunity for desocialization and the posthuman dissolution of individuality, interiority, ambivalence, critical thinking, and resistance. It is therefore no surprise that even Middle East "oil countries" (those in the Gulf Cooperation Council) now aim to achieve net zero (by around 2050)[40] while also looking to "seize the metaverse opportunity"[41] (as detailed in a fascinating document).[42]

The blind spot in the climate change discourse is that the capitalist "growth fetish" is predicated on the assumption that resources, just like capital, are infinite. "Sustainable capitalism" is therefore an oxymoron—unless, that is, we place it in a tyrannical framework. When looking at the UN's 17 Sustainable Development Goals,[43] for instance, it is tempting to read their idealism as a sinister warning of the brave new world in the making. Thus, "eradicating poverty" becomes *poverty management*; "zero hunger" becomes *rationing food*; "good health and wellbeing" becomes *compulsory vaccination*; "quality education" becomes *suppression of dissent*; "affordable and clean energy" becomes *low-energy destitution*; "decent work and economic growth" becomes *spiraling wealth inequality*; "sustainable cities and communities" becomes *urban apartheid*; "responsible consumption and production" becomes *mass immiseration*; and "peace, justice and strong institution" becomes *just wars*.

Along these lines, the fact that climate change organizations are funded by Big Money, including Big Oil itself, should at the very least give us pause. Consider the Just Stop Oil movement.[44] As detailed by *The Guardian*, Just Stop Oil has "received hundreds of thousands of dollars from the Los Angeles-based Climate Emergency Fund (CEF)," which "was started with a $500,000 donation from Aileen Getty, the granddaughter of Jean Paul Getty whose petrochemical empire made him the world's richest man, a source of some controversy in the climate activist world."[45] A billionaire oil heiress who donates millions each year to groups of in-your-face ecowarriors while she expands her financial portfolio and travels among various luxury homes by private jet should cause not merely "some controversy" but a deep sense of nausea, ideally followed by serious reflection. Instead of tackling the key issue—the criminal and destructive systemic compulsion to economic growth—we are fed yet another false binary (are we for or against climate change protesters?), which is itself based on ecology being the new "opium of the masses."

It should be clear that "low-energy capitalism" comes with significant collateral damage. The C40 Cities Climate Leadership Group, funded by a host of the usual suspects,[46] prescribes drastic consumption reductions for city dwellers in order to keep the temperature rise below 1.5 degrees and avoid "climate breakdown."[47] This is to be achieved by 2030, and it affects categories like cars, flights, appliances, and food. For instance, the C40 report recommends "the total elimination of meat and dairy products [which is] consistent with evidence that these food groups are generally associated with the highest levels of emissions and are not necessary for human health if appropriate food substitutions are made to ensure sufficient nutrient intake."[48] In short, the reduction of consumption-based emissions requires "significant behavioral changes," which effectively amounts to implementing a smart version of the Covid lockdown fraud. No wonder the 15-Minute City, initially conceived in 2016, gained popularity during the recent lockdowns. As always, the projected figures are sprinkled with irresistible humanitarian appeal, claiming that "eating less red meat and more fruit and vegetables could save 170,000 deaths per year, equivalent to $600 billion based on the economic value of life" and that "reducing dairy could save 19 billion cubic meters of freshwater per year" and "460 million square meters of land per year, equivalent to a land mass the size of Spain, or 32 billion trees," and so on.[49] As most people are defenseless when exposed to the overwhelming facticity of numbers, their commitment to "saving the planet" leads them to embrace their own coerced immiseration with gusto.

It is time to recognize that net zero is a substantial factor in the planned demolition of the current economic model. The spinning of the environmental narrative must be contextualized within the attempt to manage the monstruous debt burden of our decrepit civilization. Capitalism today continues to "thrive" by feeding liquidity into the debt-based system with one hand and stifling demand with the other. It should go without saying that this perverse strategy completely ignores the devastating internal contradiction of capitalist accumulation, which is also missed by the populist critics of globalism. Ultimately, the authoritarian attempt to manage the collapse of money as a store of value stems from the fact that value-productive labor power, the substance of capital, was made obsolete by the scientification of production over the past fifty years. It is within this wider context that we must place the current shift toward a "lower-energy capitalism" for the masses. The latter is rooted not merely in "peak oil" but more fundamentally in "peak productive labor," for value creation in capitalist terms depends on the *combustion of human energy*. In relation to peak productive labor, there is no denying that the world is increasingly populated by "useless eaters."

While the capitalist social relation is reified in anonymous markets driven by competition and a now dominant architecture of "monetary plumbing," capital's self-expansive capacity depends on labor markets, which is where the labor commodity is purchased for use as "raw material" for capitalist valorization. The "beautiful machine" must of course extract energy from raw materials as such (from fossil fuels to lithium, nickel, cobalt, etc.); however, it is primarily powered by human labor. Only by exploiting commodity-producing wage labor can the capitalist make two (real) dollars out of one. Yet, as David Graeber put it succinctly, "Automation *did*, in fact, lead to mass unemployment. We have simply stopped the gap by adding dummy jobs that are effectively made up."[50] This is why the epochal depletion of *commodity-producing* labor power is the root cause of our collapse.

Today, in many regions of the world, the system based on commodity production is already in tatters. The compensatory addiction to speculative profit now prompts a shift to an inherently oppressive ideology legitimized by irresistible, "science-based" tales of global calamities and the attendant magic bullets. The incorporation of the masses into modern citizenship was always a process of *adaptation* that forced human consciousness into the form of life organized around wage labor (capitalist and socialist alike). In this respect, modern dictatorships are by no means exceptions to democracy but manifestations of the fleeting character of democracy itself. It is now clear that democratic systems are once again unable to regulate the increasingly destructive force of the economy. In the highly financialized stage of capitalism in which we find ourselves, an ever-larger share of the citizenry is turned into an (increasingly angry) economic *surplus* to be disciplined in ways other than wage labor and the promise of social mobility. Hence, the new totalitarian character of contemporary capitalism.

With unparalleled concentrations of wealth and power, elites deploy sophisticated techniques of manipulation though which they silence and discredit dissent while simultaneously promoting "humanitarian solutions"—which, again, is what totalitarian regimes always do. Today's left, bathing in an ocean of intellectual bad conscience, contributes substantially to this new normal. If in the recent past the left was unafraid to denounce the corrupt nature of existing power relations, it now wholeheartedly embraces the "revolution of the ruling class." Only a few decades ago, the left still had the intellectual integrity to reject compliance. In 1993, for instance, Marxist political theorist Michael Parenti could still say what is plainly obvious but has become anathema to today's opportunistic left: "No ruling class could survive if it wasn't attentive to its own interests, consciously trying to anticipate, control, or initiate events at home and abroad, both overtly and secretly. It's hard to imagine a modern state in which there'd be no conspiracies, no plans, no machinations, deceptions, or secrecies within the circles of power."[51]

The left has traded in the capacity to critique the insanity of capital for a share of that very capital. If the left largely acquiesces or colludes with power, most of the remaining critical voices merely advocate for the beheading of the financial aristocracy, naively believing that this would enable the capitalist engine to once again fire on all cylinders. This is a narrow-minded view insofar as it forsakes the crucial insight into the objective dimension of capitalist reproduction—which has now clearly emerged as the compulsion through which "capital [...] works towards its own dissolution."⁵² The financial apparatus can be abolished only by overcoming capitalist relations as such. While there should be no doubt that the destructive course of our world is being steered, we should not confuse the immoral technocrats with capital's amoral drive. The global plutocracy is the subjective extension of the system's objective violence.

The decrepitude of our civilization results from the inertial self-movement of capital's centuries-old law of self-expansion. This law is *internal* and *immanent* rather than external and transcendent. While capitalist reproduction needs constant subjective validation, its aim—profitability—is a priori inscribed in its modus operandi. Whether it achieves profitability by exploiting human labor, starting wars, or speculating on financial assets is completely irrelevant from capital's blinkered perspective. This means that, strictly speaking, the current implosive process is not caused by the sociopathic elites, who are instead guilty of cynically managing it. Collapse itself is rather the consequence of a tectonic shift that undermines the system's *productive* conditions of possibility. Capital's appropriation of technology for its own misanthropic end turns a potential blessing into a catastrophic misfortune. Herbert Marcuse grasped this in 1964, at the dawn of the third industrial revolution: "It seems that automation to the limits of technical possibility is incompatible with a society based on the private exploitation of human labor power in the process of production."⁵³ As noted by Hannah Arendt a few years earlier, however, such incompatibility was likely to go unrecognized:

> Closer at hand and perhaps equally decisive is another no less threatening event. This is the advent of automation, which in a few decades probably will empty the factories and liberate mankind from its oldest and most natural burden, the burden of laboring and the bondage to necessity. [...] The modern age has carried with

it a theoretical glorification of labor and has resulted in a factual transformation of the whole of society into a laboring society. It is a society of laborers which is about to be liberated from the fetters of labor, and this society does no longer know of those other higher and more meaningful activities for the sake of which this freedom would deserve to be won. […] What we are confronted with is the prospect of a society of laborers without labor, that is, without the only activity left to them. Surely, nothing could be worse.[54]

The bitter irony is that, today, a minimum of human labor would satisfy the basic needs of all members of any society.

Conclusion

The One-Way Street of Capitalist Civilization

> What if contemporary capitalism isn't borrowing its way out of secular stagnation? What if the massive growth of global debt isn't a fragile house of cards destined to collapse? What if the "autumn of the system" doesn't spell death in the winter and rebirth in the spring, but a winter without end, a dark age doomed to permanent indebtedness?
> —Amin Samman and Stefano Sgambati[1]

> What I propose, therefore, is very simple: it is nothing more than to think what we are doing.
> —Hannah Arendt[2]

AMONG THE MANY PROPHETIC PASSAGES in Walter Benjamin's *Einbahnstraße* (One-way street)—the anthology of aphoristic meditations the German philosopher penned in the 1920s—the section "Imperial Panorama: A Tour of German Inflation" stands out as perhaps the most compelling piece of social criticism in Benjamin's entire oeuvre. Written immediately before the peak of Weimar hyperinflation in late 1923, the "tour" is composed of 14 "theses" on the deterioration of sociality as observed in Berlin by the philosopher-flaneur. Reading this section attentively from today's perspective can be an illuminating experience. It reminds us that the delusions of *Homo economicus* repeat themselves with uncanny punctuality in modern history.

As an opening gambit, Benjamin situates the socioeconomic *instability* caused by hyperinflation within a wider historical context dominated by the *stability* of decline and immiseration. The latter, he argues, escapes the "stock of phraseology that lays bare the amalgam of stupidity and cowardice constituting the mode of life of the German bourgeois." He then continues:

> The helpless fixation on notions of security and property deriving from past decades keeps the average citizen from perceiving the quite remarkable stabilities of an entirely new kind that underlie the present situation. [...] Stable conditions need by no means be pleasant conditions, and even before the war [World War I] there were strata for whom stabilized conditions amounted to stabilized wretchedness. To decline is no less stable, no more surprising, than to rise.[3]

If the immiserated masses languished in a steady condition of destitution both before and after World War I, the predicament of Berlin's urban bourgeoisie under the heavy blows of hyperinflation should be pitched against the background of *universal delusion* characterizing capitalist modernity. It is precisely because the declining middle classes are unable to see past individualism and economic self-interest that they cling to the fantasy that any loss of purchasing power is a temporary glitch awaiting systemic resolution—as though capital were an inexhaustible mode of wealth creation. The inherent myopia of the bourgeois suggests that they will comply with any ideological demand that carries the promise of socioeconomic protection, fulfilling the conservative illusion of perpetual wealth stability—which is precisely why Benjamin, in 1923, senses that a new catastrophe (World War II and the Holocaust) is on its way.

A hundred years later, Benjamin's critique rings especially true for a delusional middle class for whom the structural devaluation of fiat currencies has ushered in the chilling prospect of persistent immiseration. The same cry of frustration and incredulity regarding inflation that Benjamin recorded in 1923 can be heard all around us in 2024: "Things can't go on like this!"

At a deep existential level, most of today's middle classes still identify with the consumerist utopia of endless growth that characterized both the postwar Fordist accumulation cycle and the subsequent neoliberal financialization of the economy. The fantasy of a "Goldilocks economy" is still working in the background, as the moral majority are unwilling to reflect on the historical trajectory of capitalism as a social formation. This type of delusion requires the repression of any genuine intuition regarding the fact that capitalist decline is now both inevitable and catastrophic. At the same time, today's middle classes can hardly avoid fits of panic at the prospect of losing purchasing power and, with it, their status. And still this panic does not translate into any meaningful awareness of systemic implosion. Rather, it tends to seek redemption in the acceptance of a new normal that requires ever-increasing doses of "active ignorance" toward the unmitigated barbarism unleashed by transnational flows of capital.

If a new type of dogmatic conservatism exploded during the "pandemic," affecting nearly all self-proclaimed free and progressive voices, it descends from the obdurate attachment to a way of life that is as ingrained in our minds and bodies as it is irreversibly breaking apart. The sad lesson is that, collectively, most of us are incapable of even imagining the possibility of another world. Ultimately, behind the "picture of imbecility" that describes the people's compliance with power, one detects a desperate attachment to the capitalist gift, the stubborn echo of the original promise of socioeconomic privilege that is now quickly evaporating. The voice of authority that promised salvation from Virus is the same voice that promises salvation from economic freefall. But any ideal of solidarity mobilized by capitalist power under warlike conditions should at least appear unnatural to the reflective mind.

As Benjamin put it in *One-Way Street*, because "money stands ruinously at the center of every vital interest," the social bond is disintegrating. Benjamin also read inflation metaphorically, as the cultural or psychological attitude that accompanies the destructive logic of capital. The objective violence of German hyperinflation—the printing of banknotes to finance war reparations—is deployed as a trope to indict the increase of human "stupidity and cowardice" regarding the modern dogma of capital's self-valorization, which leads the masses to submit to despotic diktats in the hopes of retaining a modicum of economic privilege. Ultimately, the object of Benjamin's critique is the hyperinflation of herd behavior under economic duress, as expressed in a passage that could be read as a summary of today's conflation of public virtue and private vice:

> A curious paradox: people have only the narrowest private interest in mind when they act, yet they are at the same time more than ever determined in their behavior by the instincts of the mass. And more than ever mass instincts have become confused and estranged from life. […] Again and again it has been shown that society's attachment to its familiar and long-since-forfeited life is so rigid as to nullify the genuinely human application of intellect, forethought, even dire peril. So that in this society the picture of imbecility is complete: uncertainty, indeed perversion of vital instincts, and impotence, indeed decay of the intellect.[4]

The "curious paradox" of mass compliance in the name of narrow self-interest captures the folly of an entire civilization in denial, suspended between economic collapse and "totalitarian solutions."

It seems fitting to conclude with a brief reference to a seventeenth-century North American sage known as Kandiaronk. In his dialogues with French colonizer Baron de Lahontan, published in a travelogue that became very popular in the Enlightenment salons of eighteenth-century Europe, the indigenous philosopher-statesman Kandiaronk resolutely rejected the argument that the European civilization was superior to that of his native Wendat people. In dissecting the central categories (which included economics, politics, religion, and health) of what was effectively a burgeoning capitalism, Kandiaronk argued that Europe would be better off dismantling its entire social system based on money, the pursuit of material self-interest, coercive laws, the lack of mutual aid, and blind submission to authority. In this respect, his indictment of money (which the Wendat did not use, referring to it as "the French serpent") is worth quoting:

> I affirm that what you call money is the devil of devils; the tyrant of the French, the source of all evils; the bane of soul and slaughterhouse of the living. To imagine that one can live in the country of money and preserve one's soul is like imagining one can preserve one's life at the bottom of a lake. Money is the father of luxury, lasciviousness, intrigues, trickery, lies, betrayal, insincerity—all of the world's worst behaviour.[5]

While the image of the "noble savage" that Jean-Jacques Rousseau helped to popularize is no doubt a European fantasy, and while it is true that money as a general equivalent predates capital, the indigenous American's critique of the mores of the "enlightened" settler is particularly inspiring today, at a time when a system based on the compulsive pursuit of money's self-expansion heads blindly and remorselessly toward self-destruction.

Endnotes

Introduction

1 Theodor Adorno, "Late Capitalism or Industrial Society?," in *Can One Live After Auschwitz? A Philosophical Reader*, edited by Rolf Tiedemann (Stanford: Stanford UP, 2003), p. 121.
2 Jean Baudrillard, *The Agony of Power* (Los Angeles: Semiotext(e), 2010), p. 105.
3 The concept was developed by Alfred Sohn-Rethel in his classic *Intellectual and Manual Labour: A Critique of Epistemology* (Atlantic Highlands, N.J: Humanities Press, 1977 [1970]).
4 Walter Benjamin, "Kapitalismus als Religion" (Fragment), in *Gesammelte Schriften* vol. 6. (Frankfurt am Main: Suhrkamp, 1991 [1921]), pp. 100–102. For an English translation, see Walter Benjamin, *Toward a Critique of Violence*, edited by Peter Fenves and Julia Ng (Stanford: Stanford University Press, 2021), pp. 90–93 (91).
5 Jorgelina Do Rosario, "Global debt hits new record high at $313 trillion – IIF," Reuters. Available here: https://www.reuters.com/business/global-debt-hits-new-record-high-313-trillion-iif-2024-02-21/.
6 Terry Chan and Alexandra Dimitrijevic, "Global Debt Leverage: Is a Great Reset Coming?," S&P Global, January 13, 2023. Available here: https://www.spglobal.com/en/research-insights/featured/special-editorial/look-forward/global-debt-leverage-is-a-great-reset-coming.
7 Via Hegel and Marx in particular, I presented a critique of capitalism as a self-fulfilling prophecy in *Unworkable: Delusions of an Imploding Civilization* (New York: SUNY Press, 2022). The theoret-

ical framework outlined in that book is further developed here and deployed in a more directly polemical fashion.

8   See https://research.stlouisfed.org/publications/review/2023/06/02/fiscal-dominance-and-the-return-of-zero-interest-bank-reserve-requirements.

9   See https://www.usdebtclock.org/.

10 See https://www.fiscal.treasury.gov/reports-statements/financial-report/unsustainable-fiscal-path.html#:~:text=The%20debt-to-GDP%20ratio%20rises%20continuously%20in%20great%20part,both%20the%202021%20and%202020%20Financial%20Report%20projections.

11 See https://cbdctracker.org/.

12 The so-called token economy is a behavioral management system in which an individual is rewarded with tokens for demonstrating the desired conduct. Tokens are, by definition, "objects" (often virtual) whose function is to provide one with access to things such as social, economic, and cultural services.

13 See https://www.bis.org/publ/arpdf/ar2022e3.htm.

14 As detailed by Pam and Russ Martens at Wall Street on Parade, the Federal Reserve began, on September 17, 2019, an extraordinary program of repo loans to its "primary dealers" on Wall Street (including JP Morgan, Goldman Sachs, Barclays, BNP Paribas, Nomura, Deutsche Bank, Bank of America, Citibank, and other megabanks). See https://wallstreetonparade.com/2021/12/the-fed-is-about-to-reveal-which-wall-street-banks-needed-4-5-trillion-in-repo-loans-in-q4-2019/ and https://wallstreetonparade.com/2022/03/the-feds-secret-repo-loans-another-news-blackout-and-a-french-bank-scandal/. Further evidence of the repo market's persistent fragility came on July 28, 2021, when the Fed announced the creation of a "Standing Repo Facility" (SRF), consisting of $500 billion in weekly backstop credit for the Fed's primary dealers and additional counterparties. See https://www.federalreserve.gov/newsevents/pressreleases/monetary20210728b.htm. See also https://www.newyorkfed.org/markets/repo-agreement-ops-faq.

15 See https://www.newyorkfed.org/markets/OMO_transaction_data.html#rrp. One can easily calculate that the Fed grant-

ed $19.87 trillion in term loans to Wall Street trading arms and foreign megabanks in the fourth quarter of 2019 alone, followed by another $28.06 trillion in the first quarter of 2020. These staggering amounts of "money" are equal to roughly half of the world's GDP.

16 On this topic, see Geoffrey Parker, *The Military Revolution: Military Innovation and the Rise of the West, 1500–1800* (Cambridge: Cambridge University Press, 1996); Daniel R. Headrick, *Power over Peoples – Technology, Environments, and Western Imperialism, 1400 to the Present* (Princeton: Princeton University Press, 2012); Robert Kurz, "The Big Bang of Modernity," *The Futures of Work* (21), February 10, 2022 (2011). Available here: https://futuresofwork.co.uk/2022/02/10/introduction-to-kurz-war-and-wertkritik/.

17 See David Gritten, "Gaza war: Where does Israel get its weapons?," *BBC news*, April 15, 2024. Available here: https://www.bbc.co.uk/news/world-middle-east-68737412.

18 It happened in November 2023 at Barclay Primary School in Leyton, East London. Following protests from parents, the school decided to close early for the Christmas period. See https://www.trtworld.com/magazine/8-year-old-suspended-for-wearing-palestinian-badge-at-east-london-school-16346686.

19 Karl Marx, *Capital: A Critique of Political Economy*, vol. 1 (London: Penguin, 1990 [1867]), p. 919.

Chapter One

1 Jacques Camatte, *This World We Must Leave and Other Essays*, edited by Alex Trotter (New York: Autonomedia, 1995 [1976]), p. 40.

2 Jacques Lacan, *The Seminar of Jacques Lacan, book 17, The Other Side of Psychoanalysis*, trans. Russell Grigg (New York: Norton, 2007), pp. 177–78.

3 Guy Debord, *Society of the Spectacle* (London: Rebel Press, 1983 [1967]), p. 58.

4 See, for instance, David Haggith, "Repocalypse: The second coming." The Great Recession, December 23, 2019. Available here: https://thegreatrecession.info/blog/repocalypse-the-second-coming.

5   See Amin Samman and Stefano Sgambati, "Financial Eschatology and the Libidinal Economy of Leverage," *Theory, Culture & Society*, 40:3, 2023, pp. 103–21.
6   See Lily Kuo, "China confirms human-to-human transmission of coronavirus," *The Guardian*, January 21, 2020. Available here: https://www.theguardian.com/world/2020/jan/20/coronavirus-spreads-to-beijing-as-china-confirms-new-cases.
7   See https://www.macrotrends.net/countries/CHN/china/gdp-growth-rate#:~:text=China%20gdp%20growth%20rate%20for,a%200.8%25%20decline%20from%202018.
8   The texts in the agreement are no doubt fascinating reads, especially when considering the agreement's timing. They include obligations regarding technology transfer, such as China's agreement not to "disclose sensitive technical information—including trade secrets and other confidential business information," as well as an obligation for the "early resolution of potential pharmaceutical patent disputes." Available here: https://ustr.gov/phase-one#:~:text=Together%2C%20we%20are%20righting%20the,workers%2C%20farmers%2C%20and%20families.&text=The%20United%20States%20and%20China%20signed%20an%20historic%20and%20enforceable,deal%20on%20January%2015%2C%202020.
9   See https://www.bis.org/publ/arpdf/ar2019e.pdf.
10 See https://www.bis.org/publ/work804.pdf.
11 See https://www.blackrock.com/corporate/literature/whitepaper/bii-macro-perspectives-august-2019.pdf. See also https://wallstreetonparade.com/2020/06/blackrock-authored-the-bailout-plan-before-there-was-a-crisis-now-its-been-hired-by-three-central-banks-to-implement-the-plan/.
12 See Brendan Greeley, "Central bankers rethink everything at Jackson Hole," *Financial Times*, August 25, 2019. Available here: https://www.ft.com/content/360028ba-c702-11e9-af46-b09e8bfe60c0.
13 See Annie Massa and Caleb Melby, "In Fink We Trust: BlackRock Is Now 'Fourth Branch of Government,'" *Bloomberg*, May 21, 2020. Available here: https://www.bloomberg.com/news/articles/2020-05-21/how-larry-fink-s-blackrock-is-helping-the-fed-with-bond-buying?leadSource=uverify%20wall.

14 See Annie Massa, "Fed Enlists BlackRock In Its Massive Debt-Buying Programs," *Bloomberg*, March 24, 2020. Available here: https://www.bloomberg.com/news/articles/2020-03-24/fed-hires-blackrock-for-agency-cmbs-corporate-debt-programs.
15 See https://www.govinfo.gov/content/pkg/DCPD-201900631/pdf/DCPD-201900631.pdf.
16 See https://rumble.com/v1qnz5f-claudia-stauber-from-cabin-talk-vermont-usa-predicts-the-pandemic-in-sept-2.html.
17 See https://centerforhealthsecurity.org/our-work/tabletop-exercises/event-201-pandemic-tabletop-exercise.
18 See https://www.weforum.org/videos/update-wuhan-coronavirus-covid-19-davos-2020.
19 At her LinkedIn page, we can read, "Some brands that I've worked with: L'Oréal, DHL, HCLTech, WeChat, Lenovo, McLaren, Roche, Audi, LinkedIn, Vogue, P&G, AstraZeneca, J&J :) ." A truly global young leader.
20 See https://www.youtube.com/watch?app=desktop&v=CceUHgvvLS0.
21 See John Detrixhe, "Zombie companies are hiding an uncomfortable truth about the global economy," *Quartz*, March 9, 2020. Available here: https://qz.com/1812705/zombie-companies-are-spreading-as-interest-rates-fall/.
22 See Randall Wray, "$29,000,000,000,000: A Detailed Look at the Fed's Bailout of the Financial System," Levy Economic Institute, December 23, 2011. Available here: https://www.levyinstitute.org/publications/29000000000000-a-detailed-look-at-the-feds-bailout-by-funding-facility-and-recipient.
23 See Spriha Srivastava, "QE Infinity: Are we heading into the unknown?," *CNBC*, August 26, 2016. Available here: https://www.cnbc.com/2016/08/26/qe-infinity-are-we-heading-into-the-unknown.html.
24 Ellen Brown, "Another Bank Bailout Under Cover of a Virus," *The Web of Debt*, May 18, 2020. Available here: https://ellenbrown.com/2020/05/18/another-bank-bailout-under-cover-of-a-virus/.
25 "Capital itself is the moving contradiction, [in] that it presses to reduce labour time to a minimum, while it posits labour time, on

the other side, as sole measure and source of wealth." Karl Marx, *Grundrisse: Foundations of the Critique of Political Economy* (London: Penguin, 1993 [1939–41]), p. 706.

26 See Chase Peterson-Withorn, "The World's Billionaires Have Gotten $1.9 Trillion Richer In 2020," *Forbes*, December 16, 2020. Available here: https://www.forbes.com/sites/chasewithorn/2020/12/16/the-worlds-billionaires-have-gotten-19-trillion-richer-in-2020/?sh=75b6372c7386.

27 See https://www.who.int/bulletin/volumes/99/1/20-265892/en/.

28 See https://www.statista.com/statistics/257364/top-lobbying-industries-in-the-us/#:~:text=Leading%20lobbying%20industries%20in%20the%20U.S.%202020&text=In%202020%2C%20the%20pharmaceuticals%20and,million%20U.S.%20dollars%20on%20lobbying.

29 See https://www.fda.gov/vaccines-blood-biologics/vaccines/emergency-use-authorization-vaccines-explained#:~:text=Under%20an%20EUA%2C%20FDA%20may,are%20no%20adequate%2C%20approved%2C%20and.

30 As indicated earlier, I have chosen not to discuss the various lab leak, gain-of-function coronavirus theories, not only because they are beyond my field of competence but, more importantly, because they would detract from my wider argument concerning economic causality.

31 The Italian case is particularly telling. See, for instance, Simona Ravizza, "Milano, terapie intensive al collasso per l'influenza: già 48 malati gravi molte operazioni rinviate," *Corriere della Sera*, January 10, 2018. Available here: https://milano.corriere.it/notizie/cronaca/18_gennaio_10/milano-terapie-intensive-collasso-l-influenza-gia-48-malati-gravi-molte-operazioni-rinviate-c9dc43a6-f5d1-11e7-9b06-fe054c3be5b2.shtml.

32 Robert Kurz, "The apotheosis of money: the structural limits of capital valorization, casino capitalism and the global financial crisis," 1995. Available here: https://libcom.org/article/apotheosis-money-structural-limits-capital-valorization-casino-capitalism-and-global#footnoteref38_i6920p7.

33 See Mariana Mazzucato, "Avoiding a Climate Lockdown," *Project Syndicate*, September 22, 2020. Available here: https://www.project-syndicate.org/commentary/radical-green-overhaul-to-avoid-climate-lockdown-by-mariana-mazzucato-2020-09.

Chapter Two

1 There is now a vast literature on the ways technological automation impacts our "work societies." While my approach and research are inspired primarily by the theory of "value criticism" (*Wertkritik*), which draws from the Marxian tradition, the interrelations between automation and work are discussed from different angles by a growing number of contemporary authors, including the following: Jeremy Rifkin, *The End of Work: The Decline of the Global Labour Force* (New York: Putnam, 1994) and *The Zero Marginal Cost Society: the Internet of Things, The Collaborative Commons, and the Eclipse of Capitalism* (London: Palgrave-Macmillan, 2014); Jon-Arild Johannessen, *Automation, Capitalism, and the End of the Middle Class* (London and New York: Routledge, 2019); Aaron Benavav, *Automation and the Future of Work* (London and New York: Verso, 2020); Bernard Stiegler, *The Age of Disruption: Technology and Madness in the Age of Computational Capitalism* (Cambridge, Oxford, Boston: Polity, 2019); Martin Ford, *The Rise of the Robots: Technology and the Threat of Mass Unemployment* (London: Oneworld, 2016).
2 Amin Samman and Stefano Sgambati, "Financial Eschatology and the Libidinal Economy of Leverage," p. 109.
3 The following piece of UK cattle legislation increasingly applies to "human animals" too: "The Cattle Identification Regulations 2007 implement statutory requirements relating to the notification of cattle holdings, ear tagging, passports and registration of cattle, and the subsequent record-keeping requirements. Cattle need to be identified for traceability, to track disease outbreaks and to ensure the integrity of British beef. Cattle must be identified with a pair of approved ear tags and have been issued with a passport. This identity and documentation must stay with the beast throughout its life. The British Cattle Movement Service (BCMS) must be informed of any

movements and deaths." (see https://www.businesscompanion.info/en/quick-guides/animals-and-agriculture/cattle-identification).

4   It is worth adding that Chomsky, like many on the "left," completely lost the plot when he called for the segregation of the "unvaccinated," even adding that their destitution would be their own problem, "like people in jail." See https://www.youtube.com/watch?v=TzW-cP2b4uZ4.

5   See https://www.who.int/news/item/05-06-2023-the-european-commission-and-who-launch-landmark-digital-health-initiative-to-strengthen-global-health-security.

6   Mauro Bottarelli, "'No free lunch': il denaro a costo zero perenne impone Covid perenne. Punto," *Money.it*, July 8, 2012. Available here: https://www.money.it/Denaro-costo-zero-Covid-perenne.

7   See Jedidajah Otte, "'Everything will be all right': message of hope spreads in Italy," *The Guardian*, March 12, 2020. Available here: https://www.theguardian.com/world/2020/mar/12/everything-will-be-alright-italians-share-slogan-of-hope-in-face-of-coronavirus-crisis.

8   See https://www.newyorkfed.org/markets/desk-operations/reverse-repo.

9   See https://www.reuters.com/article/usa-fed-reverse-repo/fomc-raises-counterparty-limit-in-reverse-repos-to-160-bln-idUSL-1N2QO2A3.

10 For a biopolitical critique of Covid-19, see especially Giorgio Agamben, *Where Are We Now? The Epidemic as Politics* (Lanham, MD: Rowman and Littlefield, 2021).

11 See https://www.youtube.com/watch?v=rpNnTuK5JJU.

12 https://www.youtube.com/watch?v=jm15P4JgTCo.

13 See https://www.id2020.org.

14 Ennio Flaiano, *La solitudine del satiro* (Milan: Adelphi, 1996), p. 356. In truth, Flaiano was quoting painter and friend Mino Maccari, as reported in *Satira è vita* (Bologna: Pendragon, 2002), p. 44.

15 On this topic, see especially Vandana Shiva (ed.), *Philanthrocapitalism and the Erosion of Democracy: A Global Citizens Report on the Corporate Control of Technology, Health, and Agriculture* (Santa Fe: Synergetic Press, 2022).

16 Georg Wilhelm Friedrich Hegel, *Philosophy of Right* (Oxford: Oxford University Press, 2008), p. 200.
17 See David Coady, "Conspiracy Theory as Heresy," in *Educational Philosophy and Theory*, 55:7, 2021, pp. 756–59.
18 Ole Bjerg, "Conspiracy Theory: Truth Claim or Language Game?," *Theory, Culture & Society*, 2016, pp. 1–23 (6).
19 Slavoj Žižek, "Vaccinated or not, we are ALL controlled and manipulated," *RT*, November 2, 2021. Available here: https://www.rt.com/op-ed/539185-zizek-greek-covid-skeptics-scam/.
20 Slavoj Žižek, *Surplus-Enjoyment. A Guide for the Non-Perplexed* (London and New York: Bloomsbury, 2022), pp. 305 and 312.
21 Jacques Lacan, *Écrits. The First Complete English Edition*, trans. Bruce Fink (New York: W. W. Norton, 2006), p. 742.
22 Jacques Lacan, *The Seminar of Jacques Lacan, book 17, The Other Side of Psychoanalysis*, p. 110.
23 Jacques Lacan, *Freud Forever: An Interview with Panorama*, trans. Philip Dravers, *Hurly Burly* 12, 2015, pp. 13–21 (18).
24 Theodor Adorno and Max Horkheimer, *Dialectic of Enlightenment* (Stanford: Stanford University Press, 2002 [1944]).
25 Jacques Lacan, *The Seminar of Jacques Lacan, Book 11, The Four Fundamental Concepts of Psychoanalysis*, trans. Alan Sheridan (New York: W. W. Norton, 1998), p. 22.
26 From personal correspondence.
27 Jean Baudrillard, "Opposer à Le Pen la vitupération morale, c'est lui laisser le privilège de l'insolence. La conjuration des imbéciles," *Libération*, May 7, 1997. Available here: https://www.liberation.fr/tribune/1997/05/07/opposer-a-le-pen-la-vituperation-morale-c-est-lui-laisser-le-privilege-de-l-insolence-la-conjuration_206413/.
28 Jean Baudrillard, *The Agony of Power*, p. 101.
29 Jacques Camatte, *This World We Must Leave and Other Essays*, p. 42.
30 Domenico Losurdo, *Liberalism: A Counter-History* (London and New York: Verso, 2011).
31 Johann Wolfgang von Goethe, *Goethe's World View Presented in his Reflections and Maxims* (New York: F. Ungar, 1963), pp. 58–59.

32 Max Horkheimer, "The Jews and Europe," in E. Bronner and D. Kellner (eds.), *Critical Theory and Society. A Reader* (London and New York: Routledge, 1989), pp. 77–94 (78).
33 See https://www.weforum.org/events/pioneers-of-change-summit-2020/.
34 See https://www.weforum.org/agenda/2020/11/the-world-needs-corporate-activists-with-these-5-steps-you-can-become-one/.
35 Sebastian Buckup and Tomas Casas Klett, "Modern Leaders Need a Powerful Narrative," *Management Today*, November 6, 2018. Available here: https://www.managementtoday.co.uk/modern-leaders-need-powerful-narrative/reputation-matters/article/1498184.
36 See https://medium.com/world-economic-forum/welcome-to-2030-i-own-nothing-have-no-privacy-and-life-has-never-been-better-ee2eed62f710.
37 Jean Baudrillard, *Cool Memories* (London and New York: Verso, 1990), p. 127. See also, Kate Crawford, *Atlas of AI. Power, Politics, and the Planetary Costs of Artificial Intelligence* (New Haven: Yale University Press, 2022).
38 Daniel Guérin, *Fascism and Big Business* (New York and London: Pathfinder, 1973), p. 28.
39 Ibid, p. 387.

Chapter Three

1 Franco "Bifo" Berardi, *After the Future* (Edinburgh, Oakland, Baltimore: AK Press, 2011), p. 43.
2 Walter Benjamin (2003), *Selected Writings, vol. 4, 1938–1940*, ed. H. Eiland and M. W. Jennings (Cambridge, MA: Harvard UP), p. 402.
3 See Karl Marx, *Grundrisse: Foundations of the Critique of Political Economy*, pp. 105–8.
4 See Karl Marx, *Capital: A Critique of Political Economy*, pp. 253–54 and 267.
5 Karl Marx, *Capital: A Critique of Political Economy*, vol. 1, pp. 133–35.
6 Robert Kurz, *The Substance of Capital: The Life and Death of Capitalism*, trans. Robin Halpin (London: Chronos, 2016), 88 (emphasis

added). See also, Jean Baudrillard, *The Mirror of Production*, trans. Mark Poster (St. Louis, MO: Telos Press, 1975), pp. 21–51.

7   See Jacques Lacan, *From an Other to the other, Book XVI: The Seminar of Jacques Lacan* (Cambridge: Polity, 2023). I have discussed Lacan's take on Marx's concept of surplus value in various parts of my research, including *Unworkable: Delusions of an Imploding Civilisation*; *Crisi di valore. Lacan, Marx e il crepuscolo della società del lavoro* (Milano: Mimesis, 2018); and, with Heiko Feldner, *Critical Theory and the Crisis of Contemporary Capitalism* (London and New York: Bloomsbury, 2015).

8   See Walter Benjamin, "Kapitalismus als Religion."

9   "Custom is the source of our strongest and most believed proofs. It bends the automaton, which persuades the mind without its thinking about the matter." Hence, "we must kneel, pray with the lips, etc." in order to believe (Blaise Pascal, *Pensées*, New York: E. P. Dutton, 1958, p. 73).

10 Slavoj Žižek, *Pandemic! Covid-19 Shakes the World* (New York and London: OR Books, 2020), p. 31.

11 Slavoj Žižek, *Pandemic! 2. Chronicles of a Time Lost* (New York and London: OR Books, 2020), p. 113.

12 Karl Marx, *Capital: A Critique of Political Economy*, vol. 1, p. 125.

13 Fredrich Nietzsche, *Thus Spake Zarathustra* (New York: Algora Publishing, 2003), pp. 11–12 (emphasis added).

14 Ralf Dahrendorf, *Reisen nach innen und aussen. Aspekte der Zeit* (Stuttgart: Deutsche Verlags-Anstalt, 1984).

15 See, among others, Philippe Ariés, *Western Attitudes Toward Death from the Middle Ages to the Present* (Baltimore: John Hopkins UP, 1974); Jean Baudrillard, *Symbolic Exchange and Death* (New York: Sage, 1993); Norbert Elias, *The Loneliness of the Dying* (London and New York: Continuum, 2001); Robert Redeker, *L'éclipse de la mort* (Paris: Desclée de Brouwer, 2017).

16 Chuck Collins, Omar Ocampo, Sophia Paslaski, "Billionaire Bonanza 2020: Wealth Windfalls, Tumbling Taxes, and Pandemic Profiteers," *Institute for Policy Studies*, April 23, 2020. Available here: https://ips-dc.org/billionaire-bonanza-2020/.

17 For a general overview, see "Studies on Covid-19 Lethality," *Swiss Policy Research*, May 2020. Available here: https://swprs.org/studies-on-covid-19-lethality/

18 Anthony Fauci, Clifford Lane, and Robert Redfield, "Navigating the Uncharted," *New England Journal of Medicine*, 382(13): 1268–1269, March 26, 2020. Available here: https://www.ncbi.nlm.nih.gov/pmc/articles/PMC7121221/.

19 Vladimiro Giacchè, *La fabbrica del falso* (Reggio Emilia: Imprimatur, 2016).

20 Joseph Schumpeter, *Capitalism, Socialism & Democracy* (London and New York: Routledge, 2010 [1943]), p. 76.

21 Theodor W. Adorno, *Negative Dialectics* (London and New York: Routledge, 2004), p. 320.

22 Naomi Klein, *The Shock Doctrine: The Rise of Disaster Capitalism* (London: Penguin, 2008).

23 Alan Cassels, *Seeking Sickness. Medical Screening and the Misguided Hunt for Disease* (Vancouver, Toronto, Berkeley: Greystone Books, 2012).

24 Ivan Illich, *Limits to Medicine: Medical Nemesis. The Expropriation of Health* (London and New York: Marion Boyars, 2010 [1976]).

25 James Crump, "'This is like a world war': Bill Gates says the pain of coronavirus will be around for generations," *The Independent*, April 24, 2020. Available here: https://www.independent.co.uk/news/world/americas/bill-gates-coronavirus-pandemic-world-war-define-era-generations-a9482306.html. It is also worth recalling that Gates "predicted" the Covid pandemic in an interview that appeared in an episode of the Netflix show *Explained* (season 2), aired on November 7, 2019, under the title "The Next Pandemic." Here is the episode's prophetic tagline: "If you're not worried about a looming global pandemic, you probably should be."

26 David Graeber, *Bullshit Jobs. The Rise of Pointless Work and What We Can Do About It* (London: Penguin, 2018).

27 An important recent contribution to the empirical evidence that supports Marx's law regarding the tendency of the rate of profit to fall is made in Tomás Rotta and Rishabh Kumar's, "Was Marx right? Development and exploitation in 43 countries, 2000–2014,"

Structural Change and Economic Dynamics, 69: 213–23, June 2023. Available here: https://www.sciencedirect.com/science/article/pii/S0954349X23001753.
28 Jean Baudrillard, *Simulations* (Los Angeles: Semiotext[e], 1983), p. 47.
29 See Étienne de La Boétie, *Discourse on Voluntary Servitude* (Indianapolis, IN: Hackett Publishing Company, 2012 [1577]).
30 Antonio Gramsci, *Selections from the Prison Notebooks* (New York: International Publishers, 1971), pp. 275–76.

Chapter Four

1 Elena Gorokhova, *A Mountain of Crumbs* (London: Simon & Schuster, 2011), p. 181.
2 Ylan Mui, "Economists warn of inflation inequality as poor get slammed by rising prices," *CNBC*, December 29, 2021. Available here: https://www.cnbc.com/2021/12/29/economists-warn-of-inflation-inequality-in-2022.html.
3 Larry Elliot, "Global inequality 'as marked as it was at peak of western imperialism,'" *The Guardian*, December 7, 2021. Available here: https://www.theguardian.com/business/2021/dec/07/global-inequality-western-imperialism-super-rich.
4 See, for instance, Philip Inman, "Is a global recession coming? Here are seven warning signs," *The Guardian*, August 25, 2019. Available here: https://www.theguardian.com/uk-news/2019/aug/25/is-a-global-recession-coming-here-are-seven-warning-signs.
5 See https://www.youtube.com/watch?v=tB2CM2ngpQg.
6 See Silvia Amaro, "ECB faces calls to be clearer on inflation after Fed's Powell drops 'transitory,'" *CNBC*, December 2, 2021. Available here: https://www.cnbc.com/2021/12/02/powell-time-to-retire-transitory-what-it-means-for-the-ecb.html.
7 See https://www.bls.gov/cpi/notices/2021/2022-weight-update.htm.
8 See Craig Stirling and Harumi Ichikura, "Fastest Inflation in Euro's History Set to Raise Pressure on ECB," *Bloomberg*, November 26, 2021. Available here: https://www.bloomberg.com/

news/articles/2021-11-26/fastest-inflation-in-euro-s-history-set-to-raise-pressure-on-ecb?leadSource=uverify%20wall.
9. John Maynard Keynes, "Economic Possibilities for Our Grandchildren," in *Essays in Persuasion* (New York: W. W. Norton & Co., 1963), pp. 358–73.
10. Franco Berardi, "Rassegnatevi," in *Not*, December 1, 2021. Available here: https://not.neroeditions.com/rassegnatevi/ (author translation).
11. Jean Baudrillard, *The Gulf War Did Not Take Place* (Sydney: Power Publications, 1995).
12. Munsif Vengattil and Elizabeth Culliford, "Facebook allows war posts urging violence against Russian invaders," Reuters, March 11, 2022. Available here: https://www.reuters.com/world/europe/exclusive-facebook-instagram-temporarily-allow-calls-violence-against-russians-2022-03-10/.
13. See https://then24.com/2022/03/02/an-italian-university-suspended-a-course-on-dostoevsky-due-to-russias-invasion-of-ukraine/.
14. See https://www.youtube.com/watch?v=Nbj1AR_aAcE.
15. See https://www.youtube.com/watch?v=WV9J6sxCs5k.
16. Lev Golinkin, "Neo-Nazis and the Far Right Are on the March in Ukraine," *The Nation*, February 22, 2019. Available here: https://www.thenation.com/article/politics/neo-nazis-far-right-ukraine/.
17. Andriy Zagorodnyuk, Alina Frolova, Hans Petter Midtunn, Oleksii Pavliuchyk, "Is Ukraine's reformed military ready to repel a new Russian invasion?," Atlantic Council, December 23, 2021. Available here: https://www.atlanticcouncil.org/blogs/ukrainealert/is-ukraines-reformed-military-ready-to-repel-a-new-russian-invasion/.
18. See https://www.youtube.com/watch?v=hQ58Yv6kP44.
19. See https://www.whitehouse.gov/briefing-room/speeches-remarks/2023/02/21/remarks-by-president-biden-ahead-of-the-one-year-anniversary-of-russias-brutal-and-unprovoked-invasion-of-ukraine/.
20. Max Bearak, "The U.S. Is Paying Billions to Russia's Nuclear Agency. Here's Why," *The New York Times*, June 14, 2023. Available here:

https://www.nytimes.com/2023/06/14/climate/enriched-uranium-nuclear-russia-ohio.html.

21 Karen Gilchrist, "Sanctioned Western tech is still entering Russia and powering its military machine, new analysis shows," *CNBC*, January 11, 2024. Available here: https://www.cnbc.com/2024/01/11/sanctioned-western-tech-is-still-entering-russia-and-powering-its-war.html.

22 John Nye and Maria Snegovaya, "Russia is Shrugging Off Sanctions," *Foreign Policy*, November 13, 2023. Available here: https://foreignpolicy.com/2023/11/13/russia-sanctions-evasion-oil-revenue-ukraine-war/.

23 Karl Marx, *Capital: A Critique of Political Economy*, vol. 3 (London: Penguin 1991), p. 200.

24 Available here: https://resistir.info/livros/rebuilding_americas_defenses.pdf.

25 See Mike Stone, "US arms exports hit record high in fiscal 2023," Reuters, January 29, 2024.

26 See https://eda.europa.eu/news-and-events/news/2023/11/30/record-high-european-defence-spending-boosted-by-procurement-of-new-equipment.

27 Tom Fairless, "How War in Europe Boosts the U.S. Economy," *Wall Street Journal*, February 18, 2024. Available here: https://www.wsj.com/economy/ukraine-war-europe-american-economy-654ca41b.

28 Sylvia Pfeifer, Patrick Mathurin, Patricia Nilsson, "Top defence contractors set to rake in record cash after orders soar", *Financial Times*, August 27, 2024. Available here: https://www.ft.com/content/5e368d70-b6e2-4433-a747-cdcfab061f27.

29 Lorne Cook, "A top EU official calls for a new defense industry strategy with locally made arms at its heart," Associated Press, February 28, 2024. Available here: https://apnews.com/article/eu-defense-industry-ukraine-war-russia-assets-9f0c46e058122958f-621f198cd53d775.

30 Dan Sabbagh and Peter Walker, "Army chief says people of UK are 'prewar generation' who must be ready to fight Russia," *The Guardian*, January 24, 2024. Available here: https://www.theguardian.

com/uk-news/2024/jan/24/army-chief-says-people-of-uk-are-pre-war-generation-who-must-be-ready-to-fight-russia.
31 See text from UK Ministry of Defence website: https://www.gov.uk/government/speeches/defending-britain-from-a-more-dangerous-world (emphasis added).
32 See https://www.youtube.com/watch?v=_IGU_7alJ80.
33 See https://fred.stlouisfed.org/series/RRPONTSYD.
34 See https://www.federalreserve.gov/financial-stability/bank-term-funding-program.htm.
35 Alan Goldstein, "Shadow Bank Loans from US Lenders Surpass $1 Trillion in Fed Data," *Bloomberg*, February 10, 2024. Available here: https://www.bloomberg.com/news/articles/2024-02-10/shadow-bank-loans-from-us-lenders-surpass-1-trillion-in-fed-data.
36 Huw Jones, "Global regulators make tackling non-bank leverage a priority for 2024," *Reuters*, December 20, 2023. Available here: https://www.reuters.com/markets/global-regulators-make-tackling-non-bank-leverage-priority-2024-2023-12-20/.
37 Karl Marx, *Capital: A Critique of Political Economy*, vol. 1, p. 926.
38 Theodor Adorno, "Late Capitalism or Industrial Society?," p. 122.
39 Sean O'Hagan, "Jonathan Glazer on his Holocaust film *The Zone of Interest*: 'This is not about the past, it's about now,'" *The Guardian*, December 10, 2023. Available here: https://www.theguardian.com/film/2023/dec/10/jonathan-glazer-the-zone-of-interest-auschwitz-under-the-skin-interview.
40 This powerful argument was developed by Italian intellectual (and Jewish communist) Franco Fortini in his *I cani del Sinai*, penned on the occasion of the Six-Day War (1967). The book is available in English translation as *The Dogs of Sinai* (Kolkata: Seagull Books, 2014).

Chapter Five

1 Giorgio Agamben, "Il silenzio di Gaza," *Quodlibet*, October 30, 2023 (author translation). Available here: https://www.quodlibet.it/giorgio-agamben-silenzio-gaza.
2 See, for instance, Nasiru Eneji Abdulrasheed, "IDF Soldier's Instagram Video Sparks War Crimes Controversy," *BNN Breaking*, Feb-

ruary 6, 2024. Available here: https://bnnbreaking.com/politics/instagram-post-ignites-controversy-over-alleged-idf-misconduct. See also https://www.amnesty.org/en/latest/news/2023/11/israel-opt-horrifying-cases-of-torture-and-degrading-treatment-of-palestinian-detainees-amid-spike-in-arbitrary-arrests/.
3   Slavoj Žižek, "What Donald Rumsfeld Doesn't Know That He Knows About Torture and the Iraq War," *In These Times*, May 21, 2004. Available here: https://inthesetimes.com/article/what-rumsfeld-doesn-know-that-he-knows-about-abu-ghraib.
4   SMEs are being destroyed and replaced by corporate capital on a terrifyingly wide scale. This process began to accelerate with the 2008 financial crisis and continued even faster with Covid-19 and the subsequent interest rate hikes.
5   See the official chart here: https://fred.stlouisfed.org/series/H41RESPPALDKNWW.
6   See https://www.usbanklocations.com/bank-rank/derivatives.html.
7   See https://www.bis.org/publ/othp61.pdf.
8   Yanis Varoufakis, "Who's Afraid of Central Bank Digital Currencies?," *Project Syndicate*, May 15, 2023. Available here: https://www.project-syndicate.org/commentary/central-bank-digital-currency-would-upend-financial-industry-by-yanis-varoufakis-2023-05?barrier=accesspaylog.
9   Yanis Varoufakis, "Time to Blow Up the Banking System," *Project Syndicate*, April 9, 2023.
10 Richard Partington, "'Securonomics': five key business messages from Labour conference," *The Guardian*, October 10, 2023. Available here: https://www.theguardian.com/business/2023/oct/10/securonomics-five-key-business-messages-from-labour-conference.
11 See Robert Kurz, *Geld ohne Wert: Grundrisse zu einer Transformation der Kritik der politischen Ökonomie* (Berlin: Horlemann Verlag, 2012).
12 Jacques Lacan, *The Other Side of Psychoanalysis. The Seminar of Jacques Lacan, book 17* (New York: Norton, 2007), p. 110.
13 See https://watson.brown.edu/costsofwar/papers/2023/IndirectDeaths.
14 Jorge Mario Bergoglio, *Contro la guerra. Il coraggio di costruire la pace* (Milano: Solferino, 2022).

15 Insofar as crude oil is a fundamental component of the economic system and every single Wall Street bank is heavily invested in it, one should expect that it will be boosted. We should expect that more US-led military interventions in the Middle East, for instance, will cause crude oil, and energy prices overall, to move higher going forward.

16 See Clare Jim and Xie Yu, "China Evergrande ordered to liquidate in landmark moment for crisis-hit sector," Reuters, January 29, 2024. Available here: https://www.reuters.com/business/embattled-china-evergrande-back-court-liquidation-hearing-2024-01-28/.

17 On January 21, 2024, Hamas published a 16-page report highlighting the motives for its cross-border attack on Israel and its connection to the Palestinian cause while also countering Israeli allegations. See https://www.palestinechronicle.com/hamas-document-reveals-why-we-we-carried-out-al-aqsa-flood-operation-summary-pdf/.

18 Jim Garamone, "U.S. Flowing Military Supplies to Israel, as Country Battles Hamas Terrorists," U.S Department of Defense, October 10, 2023. Available here: https://www.defense.gov/News/News-Stories/Article/Article/3553040/us-flowing-military-supplies-to-israel-as-country-battles-hamas-terrorists/.

19 Also, higher stock prices at year's end means that the upper management of major corporations get their multimillion-dollar year-end bonuses, which are based on year-end stock prices.

20 See Andres Triay, Robert Legare, Jeff Pegues, "Threats in U.S. rising after Hamas attack on Israel, says FBI Director Christopher Wray," *CBS News*, October 15, 2023. Available here: https://www.cbsnews.com/news/threats-in-u-s-rising-after-hamas-attack-on-israel-says-fbi-director-christopher-wray/.

21 Ashleigh Furlong, "French minister warns of resumption of 'Islamist terrorist' threat in Europe," *Politico*, May 20, 2023. Available here: https://www.politico.eu/article/france-minister-warns-resumption-sunni-islamist-terrorism-threat-europe-gerard-darmanin/.

22 See Rajeev Sjal, "Extremists could use AI to plan attacks, Home Office warns," *The Guardian*, July 18, 2023. Available here: https://www.theguardian.com/politics/2023/jul/18/extremists-might-use-ai-to-plan-attacks-home-office-warns.

23 Amira Haas, "Arriving Again at the Cycle of Vengeance," *Haaretz*, October 10, 2023. Available here: https://www.haaretz.com/opinion/2023-10-10/ty-article/.premium/arriving-again-at-the-cycle-of-vengeance/0000018b-15d7-d2fc-a59f-d5df-4d810000?v=1697053646597.
24 Slavoj Žižek, "The Real Dividing Line in Israel-Palestine," *Project Syndicate*, October 13, 2023. Available here: https://www.project-syndicate.org/commentary/israel-palestine-hamas-and-hardliners-against-peace-by-slavoj-Žižek-2023-10?barrier=accesspaylog.
25 Miranda Cleland, "The US is complicit in Israel's campaign of genocide against children of Gaza," *Middle East Eye*, October 17, 2023. Available here: https://www.middleeasteye.net/opinion/israel-palestine-war-us-complicit-genocide-children.
26 Jean Baudrillard, *Simulations*, p. 29.
27 See https://www.youtube.com/watch?v=3x02rCeusCI.
28 See Adam Lebor, *Tower of Basel: The Shadowy History of the Secret Bank that Runs the World* (New York: PublicAffairs, 2014).
29 See Thorstein Veblen, "Review of John Maynard Keynes, *The Economic Consequences of the Peace,*" in *Political Science Quarterly*, 35 (1920), pp. 467–72.
30 Karl Marx, *Capital: A Critique of Political Economy*, vol. 1, p. 342.
31 See https://ycharts.com/indicators/us_currency_in_circulation#:~:text=US%20Currency%20in%20Circulation%20(I%3AUSCCNW)&text=US%20Currency%20in%20Circulation%20is,2.10%25%20from%20one%20year%20ago.
32 David Lawder, "World Bank chief says Gaza conflict is economic shock 'we don't need,'" Reuters, October 10, 2023. Available here: https://www.reuters.com/markets/world-bank-chief-banga-says-gaza-conflict-is-economic-shock-we-dont-need-2023-10-10/.
33 See https://www.ft.com/content/144c541a-1109-40c9-b74a-7d176ba90fc6.
34 Hugh Son, "Big banks are quietly cutting thousands of employees, and more layoffs are coming," *CNBC*, October 19, 2023. Available here: https://www.cnbc.com/2023/10/19/big-banks-cut-thousands-of-jobs-more-layoffs-coming.html#:~:text=Even%20as%20

the%20economy%20has,key%20exception%20being%20JPMorgan%20Chase.
35 Sarah Butcher, "Bank of America cut 7,500 jobs and no one noticed," eFinancialCareers, October 18, 2023. Available here: https://www.efinancialcareers.jp/news/2023/10/bank-of-america-job-cuts.
36 Saeed Azhar and Nupur Anand, "Bank of America's unrealized losses on securities rose to $131.6 bln," Reuters, October 17, 2023. Available here: https://www.reuters.com/business/finance/bank-americas-unrealized-losses-securities-rose-1316-bln-2023-10-17/.
37 Jon Kamp and Shannon Najmabadi, "More Americans Are Ending Up Homeless—at a Record Rate," *Wall Street Journal*, August 14, 2023. Available here: https://www.wsj.com/articles/homelessness-increasing-united-states-housing-costs-e1990ac7.
38 See https://www.statista.com/statistics/193215/unadjusted-monthly-number-of-inactive-labor-force-in-the-us/#:~:text=In%20August%202023%2C%20the%20inactive,16%20years%20old%20and%20over.
39 See https://www.statista.com/statistics/192417/inactive-labor-force-of-the-us-since-1990/.
40 See https://www.nasdaq.com/articles/americans-do-not-have-enough-savings.-heres-what-you-can-do-about-it.
41 See https://www.usdebtclock.org/.
42 Immanuel Kant, *Critique of Judgement*, trans. J. H. Bernard (London: Macmillan, 1914 [1790]), p. 110.

Chapter Six

1   Chef Rubio (Gabriele Rubini), "Chef Rubio a l'AD: 'A che serve dire "Palestina libera" se poi non si dice da chi è occupata,'" *L'antidiplomatico*, January 25, 2024. Available here: https://www.lantidiplomatico.it/dettnews-chef_rubio_a_lad_a_che_serve_dire_palestina_libera_se_poi_non_si_dice_da_chi__occupata/5496_52500/ (author translation). On May 15, 2024, Rubini was ambushed outside his home and violently attacked by a gang of

six in what appears to be retaliation for his pro-Palestine stance. See https://www.albawaba.com/node/italian-chef-gabriele-rubini-violently-attacked-being-pro-gaza-1566988.

2 Philip Oltermann, "Israel-Hamas war opens up German debate over meaning of 'Never again,'" *The Guardian*, November 22, 2023. Available here: https://www.theguardian.com/world/2023/nov/22/israel-hamas-war-opens-up-german-debate-over-meaning-of-never-again.

3 See Zac Larkham, "The Quiet Rise of Real-Time Crime Centers," *Wired*, July 10, 2023. Available here: https://www.wired.com/story/real-time-crime-centers-rtcc-us-police/.

4 Elliot Smith, "IMF says global economy faces 'confluence of calamities' in biggest test since World War II," *CNBC*, May 23, 2022. Available here: https://www.cnbc.com/2022/05/23/imf-economy-faces-confluence-of-calamities-in-biggest-test-since-world-war-ii.html#:~:text=In%20combining%20the%20Russia%2DUkraine,"potential%20confluence%20of%20calamities.

5 In December 2023, for instance, the Bundesbank attributed the stagnation (recession) of the German economy to global crisis shocks ("geopolitical tensions"). See https://www.bmwk.de/Redaktion/DE/nachrichtenen/Wirtschaftliche-Lage/2023/20231213-die-wirtschaft-lage-in-deutschland-im-dezember-2023.html. At the same time, hedge funds started shorting (betting against) top German companies (see Neil Callanan and Nishant Kumar, "Hedge Fund Qube Built a $1 Billion Short Bet Against Top German Companies," *Bloomberg.com*, January 24, 2024). Available here: https://www.bloomberg.com/news/articles/2024-01-24/hedge-fund-in-1bn-short-bet-against-vw-deutsche-bank-other-german-firms?embedded-checkout=true&leadSource=uverify%20wall.

6 See Robert Kurz, *Schwarzbuch Kapitalismus. Ein Abgesang auf die Marktwirtschaft* (Frankfurt: Eichborn), 2000, and *Geld ohne Wert: Grundrisse zu einer Transformation der Kritik der politischen Ökonomie*, 2012.

7 Larry Elliot, "'Apocalyptic' food prices will be disastrous for world's poor, says Bank governor," *The Guardian*, May 16, 2022. Available here: https://www.theguardian.com/business/2022/may/16/

apocalyptic-food-prices-will-be-disastrous-for-worlds-poor-says-bank-governor#:~:text=The%20Bank%20of%20England%20governor,impact%20on%20the%20world's%20poor.
8   See https://fred.stlouisfed.org/series/GFDEBTN.
9   George Orwell, *1984* (London: Penguin Classics, 2018 [1949]), p. 216.
10 Elliot Smith, "Zelenskyy, BlackRock CEO Fink agree to coordinate Ukraine investment," *CNBC*, December 28, 2022. Available here: https://www.cnbc.com/2022/12/28/zelenskyy-blackrock-ceo-fink-agree-to-coordinate-ukraine-investment.html.
11 No wonder Fink thinks that "the big winners are countries that have shrinking populations" (see https://www.youtube.com/watch?v=s-_H2IxAxeQ).
12 Damian Garde and Matthew Herper, "Pfizer and BioNTech to submit Covid-19 vaccine data to FDA as full results show 95% efficacy," *Statnews*, November 18, 2020. Available here: https://www.statnews.com/2020/11/18/pfizer-biontech-covid19-vaccine-fda-data/.
13 John P. A. Joannidis, "Infection fatality rate of COVID-19 inferred from seroprevalence data," *Bulletin of the World Health Organization*, 99 (1): 19–33.
14 Frank Chung, "Pfizer did not know whether Covid vaccine stopped transmission before rollout, executive admits," *News.com.au*, October 13, 2022. Available here: https://www.news.com.au/technology/science/human-body/pfizer-did-not-know-whether-covid-vaccine-stopped-transmission-before-rollout-executive-admits/news-story/f307f28f794e173ac017a62784fec414.
15 See https://www.ft.com/content/87ed8ea6-4913-4452-9135-498040ad338f.
16 See https://edition.cnn.com/2022/12/30/investing/dow-stock-market-2022/index.html.
17 Masaki Kondo and Garfield Reynolds, "Global Era of Negative Yields Is Ending as Japan Bond Tops Zero," *Bloomberg*, December 21, 2022. Available here: https://www.bloomberg.com/news/articles/2022-12-21/japan-two-year-yield-rises-above-zero-for-first-time-since-2015-lbwxxzr3?leadSource=uverify%20wall.

18 Jim Tyson, "Stock buybacks rise toward record $1T: Goldman Sachs," *CFO Dive*, November 4, 2022. Available here: https://www.cfodive.com/news/share-buybacks-record-1-trillion-dollars-goldman-sachs/635836/.
19 Michael Derby, "Fed reverse repo facility hits record $2.554 trillion," Reuters, December 30, 2022. Available here: https://www.reuters.com/markets/us/fed-reverse-repo-facility-hits-record-2554-trillion-2022-12-30/.
20 See https://www.bis.org/publ/qtrpdf/r_qt2212h.pdf.
21 See list here: https://www.fsb.org/2022/11/2022-list-of-global-systemically-important-banks-g-sibs/.
22 Recent hyperinflationary cycles include Bolivia (1985), Argentina (1989), Peru (1990), Nicaragua (1991), Bosnia (1992), Ukraine (1992), Russia (1992), Moldova (1992), Armenia (1993), Congo (1993), Yugoslavia (1994), Georgia (1994), Bulgaria (1997), Venezuela (2016), Zimbabwe (2007/09 and 2017), and Lebanon (2020–present).
23 Emile Cioran, *The Temptation to Exist* (Chicago: Quadrangle Books, 1968), p. 48.
24 Julian Borger, "Doomsday Clock at record 90 seconds to midnight amid Ukraine crisis," *The Guardian*, January 24, 2023. Available here: https://www.theguardian.com/world/2023/jan/24/doomsday-clock-at-record-90-seconds-to-midnight-amid-ukraine-crisis.
25 See https://www.whitehouse.gov/briefing-room/statements-releases/2022/11/16/g20-bali-leaders-declaration/.

Chapter Seven

1 See https://www.simonmichaux.com.
2 Jean Baudrillard, *Simulations*, p. 74.
3 See, for instance, Wolfgang Streeck, *How Will Capitalism End? Essays on a Failing System* (London: Verso, 2016).
4 Stefano Rebaudo, "Italy's 10-year bond yields above 4% for first time since 2014,"*Yahoo! Finance*, June 13, 2022. Available here: https://finance.yahoo.com/news/1-euro-zone-bond-yields-080040417.html?guccounter=1

5   Francesco Canepa and Balazs Koranyi, "ECB to channel cash from north to south in bid to cap spreads," Reuters, June 30, 2022. Available here: https://www.reuters.com/markets/europe/exclusive-ecb-channel-cash-north-south-bid-cap-spreads-sources-2022-06-30/.
6   https://www.ecb.europa.eu/press/pr/date/2022/html/ecb.pr220721~973e6e7273.en.html.
7   See https://www.youtube.com/watch?v=MfA4i-Oy5ak.
8   See https://www.nommeraadio.ee/meedia/pdf/RRS/Rockefeller%20Foundation.pdf.
9   A recent wave of demonstrations has come from German farmers who oppose their government's planned cuts to the agricultural sector. See Riham Alkousa and Swantje Stein, "German farmers protest with tractors against austerity measures," Reuters, December 18, 2023. Available here: https://www.reuters.com/world/europe/german-farmers-protest-with-tractors-against-austerity-measures-2023-12-18/. See also, Jon Henley and Philip Oltermann, "German farmers block roads with tractors in subsidies protest," *The Guardian*, January 8, 2024. Available here: https://www.theguardian.com/world/2024/jan/08/german-farmers-block-roads-tractors-subsidies-protest.
10 See Kim Willsher, "Macron warns of 'end of abundance' as France faces difficult winter," *The Guardian*, August 24, 2022. Available here: https://www.theguardian.com/world/2022/aug/24/macron-warns-of-end-of-abundance-as-france-faces-difficult-winter#:~:text=%E2%80%9CThis%20overview%20that%20I'm,-feel%20a%20lot%20of%20anxiety.
11 See Hannah Natanson, Fenit Nirappil and Maegan Vazquez, "A few schools mandated masks. Conservatives hit back hard," *The Washington Post*, September 7, 2023. Available here: https://www.washingtonpost.com/education/2023/09/06/school-mask-mandate-politics/.
12 See Molly Bohannon, "Mask Mandates Return At Atlanta College, Hollywood Studio As Covid Cases Start To Rise," *Forbes*, August 22, 2023. Available here: https://www.forbes.com/sites/mollybo-

hannon/2023/08/22/mask-mandates-return-at-atlanta-college-hollywood-studio-as-covid-cases-start-to-rise/.
13 See Johanna Alonso, "Another College Mandates Masks," *Inside Higher Ed*, August 28, 2023. Available here: https://www.insidehighered.com/news/quick-takes/2023/08/28/another-college-mandates-masks-two-weeks-term.
14 See Annika Kim Constantino, "U.S. will again offer free at-home Covid tests starting Monday," *CNBC*, September 20, 2023. Available here: https://www.cnbc.com/2023/09/20/us-will-again-offer-free-at-home-covid-tests-starting-monday.html?__source=androidappshare.
15 See Nicola Davis, "Covid testing to be scaled up in England as winter pressure on NHS draws near," *The Guardian*, September 4, 2023. Available here: https://www.theguardian.com/world/2023/sep/04/covid-testing-to-be-scaled-up-in-england-as-winter-pressure-on-nhs-draws-near.
16 See Alexander Butler, "Gatwick flights cancelled - latest: Calls for air traffic control chief to quit as Covid disruption continues," *The Independent*, September 27, 2023. Available here: https://www.independent.co.uk/travel/london-gatwick-flights-cancelled-easyjet-latest-b2419250.html.
17 See, for instance, https://ukhsa.blog.gov.uk/2024/01/15/should-we-be-worried-about-the-new-covid-19-variant/. See also, as an example of media scaremongering, Jamie Ducharme, "We're In a Major COVID-19 Surge. It's Our New Normal," *Time*, January 12, 2024. Available here: https://time.com/6554340/covid-19-surge-2024/.
18 See https://www.who.int/activities/prioritizing-diseases-for-research-and-development-in-emergency-contexts.
19 See "What is Disease X? WHO panel to debate on deadly virus that could kill 20 times more than Covid-19," *The Economic Times*, January 16, 2024. Available here: https://economictimes.indiatimes.com/news/science/what-is-disease-x-who-panel-to-debate-on-deadly-virus-that-could-kill-20-times-more-than-covid-19/articleshow/106886752.cms?from=mdr.

20 See https://www.who.int/news/item/14-08-2024-who-director-general-declares-mpox-outbreak-a-public-health-emergency-of-international-concern.
21 Tiffany Chan, "Oxford approves curfew to prevent EEE spread, despite protests," *CBS news*, August 22, 2024. Available here: https://www.cbsnews.com/boston/news/oxford-outdoor-ban-eee/.
22 See https://www.gov.uk/government/news/uk-emergency-alerts-test-keep-calm-and-carry-on-this-is-just-a-test.
23 See https://www.fema.gov/press-release/20230803/fema-and-fcc-plan-nationwide-emergency-alert-test-oct-4-2023.
24 Jean Baudrillard, *Simulations*, p. 111.
25 This picture is further aggravated by China and other BRICS+ countries dumping US Treasuries.
26 Karl Marx, *Capital: A Critique of Political Economy*, vol. 3, pp. 598 and 608.
27 See Maha El Dahan and Yousef Saba, "Saudi Arabia, Russia extend voluntary oil cuts to year-end, markets jump," Reuters, September 5, 2023. Available here: https://www.reuters.com/business/energy/saudi-arabia-extends-voluntary-oil-output-cut-1-mln-bpd-end-2023-2023-09-05/.
28 See Arathy Somasekhar, "U.S. emergency oil reserves tumble to lowest since 1984," Reuters, September 12, 2022. Available here: https://www.reuters.com/markets/us/crude-us-emergency-reserve-falls-lowest-since-oct-1984-2022-09-12/.
29 See https://www.morningstar.com/news/marketwatch/20230912313/oil-futures-end-at-fresh-highs-for-the-year-as-opec-forecasts-a-fourth-quarter-supply-shortfall.
30 See https://www.ranken-energy.com/index.php/products-made-from-petroleum/.
31 See Shannon Osaka, "What the world would look like without fossil fuels," *The Washington Post*, September 30, 2023. Available here: https://www.washingtonpost.com/climate-environment/2023/09/30/end-fossil-fuels-biden/.
32 See https://www.eesi.org/topics/fossil-fuels/description#:~:text=Fossil%20fuels—including%20coal%2C%20oil,percent%20of%20the%20world's%20energy.

33 See Seth Borenstein, Fatima Hussain, and The Associated Press, "Bill Gates sees 'a lot of climate exaggeration' out there: 'The climate is not the end of the planet. So the planet is going to be fine,'" *Fortune*, September 20, 2023. Available here: https://fortune.com/europe/2023/09/20/bill-gates-climate-exaggeration-bloomberg-prince-william-earthshot/.

34 See George Parker, Lucy Fisher and Jim Pickard, "Rishi Sunak announces series of U-turns on net zero pledges," *Financial Times*, September 20, 2023. Available here: https://www.ft.com/content/02ecb92e-1e67-4db1-ad73-6c0e76bdc6ca.

35 See https://spcommreports.ohchr.org/TMResultsBase/DownLoadPublicCommunicationFile?gId=28094.

36 See Natalie Grover, "BlackRock names Aramco boss to board," Reuters, July 18, 2023. Available here: https://www.reuters.com/business/blackrock-names-aramco-boss-board-2023-07-17/.

37 See Isla Binnie, "BlackRock's Fink says he's stopped using 'weaponised' term ESG," Reuters, June 26, 2023. Available here: https://www.reuters.com/business/environment/blackrocks-fink-says-hes-stopped-using-weaponised-term-esg-2023-06-26/.

38 Mark Fisher, *Capitalist Realism. Is There No Alternative?* (Zero Books, 2009), p. 27.

39 As per the 2006 "Stern Review." See https://www.lse.ac.uk/granthaminstitute/publication/the-economics-of-climate-change-the-stern-review/.

40 See https://epc.ae/en/details/featured/managing-climate-change-in-the-gulf-challenges-policies-and-the-way-forward.

41 See https://www.strategyand.pwc.com/m1/en/strategic-foresight/functional-expertise/digital-capabilities-and-offerings/metaverse.html.

42 See https://www.strategyand.pwc.com/m1/en/strategic-foresight/functional-expertise/digital/metaverse/middle-east-perspective-on-the-metaverse.pdf.

43 See https://www.undp.org/sustainable-development-goals.

44 Here is its website: https://juststopoil.org.

45 See Damien Gayle, "Just Stop Oil's 'spring uprising' protests funded by US philanthropists," *The Guardian*, April 29, 2022. Available

here: https://www.theguardian.com/environment/2022/apr/29/just-stop-oils-protests-funded-by-us-philanthropists.
46 See https://www.c40.org/funders-partners/.
47 See https://www.c40.org/news/consumption-emissions-report-spotlight/.
48 See https://c40.my.salesforce.com/sfc/p/#36000001En-hz/a/1Q000000Zih4/lPIbXzPbAkJBPhjw3YxkDk8yeWmUL-cONTXUCcVork_8.
49 See https://www.c40knowledgehub.org/s/article/In-Focus-Addressing-food-related-consumption-based-emissions-in-C40-Cities?language=en_US.
50 David Graeber, *Bullshit Jobs*, p. 265.
51 A recording of Parenti's lecture can be accessed here: https://www.youtube.com/watch?v=t21UZxRYYA4.
52 Karl Marx, *Grundrisse: Foundations of the Critique of Political Economy*, p. 700.
53 Herbert Marcuse, *The One-Dimensional Man* (London and New York: Routledge 1991 [1964]), p. 39.
54 Hannah Arendt, *The Human Condition*, (Chicago and London: The University of Chicago Press, 1998 [1958]), pp. 4–5.

Conclusion

1 Amin Samman and Stefano Sgambati, "Financial Eschatology and the Libidinal Economy of Leverage," p. 111.
2 Hannah Arendt, *The Human Condition*, p. 5.
3 Walter Benjamin, *One-Way Street* (Cambridge, MA and London: Harvard University Press, 2016), pp. 32–33.
4 Ibid, p. 34.
5 Quoted in David Graeber and David Wengrow, *The Dawn of Everything. A New History of Humanity* (London: Penguin Books, 2021), pp. 54–55.

www.ingramcontent.com/pod-product-compliance
Lightning Source LLC
Chambersburg PA
CBHW060456030426
42337CB00015B/1614